D1158703

American Jewish Thought Since 1934

THE TAUBER INSTITUTE SERIES FOR
THE STUDY OF EUROPEAN JEWRY
Jehuda Reinharz, General Editor
ChaeRan Y. Freeze, Associate Editor
Sylvia Fuks Fried, Associate Editor
Eugene R. Sheppard, Associate Editor

THE BRANDEIS LIBRARY OF MODERN JEWISH THOUGHT
Eugene R. Sheppard and Samuel Moyn, Editors

This library aims to redefine the canon of modern Jewish thought by publishing
primary source readings from individual Jewish thinkers or groups of thinkers in reliable
English translations. Designed for courses in modern Jewish philosophy, thought, and
intellectual history, each volume features a general introduction and annotations to
each source with the instructor and student in mind.

FOR THE COMPLETE LIST OF BOOKS THAT ARE FORTHCOMING
IN THE SERIES, PLEASE SEE HTTP://WWW.BRANDEIS.EDU/TAUBER

American Jewish Thought Since 1934

Edited by
Michael Marmur and
David Ellenson

WRITINGS ON IDENTITY, ENGAGEMENT, AND BELIEF

Brandeis University Press

Waltham, Massachusetts

BRANDEIS UNIVERSITY PRESS

© 2020 Brandeis University Press

All rights reserved

Manufactured in the United States of America

Designed by Eric M. Brooks

Typeset in Albertina and Verlag by Passumpsic Publishing

For permission to reproduce any of the material in this book,
contact Brandeis University Press, 415 South Street, Waltham MA 02453;
or visit brandeisuniversitypress.com

Library of Congress Cataloging-in-Publication Data
available upon request
Hardcover ISBN: 978-1-68458-013-2
Paperback ISBN: 978-1-68458-014-9
Ebook ISBN: 978-1-68458-015-6

5 4 3

"Listen to your parent's guidance,

pay attention and gain understanding"

(Proverbs 4:1)

To Dow and Fredzia Marmur, with love and gratitude

Michael Marmur

"May you live to see your children's children"

(Psalms 128:6)

To Lily, Rose, Shai, and those yet to come

David Ellenson

Contents

III | **Spirituality** 85

IV | **Hermeneutics and Politics** 123

V | **The Holocaust and Israel** 167

VI | **Feminism, Gender, and Sexuality** 213

VII | **Peoplehood** 257

Foreword

What role do Judaism and Jewish existence play in America? Conversely, what role does America play in matters Jewish there? Michael Marmur and David Ellenson have taken on the monumental task of allowing us to listen to distinctive voices in the cacophony of those who have shaped the bold and shifting soundscape of American Jewish thought over the last few generations. *American Jewish Thought Since 1934: Writings on Identity, Engagement, and Belief* takes Mordecai Kaplan's *Judaism as a Civilization* (1934) as the "Archimedean point" thanks to which Jewish thought in America acquires a distinctive set of characteristics. The present volume engages theological questions; loyalty and belonging; the significance of halachic, spiritual, and ritual practice; secularization and its discontents; and the creative recasting of Jewish peoplehood. Marmur and Ellenson are careful to point out how a plurality of approaches emerged in response to the fundamental ruptures and challenges of continuity posed by the Holocaust, the establishment of the state of Israel, and the twentieth-century civil rights movement. This volume includes representative figures from a wide swath of the most distinctive currents and movements evident in North American Jewish thought over the last eighty years: post-Holocaust theology, secular forms of Jewish spirituality, ultra-orthodoxy, American neo-orthodoxy, neo-Hasidism, feminism and queer theory, diasporic critiques of Zionism, and unrestrained Zionist militancy. It serves as a reminder of the creativity of American Jewish thought and of the possibilities of its still-unwritten future.

Eugene R. Sheppard and Samuel Moyn, Editors
The Brandeis Library of Modern Jewish Thought

Acknowledgments

We would like to express special gratitude to Sylvia Fuks Fried, executive director of the Tauber Institute for the Study of European Jewry at Brandeis University, as well as Samuel Moyn and Eugene Sheppard, for inviting us to undertake this project. They have been invaluable sources of counsel throughout, and we thank them for their support, advice, and constructive comments. Whatever merits this volume possesses are in no small part due to them.

During the three years of coediting this book and choosing the selections for it, Michael Marmur worked at Hebrew Union College–Jewish Institute of Religion, and David Ellenson taught primarily at Brandeis University. In 2018–19, however, David, who had served as President of HUC-JIR from 2001 to 2013, was called back to serve as Interim President after the tragic death on May 5, 2018, of beloved colleague Rabbi Aaron Panken, who served as President of HUC-JIR from 2014 to 2018. Michael had served as Provost at HUC-JIR under Aaron, and David had worked for years with Aaron during his time as President. We both loved and treasured Aaron as a colleague and a friend. We miss him greatly, and we acknowledge that the academic leadership and vision he provided at HUC-JIR when this book was conceived and compiled allowed for its completion. Our debt to him is profound, and our sadness at his passing remains acute.

A work like this cannot be written without the advice and efforts of many. While there are many names we might list here, we are particularly aware of the insights and recommendations we have received from a number of senior colleagues in the field, at a Scholars Workshop in American Jewish Thought held at New York University in December 2016. Professors Michah Gottlieb and Eugene Sheppard organized the workshop. Professor Judith Plaskow also provided invaluable assistance, as did a number of other colleagues in informal conversations in the course of the last several years. We are very grateful for their encouragement and suggestions.

We also express our deepest thanks to Yoram Bitton, Director of Libraries at HUC-JIR; Sheryl Stahl, Director of the Frances-Henry Library at HUC-JIR, Los Angeles; Laurel Wolfson, Director of the Klau Library at HUC-JIR,

Cincinnati; Tamar Duvdevani, Director of the Abramov Library at HUC-JIR, Jerusalem; and Tina Weiss, Senior Associate Librarian at HUC-JIR, New York. Along with the other members of the HUC-JIR library system past and present, they provided constant bibliographical support. We also wish to thank James Rosenbloom, Judaica Librarian at Brandeis University, and Brandeis graduate students Bar Guzi and Iddo Haklai for their indefatigable and unfailingly courteous assistance in obtaining the sources we required for the publication of this book. We express our appreciation to Iris Ben-Zvi, Assistant to the Dean at HUC-JIR, Jerusalem; Abby Huber, former Senior Department Coordinator of the Schusterman Center for Israel Studies at Brandeis University; and Nicole Vandestienne, Executive Administrator, Office of the President at HUC-JIR; for all their aid. This book was surely facilitated by each of these individuals, and we thank them all.

We would also like to acknowledge the generous support of Steven L. Rachmuth, an alumnus of Brandeis from the class of 2014. He has believed in the importance of this project and we are grateful for his generous financial commitment to the publication of this book, which is made in memory of Carl, Lotty, David, and Otto Rachmuth, and Gilda and Mayer Milstoc.

David has also had the great pleasure over the past five years of teaching a monthly class on Jewish topics to a remarkable group of women: Karen Adler, Barbara Friedman, Mary-Joan Gerson, Billie Gold, Susan Lipton, Phyllis Friedman Perkins, Susan Schlechter, Lynn Schusterman, and Nicki Tanner. He and Michael would like to thank them all and acknowledge their generosity and support in underwriting some of the costs of this book.

We also offer thanks to our families. Our wives, Sarah Bernstein and Jacqueline Koch, encouraged us to engage together in this project, and our children offered us numerous suggestions and served as sounding boards for many of our ideas and selections for this book. On occasion, these discussions were explicit, but even when they were not, we have considered the ideas in this volume with our children constantly in mind. To Miriam, Nadav, and Gaby Marmur; Ruth Andrew Ellenson and Lorne Manly; Micah and Sarah Ellenson; Hannah Ellenson and Becca Israel; Nomi Ellenson and Alex Silver; and Rafi Ellenson—thank you.

Finally, we are mindful, in thanking our spouses and our children, that we ourselves are links in the chain of generations that mark the Jewish people. We are neither the first nor the last generation of our people, and our work in this volume and elsewhere would not be possible without our awareness of and gratitude for this fact. Michael therefore dedicates this work to his parents, who lovingly bequeathed this Jewish heritage to him, and David dedicates this work to his grandchildren, to whom this legacy will be transmitted. The lives of our dedicatees span the historical period covered in this volume, from the mid-1930s to the present day. In dedicating this book to them, we express our faith in *netzach yisrael*—the eternality of the Jewish people and its quest for meaning.

Introduction

The year 1934 saw the publication of Mordecai Kaplan's *Judaism as a Civilization*, a foundational work of American Jewish thought. Another book published that year was entitled *The Future of Judaism in America*, authored by Eugene Kohn, a colleague of Kaplan's. A sentence from that forgotten work may serve as a watchword for the present volume:

> The conditions under which Judaism must maintain itself, if it is to survive in the modern American environment, are so different from those that have confronted the Jewish people in other times and places that Jews naturally ask themselves what sort of Judaism will emerge as a result of Jewish efforts at adaptation.[1]

Decades of tumult, tragedy, and triumph separate us from this American Jew of 1934, peering with confidence into an uncertain future. His assumptions that the American context demands of Judaism a unique response if it is to adapt and survive, and that the efforts of that response will yield a new Judaism, relate not only to the deployment of institutional resources and the insights of sociological analyses. In order for Judaism to adapt to America, new kinds of thinking are necessary. This volume is devoted to some of the finest and most distinctive examples of American Jewish thought. It aims to orient readers to key topics and major figures by charting the development of responses to Kohn's question: What kind of Judaism, what forms of Jewish life, have been imagined in America in the decades that have elapsed?

Warp and Weft

Jewish thought has been generated wherever Jews, informed by their tradition and committed to the future, have attempted to articulate their concerns and insights. Its fabric is characterized as much by the pores through which influence passes as by the raw materials of which it is constituted. In the texts and textures of Judaism, the warp of perennial concerns and commitments is interwoven with the weft of specific, contextual ingredients gleaned from the events, environments, and cultures surrounding the Jews in their travels through time and space. This process yields both contemporary perspectives on the lasting questions of Jewish existence and Jewish insights on the great issues of the hour.

The impact of the larger world upon Jewish expression has been significant in every time and place where Jews have dwelt throughout Jewish history. The human quest for meaning and community, in which all modern Jewish thinkers are involved, cannot escape the contours of the sociological and historical context in which American Jews find themselves. American Jewish thought, therefore, does more than draw upon Jewish religious tradition for its tropes and substance. It is also informed by the philosophical, theological, historical, and sociological trends of the time. With rare exceptions, the men and women whose thought is represented in this volume have attempted to capture the conceptual integrity of what it means to be a modern American Jew within the larger vista of modern Jewish history. This context poses challenges even as it provides tools with which to respond to them.

Jewish and Modern

Systematic religious thought tends to reflect upon life and beliefs as lived and affirmed by a faith community. However, by shattering traditional Jewish society and the religious-cultural and political-social structures that facilitated such reflection, modernity has made the articulation of Jewish thought and belief in the modern world a strenuous exercise at best. These conditions have certainly destroyed the possibility of a univocal contemporary Jewish theology that is affirmed by all, or even most, Jews. This is why the writing of Jewish religious thought in the modern world has been a scattered and diverse enterprise in search of novel modes of expression—particularly for the majority of Jews whose acculturation has forced them to articulate a solution to the existential dilemma of being authentically Jewish and simultaneously modern.

This last point must be underscored in the examination and presentation of the writings in this volume. For the individual Jew, there exists a number of different methods for adjudicating between the demands of tradition and the facts of contemporary life. Indeed, all of modern Jewish thought is in large measure an attempt to respond to this problem, which has faced Jews since their emancipation.

In Franz Rosenzweig's opening address at the Frankfurt Lehrhaus in 1921,[2] he asserted that Jewish thought and learning in the modern period must begin with where most individual Jews are: at the periphery of Jewish life. Such thought would then aim to bring the Jew back toward the center. Rosenzweig attempted to devise approaches to revelation necessitating a dynamic encounter with Jewish sources and Jewish time. As a modern individual, Rosenzweig insisted that the task of the Jew was to transform Law (*Gesetz*), which he understood as being impersonal and static, into commandment (*Gebot*),* which he saw as a personal address by God to the individual Jew, as well as to the Jewish community. In this way, individual autonomy—a modern concept—could be retained, while maintaining a sense of commitment to both the tradition and the community.

From the particularities of their own personal perspectives, the writers included in this volume have responded to modernity's varied challenges to Jewish continuity.

The American Setting

Much divides the men and women in this volume in terms of ideological orientation and sphere of interest. But all are linked in one way or another by a factor which has had a unique impact on the shaping of contemporary Jewish discourse: America.

The Jewish community in the United States has flourished in a setting possessing no medieval past.[3] Its advantages and blessings notwithstanding, this fact has denied North American Jews even a memory of what communal life, practice, and belief were before the challenges of modernity appeared. This was not a problem of Jewish thinkers in Europe, who had millennium-old communal traditions and boundaries within which they shaped their thought.

In addition, American Jews have had to deal with the reality of a community at the beginning of the twentieth century that was composed predominantly of immigrants. Beset by factionalism and denominationalism, this community was anxious to acculturate into the American milieu. Lacking self-confidence and insecure in their new home, Jewish religious writers in the first half of the century generally wrote ideologically oriented essays and books designed to reconcile and adjust Judaism to its American setting.[4] Exhortative in tone, most of these works drew haphazardly in loose conceptual patterns upon the storehouse of symbols and images contained in traditional Judaism to provide a desired fit between American culture and Judaism. Kaufmann Kohler's *Jewish Theology* stands out as an exception that indicates how rare anything approaching systematic Jewish theological reflection was in the United States during this period.[5]

---

*We recognize that other scholars understand Rosenzweig's use of *Gesetz* and *Gebot* in different ways. See, for example, the selection by Benjamin Sommer in this volume.

This situation began to change in North America after World War II.[6] If the writings of American Jewish thinkers of a previous era had generally been somewhat apologetic and therefore outwardly directed, a younger group of Jewish intellectuals and theologians, "[m]ore secure and self-confident as Jewish-Americans than the previous generation,"[7] began to author more inwardly directed works. They enmeshed their Jewish readers within the warp and weft mentioned above, namely the perennial concerns of Jewish religion alongside responses to new developments. These men, trained in European and American university settings, were open to dialogue about matters of theological substance across Jewish denominational and interreligious lines. Anxious to draw upon the entirety of Jewish tradition and other modern European Jewish thinkers in their writings, they also incorporated insights derived from non-Jewish religious thinkers such as Karl Barth, Paul Tillich, and Reinhold Niebuhr, as well as American philosophers and thinkers like John Dewey and William James, to inform their discussions of Judaism.

Robert Goldy employed the sociological insights of Peter Berger to frame the secular context in which these thinkers emerged. Berger argued over and over again in his voluminous writings that this was a period in which secularization appeared dominant. This does not mean that religion disappeared during this era. Rather, religion came to inform and direct fewer and fewer areas of life for most people, thereby leading to the compartmentalization of religion into distinct precincts and the diminution of its influence in the public square. The compartmentalized nature of this modern American world and the pluralistic character of the American setting in which Judaism had to cope with its voluntary status contributed to the dearth of Jewish theology in the first decades of the twentieth century.

At the same time, the reality of this secular world, combined with the emergence within this environment of modern religious and philosophical trends such as existentialism and pragmatism, helped to create the frameworks for the arguments and writings of many outstanding figures of American Jewish thought. Mordecai Kaplan completed *Judaism as a Civilization* in this milieu, and Will Herberg played a central role shortly after World War II, in a renewed call for Jewish theology. Furthermore, the arrival on American shores of serious thinkers such as Emil Fackenheim, Abraham Joshua Heschel, Jakob Petuchowski, and Joseph Soloveitchik—all educated in Europe, but attuned to the reality of the American Jewish scene—played a crucial part in creating serious Jewish theological thought on the American continent. Soon these thinkers were joined by

American-born intellectuals such as Eugene Borowitz, David Hartman, Irving (Yitz) Greenberg, Emanuel Rackman, and Milton Steinberg to expand the range and depth of American Jewish theological and religious writing that appeared from 1945 to 1980. These persons created an atmosphere that has continued to encourage serious theological writing among Jews. The writing of American Jewish thought, as seen in their works and those of several others, has continued flourishing in the American setting over the last four decades.

If Peter Berger could declare in 1967 that "secularization has resulted in a widespread collapse of the plausibility of traditional religious definitions of reality,"[8] almost fifty years later he was moved to conclude that "so-called secularization theory was mistaken in the assumption that modernity necessarily leads to a decline in religion."[9] In his later work, Berger argues that the pluralism and fragmentation that mark the modern social condition have led to the resurgence of traditional religion and a renewed quest for spiritual expression and meaning in a modern pluralistic context. These developments are the backdrop to the emergence of modern American Jewish thought in all its vigor and diversity.

The multitextured, dissimilar, and overlapping nature of the books and essays produced by the individuals included in this volume and many others testify to an efflorescence of creativity in contemporary American Jewish life. They reflect the multivocal character of the American Jewish community in the past century. This book presents a representative range of thinkers and concerns in order to understand the past course of and current directions in American Jewish thought.

Contours of the Field

In asking what kind of writing might be considered American Jewish thought, we have had to consider questions of geography, chronology, and genre. We have understood "American" to mean North American, hence the inclusion of some Canadians. To have limited the volume to those born in or permanently resident in North America would have been unnecessarily restrictive. We have instead included men and women whom we deem to have made signal contributions to American Jewish thought, and who in the course of their lives have themselves been significantly impacted by the experience of America.

Our decision to begin this collection of readings in 1934 deserves some explanation. There are two main reasons for our choice of this particular year as our starting point. First, it is the year of publication of Mordecai Kaplan's *Judaism as a Civilization*, which we take to be a foundational work of American Jewish thought. Kaplan, described by Susannah Heschel as representing "a new stage in American Jewish thought,"[10] was 53 years old in the year of that book's publication and had already achieved much. Arriving in the United States from Lithuania at the age of eight, his intellectual formation involved both an extensive grounding in traditional Judaism and intensive exposure to major currents in Western, and specifically American, thought. Kaplan's American Judaism was forged at Yeshivat Etz Chaim, the City College of New York, the Jewish Theological Seminary, and Columbia University. By the early years of the twentieth century, he had become part of a circle of scholars, thinkers, and activists who lay the foundations of many institutions and attitudes destined to characterize the American Jewish community for decades. Kaplan's 1934 work is a remarkable expression of this intellectual and religious ferment, reflecting both the uniqueness of Kaplan's approach and the richness of the milieu in which the book was written.

Judaism as a Civilization marks the first mature statement of American Jewish thought. With all that had preceded it, this work could only have been produced as a result of profound engagement with some of the key trends in contemporary American philosophy and social theory. In Kaplan, we see epitomized a new moment in American Judaism. Born and raised an Orthodox Jew, he came to be fully at home with the thought of Horace Kallen and John Dewey. His cultural influences and philosophical commitments denoted a new chapter in American Judaism that allowed him to articulate more brilliantly and insightfully than any of his predecessors the problems and trials that America posed for Jewish religious thought and life. Kaplan's understanding of the challenges to Judaism inherent in the American project is palpable in his still-unsurpassed introduction to *Judaism as a Civilization*, in which he defines the ruptures that Emancipation and the Enlightenment created in modern Jewish existence. He drew upon both internal Jewish sources and external philosophical and sociological writings in laying out the parameters and scope of his own thought. While his rationalistic formulation of Reconstructionist Judaism satisfied his urge to reconcile his traditional loyalty to Jewish practice and community with his own modern philosophical and cultural commitments, his attempt at such reconciliation could not satisfactorily resolve this problem for all American Jews. Nonetheless, Kaplan stands as an Archimedean point in all that followed in American Jewish thought.

It would have been defensible to take 1945 as the starting point for this book, since there is obvious justification for seeing the Shoah as the defining caesura of contemporary Jewish life. By beginning earlier, however, we find American Jews engaging with formidable challenges at home and ominous developments abroad. In 1934, America was still in the throes of the Great Depression. It was the year in which the German-American Bund staged a pro-Nazi rally in Madison Square Garden. Henry Roth's *Call It Sleep*, published that year, provided a stirring evocation of the immigrant Jewish experience in New York's Lower East Side in the early years of the twentieth century. In the 1930s, the Jews of America were busy formulating responses to modernity before having to formulate a response to cataclysmic change. The question posed by Eugene Kohn that year —what sort of Judaism will emerge?—was to take on a dramatic new urgency in the years to come.

Questions of genre have also provided us with some interesting challenges. There are compelling American Jewish ideas to be found in poetry, fiction, film, theater, television, comedy, and songwriting. These media and others, including the plastic arts and online platforms, all testify to the variety of Jewish creativity in our day. We note these riches, just as we affirm that our emphasis is on material disseminated in books and articles, both academic and popular.

Canons and Their Limitations

None of the three thinkers arguably at the fulcrum of Jewish thought in America—Abraham Joshua Heschel (1907–72), Mordecai Kaplan (1881–1983), and Joseph B. Soloveitchik (1903–93)—were born in the United States or Canada. All three hailed from Orthodox Jewish families in Eastern Europe. Kaplan was a boy when he arrived and was to become thoroughly at ease in the intellectual and cultural milieu of America. Heschel and Soloveitchik were 32 and 29 upon arrival, heirs to the intellectual elites of Polish Hasidic and Lithuanian Mitnagdic Orthodoxy respectively, and both were graduates of German universities. They were less "all-American" than Kaplan, certainly less so than American Jews who were generations removed from Europe. But they were American nonetheless.

It is difficult to compare work produced in recent years with some of the classics of American Jewish thought. Proximity to the publication of the latest work increases the risk that we will mistake the faddish for the significant. Nonetheless, we have been struck by the productiveness of American Jewish thinkers in recent years, and we include some of this contemporary work in this collection. The judgment of posterity has not been generous to all the thinkers included in our book. To offer but one example, Milton Steinberg lauded Will Herberg's *Judaism and Modern Man* as "the book of the generation on the Jewish religion."[11]

However, the generation following that work's publication in 1959 has hardly returned to it, or, for that matter, to any of Herberg's other work.[12] In the ebb and flow of Jewish discourse he and others whose voices are to be found here may be rediscovered by a later generation. As for the writings of twenty-first century thinkers, the coming decades will determine which of them will help redefine American Jewish thought and who will be confined to a footnote.

Two canons continue to exercise influence on the developing field of American Jewish thought. First, there is a pantheon of Jewish thinkers, most of them European men born within a few decades and miles of each other, whose work has been foundational in the teaching of Jewish thought on the North American continent. Their names appear in the anthologies of modern Jewish thought published in English, in the dissertations undertaken by young scholars in the field, and in numerous books and articles. This list is not restricted to but certainly does include (listed in order of birth): Moses Mendelssohn, Nachman Krochmal, Samson Raphael Hirsch, Abraham Geiger, Hermann Cohen, Ahad Ha'am, Abraham Isaac Kook, Leo Baeck, Martin Buber, Franz Rosenzweig, and Emmanuel Levinas. Most of the teachers and exponents of Jewish thought in America were brought up on this diet, with variations allowing for ideological orientation and the ebb and flow of reputations—Levinas, for example, was largely unknown in America until the 1980s, when translations of his French-language work began to appear.

Listing leading exponents of American Jewish thought is a precarious activity. Canons can implode and lose relevance. Nonetheless, an examination of course descriptions, previous anthologies, and other works does make possible a broad sketch of the field as it is often imagined and taught. The three men mentioned above—Heschel, Soloveitchik, and Kaplan—have cast a long shadow since the middle of the twentieth century. To these names can be added Rachel Adler, Bradley Shavit Artson, Eliezer Berkovits, Eugene B. Borowitz, Arthur A. Cohen, Elliot Dorff, Arnold Eisen, Emil Fackenheim, Marcia Falk, Arthur Green, Irving "Yitz" Greenberg, David Hartman, Shaul Magid, Michael Morgan, David Novak, Peter Ochs, Vanessa Ochs, Jakob Petuchowski, Judith Plaskow, Tamar Ross, Richard Rubenstein, Norbert Samuelson, Zalman Schachter-Shalomi, Steven Schwarzschild, Milton Steinberg, Ellen Umansky, and Michael Wyschogrod. These men and women, and of course several others who would have a strong claim to be included in a list such as this, have written persuasively about some of the major questions of contemporary Jewish existence, and we have attempted to distill these into the seven parts of this book. Most of these thinkers appear in this anthology, and all of them figure either within the selections in this anthology or in the list of recommended reading we have included at the end of the book.

It is worthwhile to consider who is underrepresented or invisible on this list. Of the hundreds of names arising out of an examination of publications on Jewish thought in America, women do not represent even 10 percent of the total. By way of example, it is instructive to mention a symposium on belief held twice by *Commentary*, once in 1966 and a second time thirty years later. The original questionnaire was sent to fifty-five rabbis, of whom thirty-eight responded from across the three main denominations of American Jewish life. Given the chosen recipients of the original request, it was inevitable that all the respondents were men. By 1996, women were beginning to enter the rabbinate, and in any case the editors of *Commentary* broadened their scope and turned to communal leaders and nonrabbinical academics, too. Of the forty-five individuals whose responses were published in the later work, six were women.[13]

It would be comforting to think that this imbalance is being corrected, and there is some evidence that this is the case. Nevertheless, the twenty volumes comprising The Library of Contemporary Jewish Philosophers,[14] completed in the second decade of the twenty-first century, includes two works by women: Tamar Ross and Judith Plaskow. A 2010 work entitled *Jewish Theology in Our Time* includes the thoughts of twenty males and three females.[15] The reasons for this imbalance may be debated, but the fact of that imbalance is beyond doubt.

Most of the Orthodox figures on this list have been identified with the branch of Judaism usually known as modern Orthodoxy, but in the ultraorthodox world a number of men have had a significant impact as thinkers: Yitzhok Hutner, Aaron Kotler, and Menachem Mendel Schneerson are three such men. One looks in vain for any non-Ashkenazi voices within the accepted canon of American Jewish thought; here the name of Jose Faur certainly deserves mention, and others are likely to find their place in future syllabi and anthologies. Other voices, including those posing questions of Jewish thought through an LGBTQ prism, along with those of avowed secularists and Yiddishists, are marginalized or minimized in the current canon. We both predict and hope that this will change in the near future.

Our wish is that this present volume plays a role in the loosening of a fixed canon. While we know that any attempt to predict which particular thinkers and works will stand the test of time is a hazardous undertaking, the process of broadening the conversation seems irreversible to us, and we welcome it with the familiar Jewish combination of trepidation, curiosity, and enthusiasm.

In the course of preparing this book, our own perception of the canon has changed. We are products of our own educations and vulnerable to our own predilections, but as we have explored different aspects of the field, our appreciation for its variety and versatility has grown.

In attempting to marshal sources into a manageable form, some surprising commonalities have emerged. We were struck, for example, by how many of these thinkers turn to the image of Yavneh, the town in Judea in which Judaism was reconstituted following the destruction of the Second Temple. They interpret Yavneh differently, some emphasizing the need to "circle the wagons" in the wake of cataclysm, and others embracing the possibility of new paradigms. But a remarkable number of them see Yavneh in American Jewish terms.

Other insights have also emerged. We have come to see that what sets apart scholars and practitioners of Jewish thought is hard to define. The distinction is difficult to maintain, despite the model of academic objectivity that itself was a feature of the Jewish encounter with modernity. Most individuals who have been regarded as Jewish thinkers have engaged in scholarship, and a number of leading scholars are motivated by something other than disembodied intellectual curiosity.

We have in fact been moved by the process of conversing together about American Jewish thought for the last several years. To be sure, our insights and explanations have shifted—we conceive of the field differently than we previously did. But we have also been moved in another sense: it is stirring to witness Jewish individuals directing their prodigious energies and talents to fundamental questions of Jewish existence.

The Structure of This Book

We have divided these excerpts, representing over seventy men and women who have made significant contributions to American Jewish thought since the 1930s, into seven parts, each of which highlights a central theme or themes. A concise introduction attempts to place each part of the book in an understandable context, after which a number of excerpts are included from the authors, each of whom is briefly presented.

We begin with a perennial question of Jewish thought, and perhaps the eternal question: God. After surveying a number of approaches to God, we examine some ways in which American Jewish thinkers have responded to God's word (Revelation and Commandment), and ways in which God's presence has been sought (Spirituality). The fourth part, Hermeneutics and Politics, straddles text and context, interpretation and activism, and at its heart explores a quintessential theme of the American Jewish experience: pluralism. Part Five, The Holocaust and Israel, includes some key responses to two epoch-making events of twentieth-century Jewish history that have been linked together in the canon of American Jewish thought and have rightly garnered significant attention from American Jewish thinkers. Part Six, Feminism, Gender, and Sexuality, relates to other foundational transformations in contemporary Jewish, and indeed human, experience. We conclude with the theme at the heart of Kaplan's *Judaism as a Civilization* and with the evolving term that he coined: Peoplehood. The parts of this book move, then, from the God of Israel to the people Israel.

We do not know what the coming decades of American Jewish life will yield, but we are confident that these conversations—about God, commandment, spirituality, hermeneutics, politics, the Holocaust, Israel, feminism, gender, sexuality, identity, and peoplehood—will play their part.

Readers are advised to make use of this volume's index. While we believe that the seven parts of the book provide a way of navigating some of the complexities of American Jewish thought, a number of motifs run through more than one part of the collection. This overlap is inevitable, and it reflects the ways in which the various categories of discourse—theological and political, timeless and contemporary, the warp and weft we describe above, are inextricably bound up with each other. For similar reasons, the books and articles included at the end of the book for further reading are not divided according to categories, but rather simply listed alphabetically. Readers will discover that much of what is included on that list cuts across categories.

Our decision to include relatively short excerpts from a large number of thinkers (we are acutely aware of other significant voices we have omitted) stems both from pedagogic considerations and from our reading of the field. We have cropped these sources tightly to keep the book a manageable size, and resorted to ellipses to give the reader the gist of the argument being made as we understand it. By providing a number of excerpts from many thinkers, we believe that we have captured the effervescence and vitality of our subject, and we hope that an engaged reader will be encouraged to delve more deeply into the thought of those who appear in these pages, and that of others as well. Cutting short the arguments of fine thinkers is not to be undertaken lightly. If the result is that readers are given a grounding and an interest to delve further, we believe that the balancing act will have proven successful.

In considering the last eighty years of American Jewish thought, we hope to provide readers with a sense of the diverse ways in which a host of American Jewish thinkers have understood and expressed the nature and essence of Jewish life and belief, and how they have sought personal and communal meaning for themselves and their fellow Jews during a period of unprecedented change and ferment in Judaism's long history. The fabric of American Jewish thought is distinct to its place and time. Its meshing of warp and weft, the perennial with the particular, places it in a far longer tradition of Jewish thought. Millennia-old Jewish discussions are playing out in a remarkable setting where Jews enjoy an extraordinary degree of access and agency, and Judaism is charged with responding to the opportunities, seductions, and risks posed by this situation.

Eugene Kohn's 1934 question is the question asked by Jews in every place and at every time: what happens next for those who strive for some interaction between tradition and the contemporary? The European, and most distinctly German, influence on American Jewish thought has been enormous, and it may be that this will decrease in coming generations.[16] The impact of Jewish thought in Israel on the North American scene in the years to come is a fascinating and impenetrable question. Will postmodern forms of discourse prevail, or will modernism rediscover its confidence? Put differently, will Jewish thinkers seek to underline rationality and enlightenment or to undermine their dominance? Will American and Jewish exceptionalism fade or grow? Will American Post-Judaism be the norm?[17] The men and women in this volume offer responses—provocative or predictable, radical or reactionary—to questions Eugene Kohn articulated in an American tenor in 1934: How does America change Jewish thought, and how might Jewish thought change America? In short, what sorts of Judaisms will emerge?

Notes

1. Eugene Kohn, *The Future of Judaism in America* (New Rochelle, NY: The Liberal Press, 1934), 9.

2. Franz Rosenzweig, *On Jewish Learning*, ed. Nahum N. Glatzer (New York: Schocken, 1965), 55–71. For a different perspective on the use made of Rosenzweig in contemporary theological discourse, see Mara H. Benjamin, "Agency as Quest and Question: Feminism, Religious Studies, and Modern Jewish Thought," *Jewish Social Studies* 24, no. 2 (2018): 7–16.

3. See Marshall Sklare, *Observing America's Jews* (Hanover, NH: Brandeis University Press, 1993), 24. For an authoritative survey of the history of the American Jewish experience from its earliest stirrings, see Jonathan D. Sarna, *American Judaism: A History* (New Haven, CT: Yale University Press, 2004).

4. See Arnold M. Eisen, *The Chosen People in America: A Study in Jewish Religious Ideology* (Bloomington: Indiana University Press, 1983), especially 3–22.

5. Kaufmann Kohler, *Jewish Theology Systematically and Historically Considered* (New York: Macmillan, 1918); see also Jacob Haberman, "Kaufmann Kohler and His Teacher Samson Raphael Hirsch," *Leo Baeck Institute Year Book* 44, no.1 (1998): 73–100.

6. For a historical overview since 1945, see Dana Evan Kaplan, *Contemporary American Judaism: Transformation and Renewal* (New York: Columbia University Press, 2009), 7–55. See also Michael L. Morgan, *Dilemmas in Modern Jewish Thought: The Dialectics of Revelation and History* (Bloomington: Indiana University Press, 1992), 146–55; and Byron Sherwin, "Thinking Judaism Through: Jewish Theology in America," in *The Cambridge Companion to American Judaism*, ed. Dana Evan Kaplan (New York: Cambridge University Press, 2005), 117–32.

7. Robert G. Goldy, *The Emergence of Jewish Theology in America* (Bloomington: Indiana University Press, 1990), 48.

8. Peter L. Berger, *The Sacred Canopy: Elements of a Sociological Theory of Religion* (New York: Doubleday, 1967), 127.

9. Peter L. Berger, *The Many Altars of Modernity: Toward a Paradigm for Religion in a Pluralist Age* (Boston: de Gruyter, 2014), 51. For an acute analysis of the fate of Jewish secularization theory, see Naomi Seidman, "Religion/Secularity," in *The Routledge Handbook of Contemporary Jewish Cultures*, ed. Laurence Roth and Nadia Valman (New York: Routledge, 2015), 151–61.

10. Susannah Heschel, "The Myth of Europe in America's Judaism," in *Writing a Modern Jewish History: Essays in Honor of Salo W. Baron*, ed. Barbara Kirshenblatt-Gimblett (New Haven, CT: Yale University Press, 2006), 96.

11. Will Herberg, *Judaism and Modern Man: An Interpretation of Jewish Religion* (Philadelphia: Jewish Publication Society, 1951). This encomium is featured on the cover of Herberg's book.

12. For some appreciations of Herberg, see Seymour Siegel, "Will Herberg (1902–1977): A Ba'al Teshuvah Who Became Theologian, Sociologist, Teacher," *American Jewish Year Book* 78 (1978): 529–37; and David G. Dalin, "Will Herberg's Path from Marxism to Judaism: A Case Study in the Transformation of Jewish Belief," in *The Americanization of the Jews*, ed. Robert M. Seltzer and Norman J. Cohen (New York: New York University Press, 1995), 119–32.

13. *Commentary* 42, no. 2 (1966): 71–160; *Commentary* 102, no. 5 (1996): 18–96.

14. This important series is published by Brill and edited by Hava Tirosh-Samuelson and Aaron W. Hughes. For an appreciation of this project and a discussion of who is included and who is left out, see Warren Zev Harvey, "The Versatility of Contemporary Jewish Philosophy," in *The Future of Jewish Philosophy*, ed. Hava Tirosh-Samuelson and Aaron W. Hughes (Leiden: Brill, 2018), 41–59.

15. Elliot N. Cosgrove, ed., *Jewish Theology In Our Time: A New Generation Explores the Foundations and Future of Jewish Belief* (Woodstock, VT: Jewish Lights, 2010).

16. For some perspectives on this question, see Leora Batnitzky, "Coming After: American Jewish Thought in Light of German Judaism," in *Jewish Philosophy: Perspectives and Retrospectives*, ed. Raphael Jospe and Dov Schwartz (Boston: Academic Studies Press, 2012), 20–32; Zachary J. Braiterman, "After Germany: An American Jewish Philosophical Manifesto," in *Jewish Philosophy for the Twenty-First Century: Personal Reflections*, ed. Hava Tirosh-Samuelson and Aaron

W. Hughes (Leiden: Brill, 2014), 42–60; Eugene Sheppard, "I Am A Memory Come Alive: Nahum Glatzer and the Legacy of German Jewish Thought in America," *Jewish Quarterly Review* 94, no.1 (2004): 123–48. This last article also provides insights into the works of one of the great anthologizers of Jewish thought, Nahum Glatzer.

17. See Shaul Magid, *American Post-Judaism: Identity and Renewal in a Postethnic Society* (Bloomington: Indiana University Press, 2013).

1 | God

Attempts to speak about God refer to that which lies beyond time and context, but they inevitably reveal much about their own times and contexts. As every generation strives to imagine the excellent, something of its self-understanding is exposed. Articulation of a God concept, or for that matter rejection of any such concept, reflects core political and cultural assumptions.

American forays into Jewish theology are no exception to this general rule. Some major figures in American Judaism have advanced a version of belief in God they themselves have regarded as unchanged from the faith of the ages. An acute expression of this approach can be found in the statement by Menachem Mendel Schneerson (1902–94): "Everyone agrees that it is a fundamental principle in our faith and in our Torah to be certain that the One on High is Omnipotent—and not only in the Seventh Heaven, but also in this material and physical world, including the United States of America."[1]

Throughout much of Jewish history, the "fundamental principle" of divine authority has been posited rather than explored or explained. In some American Jewish expositions of Jewish belief, this axiomatic approach, asserting God's existence and agency instead of pondering the meaning of that assertion, is evident. A good example comes from one of the most popular books about Judaism ever published. Herman Wouk's 1959 work *This Is My God* continues to be popular six decades after its publication. Despite its theocentric title, the book's section on God is five paragraphs in length, and God is mentioned in less than a fifth of the work's pages. As Wouk (1915–2019) himself comments, "Our religion assumes that God exists. . . ."[2] Often this assumption is not explored or questioned.

*Editors' notes appear in square brackets to distinguish them from notes in the original.

1. [Menachem M. Schneerson, "#89: When One Has Trust in the One on High, One Also Has Trust in One's Fellow Jews," extracts from a talk delivered 19 Kislev 5731 (December 17, 1970). https://www.chabad.org/therebbe/article_cdo/aid/2313698, accessed January 1, 2019.]

2. [Herman Wouk, *This Is My God* (New York: Doubleday, 1959), 86. For an insightful article on the influences that shaped Wouk and his thought, see Zev Eleff, "The Jewish

Part One is devoted to some expressions of American Jewish thought that have not settled for axiomatic assumptions but have asked: what do we mean when we speak of God? How, if at all, may we speak of God today?

Contemporary Jews express a wide range of opinions and apply a variety of prisms in their theological musings. Some engage in a vigorous defense of what they take to be normative, traditional approaches to Jewish belief. For a number of American Jewish thinkers, the concept of the covenant has proven particularly resonant, while others have explored the notion of God as process, either from a rationalist or a neomystical perspective. In response to this immanentist turn, a number of thinkers have spoken up for divine transcendence or divine personality, or both.

Feminism has had a profound impact on theological discourse. The image of God as healer has also attracted attention. A number of Jewish thinkers have considered God from an avowedly nontraditional perspective, and their voices also deserve attention. In addition, a number of biblical scholars have blurred the distinction between research and theology, while some activists have placed their concept of God at the heart of a vision for societal change.

The ten excerpts here are interconnected in various ways, but it may be helpful to consider them in three broad categories. First, Mordecai Kaplan, Abraham Joshua Heschel, and Hans Jonas set out explicit and contrasting theological manifestos. Kaplan's is rationalist and naturalist, as he offers an understanding of God congruent with and complementary to his worldview. Heschel's moves beyond the rational and provides a phenomenological description of the experience of God (most probably his own). Jonas challenges the doctrine of divine omnipotence.[3] The next three sources offer contrasting approaches to a concept prevalent in the 1960s: the death of God. Richard Rubenstein, Eliezer Berkovits, and Erich Fromm each relate to this notion from within a different network of religious commitments and intellectual proclivities. Rubenstein was strongly engaged with the postwar milieu in which "death of God" thinking flourished. He offered a Jewish response to this thinking, to some degree a Jewish version of it, while Berkovits rejected it robustly, arguing that it is inimical to Jewish conceptions

Center, Herman Wouk, and the Origins of Orthodox Triumphalism," in Zev Eleff, ed., *A Century at the Center: Orthodox Judaism and The Jewish Center* (New Milford, CT: Toby Press, 2018), 279–99.]

3. [For a highly popular and influential version of a similar theological position, see Harold S. Kushner, *When Bad Things Happen to Good People* (New York: Schocken, 1989).]

of God. Fromm offers a different perspective reflecting his stance of "non-theistic mysticism."

A third group of sources relates to the language about and imagery of God that ought to be employed. A debate about God language that rose to prominence in the 1980s is represented here by an excerpt from Marcia Falk and a direct rejoinder from Edward Greenstein. Sandra Lubarsky addresses these questions by combining insights from process theology and feminist thought, while Rebecca Alpert discusses issues of language, suggesting that the grammar of our discourse on God deserves attention. In doing so, she makes specific reference to the concept of "predicate theology" promulgated by the Conservative rabbi Harold Schulweis (1925–2014).

As a medieval poem asserts, many have described God, but not according to God's essence. It is rather something of the essence of the American Jewish experience that is highlighted in these excerpts: approaches to authority and agency, particularism and universalism, coherence and meaning.

Mordecai M. Kaplan, *The Future of the American Jew*

In the course of his long life, Mordecai Kaplan (1881–1983) contributed a new vocabulary and inspired a new denomination in American Jewish life. Arriving from Lithuania as a child, Kaplan was educated at the City College of New York and Columbia University and received rabbinical ordination from the Jewish Theological Seminary of America, as well as private Orthodox semicha (ordination). He was deeply influenced by contemporary intellectual currents before taking a position as an Orthodox rabbi in Manhattan. Resigning his position as rabbi of the Jewish Center of Manhattan, he established the Society for the Advancement of Judaism. He joined the faculty of the Jewish Theological Seminary in 1909 at the invitation of Solomon Schechter and taught at JTS for over fifty years, writing several books and countless articles. His impact on American Judaism was transformational.

Mordecai M. Kaplan, *The Future of the American Jew* (New York: Macmillan, 1949), 171–80.

The objective study of religion the world over has proved beyond a doubt that the belief in God originated neither in speculative reasoning nor in any supernatural revelation. *Gods have to be believed in before they can be beheld, imagined or proved to exist.* Had this fact been recognized centuries ago, thinkers would have been spared an immense amount of mental effort to prove the existence of God. All that effort apparently was in vain, since unbelievers seldom became believers as a result of logical arguments.

To find the root of men's belief in God we have to note how man's will to live progresses from blind instinct to highly articulate purpose. In all living beings that will to live manifests itself in various hungers or drives for sustenance, shelter, a mate, migration, etc. Man, however, possesses the mental capacities which enable him to be aware of ends and means, of whole and part, of self and not-self. Thus he has come to think in general and abstract terms. This heightened awareness augments his chances for life, and brings to the fore of his consciousness his entire struggle for existence.

By the same token that man becomes aware of himself as a person engaged in a struggle against dangers and difficulties, he also becomes cognizant of the help of a Power or powers to conquer obstacles. That awareness finds expression in ideas. What is most distinctive about himself as a person is termed "soul," and what is most distinctive about the Power or powers upon whom he depends is termed "God." The correlation between ideas concerning soul and ideas concerning God explains why, with the changes in our conception of human personality, we necessarily change our conception of God. As men, for example, learn to think of the soul as independent of the body, they also learn to conceive an over-soul, or super-ego, or God as independent of visible reality.

In time, man's capacity to generalize, which itself is a manifestation of the will to live, led him to conceive of God as a universal God. This is the correlative of man's will to live in its most generalized form, in the same way as the individual deities or divine beings are the correlatives of his specific hungers or wants.

Simultaneous with progress from the notion of "gods" to that of "God," and from specific independent urges to the whole of the will to live there has been an advance from *haphazard* attempts to *consciously directed* efforts to satisfy that will. Man becomes progressively aware of his goal, and of having to choose between more and less desirable objectives and between right and wrong methods of attainment. Thus emerges gradually an awareness of a generalized will not merely to live, but to live abundantly, that is with a maximum fullness. The philosophers designate such an objective as the ultimate good, or happiness. The theologians call it salvation. Thus, simultaneously with awareness of the generalized will to the ultimate good, to happiness, or to salvation, arises awareness of the generalized idea of God.

Both the will to live and the belief in God are phases of one vital process. The belief in God is not logically inferred from the will to live. It is the psychic manifestation of the will to live. We may state, therefore, that *belief in God is the belief in the existence of a Power conducive to salvation which is the fulfilment of human destiny*. We must remember, however, that grounds for belief are not derived from speculative reason, but directly from man's actual strivings for maximum life or salvation. The inference from the striving for happiness or salvation to the existence of God is not a logical, but a soterical inference (Gr. soterios = saving). The biological will to live implies the existence of conditions that are propitious to life. The will to live abundantly and achieve one's human destiny, likewise implies the existence of conditions that favor abundant life, or salvation. The taking for granted that such conditions exist is the basis of the religious conception of God.

The religious conception of God is thus not the conception of a first cause, or of an ordering principle in the universe, but of a Power predisposing man to his ultimate good, salvation or self-fulfillment.

Religion is thus man's conscious quest for salvation or the achievement of his human destiny. The quest itself, apart from its objective, is emotionally rewarding, in that it enables one to experience the whole of the life process as having permanent worth or holiness. To believe that life is worthwhile implies that life as a whole has a purpose, and that the universe is so conditioned as to fulfil that purpose. Purpose is used here not in the sense of some end capable of being grasped by the human mind, but as the antithesis of blind chance. It is a synonym for meaning. When we see a radio, we are sure it has a purpose or meaning, though we are completely ignorant of how it works, or of the principles which underlie its functioning. Analogous is the religious person's feeling about the universe. He is sure it is not a chance happening. He is even certain that, if all men will cooperate with the inherent nature of that universe, they will achieve salvation. It is this conviction that constitutes belief in God....

To experience life as worthwhile means to have faith in its power to overcome the evils that threaten to frustrate it—disease, poverty, strife, cruelty and death. That faith presumes that life, as we know it, by no means represents its totality. Indeed, what we behold is merely the agitated surface of the boundless deep of Being, whence will in time emerge that potential good which will transform the face of human existence. To base one's life on such confidence is to activate that potential good. The existence of that potential good is what man affirms not merely in thought, but in will, every time he looks to a superhuman power for the fulfillment of his human aims. On this he builds his faith that his ideals are not will-o'-the-wisps, but a divine light illuminating the path to fulfillment. Every religion is thus a complex of values, of beliefs and of practices which center in the idea of God. *Whatever a civilization values highly it views as, in some measure, a manifestation of God in human life....*

On the assumption that God is the Power predisposing mankind to salvation and that He operates through the conditions which are essential to salvation, we should select from among the present day social and cultural interests those which aim at salvation as understood nowadays, and base our religion upon them. Why continue practices that aimed at salvation as understood in ancient times?

The answer is that, as Jews, we feel impelled to maintain the continuity and growth of the Jewish people. There can be no ultimate good or salvation for us, either as individuals or as a group, unless we are permitted to express ourselves creatively as Jews. The conditions essential to our salvation must therefore *in-clude* those which enable us to experience continuity with the Jewish past, as well as make possible a Jewish future. That continuity cannot be maintained without actually reliving the ancient experience of the will to live abundantly. There is no other possible way of reliving that experience than by giving the ancient Jewish *sancta*[4] a new lease on life, which can be done by reinterpretation. Those elements in the traditional *sancta* which can still be proved to have an intrinsic connection with ultimate good or salvation, as we now conceive it, should be singled out and treated as social and mental requirements without which salvation is for us impossible.

Thus, for example, freedom or liberation from all manner of bondage, is the central theme in the celebration of the Passover festival. By observing that festival, the Jew remembers freedom as an indispensable condition of salvation, conceived in terms that are objective, this-worldly and, simultaneously, spiritual and ethical. On the basis of this reinterpretation, God comes to be believed in as the Power that brings about freedom and redemption from bondage. All institutions, laws and tendencies that help to free men should, therefore, be treated as *sancta*, or as media which reveal God's will and holiness.

4. [Kaplan uses the Latin term *sancta* to refer to the persons, events, texts, places, concepts, and actions sanctified by a particular civilization.]

Born in Poland, Abraham Joshua Heschel (1907–72), after living in Germany and receiving his doctorate at the University of Berlin, arrived in the United States at the beginning of the Second World War to teach at Hebrew Union College in Cincinnati. From 1945 he was a member of the faculty of the Jewish Theological Seminary. Descended from important Hasidic dynasties, he brought many Hasidic concepts into currency in postwar America. To some degree, he and Mordecai Kaplan can be seen as representing an American iteration of the long-standing tension between Lithuanian intellectualism and Hasidic piety. His many books and articles have been read and discussed more intensively than perhaps any other Jewish thinker in America, and his social activism is legendary.

Abraham Joshua Heschel, *Man Is Not Alone: A Philosophy of Religion*
(Philadelphia: The Jewish Publication Society of America, 1951), 76–78,
108–9, 128.

What gives birth to religion is not intellectual curiosity, but the fact and experience of our being asked. As long as we frame and ponder our own questions, we do not even know how to ask. We know too little to be able to inquire. Faith is not the product of search and endeavor, but the answer to a challenge which no one can forever ignore. It is ushered in not by a problem, but by an exclamation. Philosophy begins with man's question; *religion begins with God's question and man's answer.*

He who chooses a life of utmost striving for the utmost stake, the vital, matchless stake of God, feels at times as though the spirit of God rested upon his eyelids—close to his eyes and yet never seen. He who has realized that sun and stars and souls do not ramble in a vacuum will keep his heart in readiness for the hour when the world is entranced. For things are not mute: the stillness is full of demands, awaiting a soul to breathe in the mystery that all things exhale in their craving for communion. Out of the world comes a behest to instill into the air a rapturous song for God, to incarnate in stones a message of humble beauty, and to instill a prayer for goodness in the hearts of all men.

The world in which we live is a vast cage within a maze, high as our mind, wide as our power of will, long as our life span. Those who have never reached the rails or seen what is beyond the cage know of no freedom to dream of and are willing to rise and fight for civilizations that come and go and sink into the oblivion, an abyss which they will never fill.

In our technological age man could not conceive of the world as anything but material for his own fulfilment. He considered himself the sovereign of his destiny, capable of organizing the breeding of races, of adapting a philosophy to his transient needs and of creating a religion at will. He postulated the existence of a Power that would serve as a guarantee of his self-fulfillment, as if God were a henchman to cater to man's aspirations and help him draw the utmost out of life.

But even those who have knocked their heads against the rail of a cage and discovered that life is involved in conflicts which they cannot solve; that the drive of possessiveness, which fills streets, homes and hearts with its clamor and shrill, is constantly muffled by the irony of time; that our constructiveness is staved in by self-destructiveness—even they prefer to live on the sumptuous, dainty diet within the cage rather than look for an exit to the maze in order to search for freedom in the darkness of the undisclosed.

Others, however, who cannot stand it, despair. They have no power to spend on faith any more, no goal to strive for, no strength to seek a goal. But, then, a moment comes like a thunderbolt, in which a flash of the undisclosed rends our dark apathy asunder. It is full of overpowering brilliance, like a point in which all moments of life are focused or a thought which outweighs all thoughts ever conceived of. There is so much light in our cage, in our world, it is as if it were suspended amidst the stars. Apathy turns to splendor unawares. The ineffable has shuddered itself into the soul. It has entered our consciousness like a ray of light passing into a lake. Refraction of that penetrating ray brings about a turning in our mind: We are penetrated by His insight. We cannot think any more as if He were there and we here. He is both there and here. He is not a *being*, but *being in and beyond all beings*.

A tremor seizes our limbs; our nerves are struck, quiver like strings; our whole being bursts into shudders. But then a cry, wrested from our very core, fills the world around us, as if a mountain were suddenly about to place itself in front of us. It is one word: GOD. Not an emotion, a stir within us, but a power, a marvel beyond us, tearing the world apart. The word that means more than universe, more than eternity, holy, holy, holy; we cannot comprehend it. We only know it means infinitely more than we are able to echo. Staggered, embarrassed, we stammer and say: He, who is more than all there is who speaks through the ineffable, whose question is more than our mind can answer; He, to whom our life can be the spelling of an answer. . . .

God cannot be distilled to a well-defined idea. All concepts fade when applied to His essence. To the pious man knowledge of God is not a thought within his grasp, but a form of thinking in which he tries to comprehend all reality. It is the untold secret of the soil in which all knowledge becomes a seed of sense, a secret by which we live and which we never truly understand; a soil from which the roots of all values derive perpetual vitality. Over and against the split between man and nature, self and thought, time and timelessness, the pious man is able to sense the interweaving of all, the holding together of what is a part, the love that hovers over acts of kindness, mountains, flowers, which shine in their splendor as if looked at by God.

How do we identify the divine?

Divine is a message that discloses unity where we see diversity, that discloses peace when we are involved in discord. God is He who holds our fitful lives together, who reveals to us that which is empirically diverse in color, in interest, in creeds—races, classes, nations—is one in His eyes and one in essence.

God means: No one is ever alone; the essence of the temporal is the eternal; the moment in an image of eternity in an infinite mosaic. God means: *Togetherness of all beings in holy otherness.*

God means: What is beyond our soul is beyond our spirit; what is at the source of our selves is at the goal of our ways. He is the heart of all, eager to receive and eager to give.

When God becomes our form of thinking we begin to sense all men in one man, the whole world in a grain of sand, eternity in a moment. To worldly ethics one human being is less than two human beings, to the religious mind if a man has caused a single soul to perish, it is as though he had caused a whole world to perish, and if he has saved a single soul, it is as though he had saved a whole world.[5]

If in the afterglow of a religious insight I can see a way to gather up my scattered life, to unite what lies in strife; a way that is good for all men as it is for me —I will know it is His way. . . .

Thinking of God is made possible by His being the *subject* and by our being His *object*. To think of God is to expose ourselves to Him, to conceive ourselves

5. Mishnah Sanhedrin 4:5.

as a reflection of His reality. He cannot be limited to a thought. To think means to set aside or to separate an object from the thinking subject. But in setting Him apart, we gain an idea and lose Him. Since He is not away from us and we are not beyond Him, He can never become the mere object of our thought. As, in thinking about ourselves, the subject cannot be detached from the object, so in thinking of God the subject cannot be detached from the object. In thinking of Him, we realize that it is through Him that we think of Him. Thus, we must think of Him as the subject of all, as the life of our life, as the mind of our mind.

Hans Jonas, "The Concept of God After Auschwitz: A Jewish Voice"

As a student of philosophy in Germany, Hans Jonas (1903–93) studied under Edmund Husserl, Rudolf Bultmann, and Martin Heidegger, and alongside his lifelong friend Hannah Arendt. He moved to Canada in 1950, and from there to New York five years later. He taught at the New School for Social Research for over twenty years. His broad range of interests included Gnosticism, philosophical biology, and environmental ethics.

Hans Jonas, "The Concept of God after Auschwitz: A Jewish Voice," *Journal of Religion* 67, no. 1 (1987): 7–12.

Bound up with the concepts of a suffering and a becoming God is that of a *caring* God—a God not remote and detached and self-contained but involved with what he cares for. Whatever the "primordial" condition of the Godhead, he ceased to be self-contained once he let himself in for the existence of the world by creating such a world or letting it come to be. God's caring about his creatures, of course, is among the most familiar tenets of Jewish faith. But my myth stresses the less familiar aspect that this caring God is not a sorcerer who in the act of caring also provides the fulfillment of His concern: He has left something for other agents to do and thereby has made His care dependent on them. He is therefore also an endangered God, a God who runs a risk. Clearly that must be so, or else the world would be in a condition of permanent perfection. The fact that it is not bespeaks one of two things: that either the One God does not exist (though more than one may), or that the One has given to an agency other than Himself, though created by Him, a power and a right to act on his own and therewith a scope for at least codetermining that which is a concern of His. That is why I said that the caring God is not a sorcerer. Somehow he has, by an act of either inscrutable wisdom or love or whatever else the divine motive may have been, foregone the guaranteeing of his self-satisfaction by his own power, after he has first, by the act of creation itself, foregone being "all in all."

And therewith we come to what is perhaps the most critical point in our speculative, theological venture: This is not an omnipotent God. We argue indeed that, for the sake of our image of God and our whole relation to the divine, for the sake of any viable theology, we cannot uphold the time-honored (medieval) doctrine of absolute, unlimited divine power. Let me argue this first, on a purely logical plane, by pointing out the paradox in the idea of absolute power. The logical situation indeed is by no means that divine omnipotence is the rationally plausible and somehow self-recommending doctrine, while that of its limitation is wayward and in need of defense. Quite the opposite. From the very concept of power, it follows that omnipotence is a self-contradictory, self-destructive, indeed, senseless concept. The situation is similar to that of freedom in the human realm: Far from being where necessity ends, freedom consists of and lives in pitting itself against necessity. Separated from it, freedom loses its object and becomes as void as force without resistance. Absolute freedom would be empty freedom that cancels itself out. So, too, does empty power, and absolute, exclusive power would be just that. . . .

But besides this logical and ontological objection, there is a more theological, genuinely religious objection to the idea of absolute and unlimited divine omnipotence. We can have divine omnipotence together with divine goodness only at the price of complete divine inscrutability. Seeing the existence of evil in the world, we must sacrifice intelligibility in God to the combination of the other two attributes. Only a completely unintelligible God can be said to be absolutely good and absolutely powerful, yet tolerate the world as it is. Put more generally, the three attributes at stake—absolute goodness, absolute power, and intelligibility—stand in such a logical relationship to one another that the conjunction of any two of them excludes the third. The question then is, Which are truly integral to our concept of God, and which, being of lesser force, must give way to their superior claim? Now, surely, goodness is inalienable from the concept of God and not open to qualification. Intelligibility, conditional on both God's nature and man's capacity, is on the latter count indeed subject to qualification but on no account to complete elimination. The *Deus absconditus*, the hidden God (not to speak of an absurd God) is a profoundly un-Jewish conception. Our teaching, the Torah, rests on the premise and insists that we can understand God, not completely, to be sure, but something of Him—of His will, intentions, and even nature—because He has told us. There has been revelation, we have His commandments and His law, and He has directly communicated with some —His prophets—as His mouth for all men in the language of man and their times: refracted thus in this limiting medium but not veiled in dark mystery. A completely hidden God is not an acceptable concept by Jewish norms.

Richard Rubenstein was born in 1924. Educated at Hebrew Union College, the Jewish Theological Seminary, and Harvard University, he worked at B'nai Brith Hillel at the University of Pittsburgh before taking a position at Florida State University, where he taught for some twenty-five years. In the course of the 1960s, he became a leading Jewish theological voice and cultural commentator.

Richard L. Rubenstein, "The Symbols of Judaism and the Death of God," and "Death of God Theology and Judaism," in Richard L. Rubenstein, *After Auschwitz: Radical Theology and Contemporary Judaism* (Indianapolis: Bobbs-Merrill Educational Publishing, 1966), 237–39, 241.

Finally, there is the problem of the God after the death of God. The focus of the synagogue upon the decisive events and seasons of life gives us a clue to the meaning of God in our times. At one level, it is certainly possible to understand God as the primal ground of being out of which we arise and to which we return.[6] I believe such a God is inescapable in the time of the death of God. The God who is the ground of being is not the transcendent, theistic God of Jewish patriarchal monotheism. Though many still believe in that God, they do so ignoring questions of God and human freedom and God and human evil. For those who face these issues, the Father-God is a dead God. Even the existentialist leap of faith cannot resurrect this God after Auschwitz.

Nevertheless, after the death of the Father-God, God remains the central reality against which all partial realities can be measured. I should like to suggest that God can be understood meaningfully not only as ground of being but also as the *focus of ultimate concern*.[7] As such He is not the old theistic Father-God. Nor is He Reconstructionism's "power that makes for salvation in the world." He is the infinite measure against which we can see our own limited lives in proper perspective. Before God it is difficult for us to elevate the trivial to the central in our lives.

6. [The notion of God as the "ground of being" was particularly associated with the thought of the German-American Lutheran theologian Paul Tillich (1886–1965).]

7. ["Ultimate concern" is also a concept associated with Tillich.]

The old Hebraic understanding of the meaning of idolatry is important for an understanding of the meaning of God as the focus of ultimate concern. Idolatry is the confusion of a limited aspect of things with the ground of the totality. This is not the occasion to catalogue the idolatries of our time. That task has been well done by others. If an awareness of God as the ground of being does nothing more than enable us to refrain from endowing a partial and limited concern with the dignity and status reserved for what is of ultimate concern, it will have served the most important of all tasks. The ancient Hebrews regarded idolatry as a special form of enslavement. Nothing in our contemporary idolatries makes them less enslaving than their archaic counterparts. God can truly make us free.

We live in a culture which tends to stress what we can do rather than what we can become. A few examples will suffice to illustrate the encouragements to idolatry and self-deception with which our culture abounds. We are forever encouraged to deny the passing of time in our overestimation of the importance of both being and looking young. One of our greatest needs is to acknowledge our temporality and mortality without illusion. By so doing, we are not defeated by time. We establish the condition of our *human* mastery over it. As the focus of ultimate concern the timeless God reflects our seriousness before our human temporality.

Another decisive contemporary need is to learn how to dwell within our own bodies. That is not so easy as it may seem. Fewer capacities come harder to Americans than the capacity to dwell within their own bodies with grace, dignity, and gratification. We become caricatures of our human potentialities when we fail to acquire this wisdom. By coming to terms with the biological nature of the timetable of life, we experience an enormous liberation yet develop the capacity for equally great renunciations when necessary. In the presence of God, as the focus of ultimate concern, we need no deceptive myths of an immortal soul. We are finite. He is eternal. We shall perish. He remains ever the same. Before Him we confront our human nakedness with truth and honesty.

God as the focus of ultimate concern challenges us to be the only persons we realistically can be, our authentic, finite selves in all of the radical insecurity and potentiality the life of mortal man affords.

One cannot pray to such a God in the hope of achieving an I-Thou relationship.[8] Such a God is not a person over against man. If God is the ground of being,

8. [The notion of an I-Thou relationship was made popular by Martin Buber (1878–1965).]

He will not be found in the meeting of I and Thou but in self-discovery. That self-discovery is not necessarily introspective. The whole area of interpersonal relations is the matrix in which meaningful and insightful self-discovery can occur. Nor can the I-Thou relation between man and God be achieved through prayer. This does not do away with worship. It sets worship in proper perspective. Even Buber admits, in his discussion of the eclipse of God,[9] the contemporary failure of personal prayer. While prayer as address and dialogue has ceased to be meaningful, the burden of this paper has been to suggest some of the ways in which religious ritual has retained its significance. Ritual is more important today than prayer save as prayer is interwoven with ritual. Our prayers can no longer be attempts at dialogue with a personal God. They become aspirations shared in depth by the religious community. As aspiration there is hardly a prayer in the liturgy of Judaism which has lost its meaning or its power. Worship is the ultimate concern by the community before God, the focus of ultimate concern.

Paradoxically God as ground does everything and nothing. He does nothing in that He is not the motive or active power which brings us to personal self-discovery or to the community of shared experience. Yet He does everything because He shatters and makes transparent the patent unreality of every false and inauthentic standard. God, as the ultimate measure of human truth and human potentiality, calls upon each man to face both the limitations and the opportunities of his finite predicament without disguise, illusion or hope.

God stands before us no longer as the final censor but as the final reality before which and in terms of which all partial realities are to be measured.

The last paradox is that in the time of the death of God we have begun a voyage of discovery wherein we may, hopefully, find the true God.

9. [See, for example, Martin Buber, *Eclipse of God* (New York: Harper and Row, 1952).]

Eliezer Berkovits (1908–92) was born in Austria-Hungary. His Orthodox rabbinical studies were undertaken at (among other places) the Hildesheimer Seminary in Berlin, where he was ordained by Rabbi Yechiel Yaakov Weinberg. He completed his PhD at the University of Berlin. From 1934 through 1950, he served congregations in Berlin, Leeds, and Sydney. Berkovits came to Boston in 1950, then moved to Chicago where he served as Professor of Jewish Thought at the Hebrew Theological College for the bulk of his career. He emigrated to Israel in 1975. Berkovits wrote extensively on topics of Jewish law, as well as on Jewish theology.

Eliezer Berkovits, *Faith after the Holocaust* (New York: Ktav, 1973), 51–53, 65–66.

To maintain that the scientific interpretation of the universe renders the idea of a Creator unnecessary shows no sign of either philosophical or theological sophistication. It may be so or it may not be so, but one should not affirm it axiomatically, as is done by the radical theologians, without ever entering onto a significant discussion of the philosophical or theological issues involved in the assertion. Finally, that the absence of God, the lack of personal experience of His presence means the death of God, be it the death of faith in God or—as some would have it—God's death in a very real sense as an event happening in time, is a most superficial way of meeting the problem of the *deus absconditus* of metaphysics or of the *El Mistater*, the hiding God of the prophets of Israel.

We believe that the "radical theology" is neither a theology nor a philosophy. In its essence it is an attitude. Its thought content is a rationalization of the attitude....

What surprises a Jew most is, I believe, the realization that for the radical theologian modern man is God's competitor. God and man face each other as enemies. It is either God or man. The radical theologian does not only say that because of the scientific interpretation of the universe there is no need for a Creator, but he also adds that since man has no more need of God, he himself becomes the creator.[10] It is not only that man has come of age and accepts re-

10. William Hamilton and Thomas J. J. Altizer, *Radical Theology and the Death of God* (New York: The Bobbs-Merrill Co., 1966), 99.

sponsibility, but man may accept responsibility for his life, for the world, only now that God is dead.[11] Especially at this point the radical theologian leans heavily on Nietzsche and Camus. This relationship of competition to the death of God between God and man is again succinctly delineated in the words of Eliade when he says: "Man cannot be free until he kills the last God."[12] "Radical theology" implies—as its positive aspect—"the turning from the cloister to the world."[13] Strangely enough, only now that God has died in man's "existence" can man leave the cloister and turn to the world; only now, because he lost his God, can he live in the secular city in freedom and responsibility. We have mentioned earlier that some of the radical theologians speak of a new optimism of trusting man and the world. It is, however, noteworthy that for them optimism is a direct result of God's death. Thus, William Hamilton, for instance, maintains: "I am persuaded that the death of God made the new optimism possible."[14] This competitive relationship between God and man is utterly foreign to the Jewish mentality. That the scientific interpretation requires no God hypothesis may be right or wrong; it has been held by numerous Jews. However, the idea that the throne vacated by God really belongs to Man the Creator, is clearly not a logical thought but one aspect of modern man's "existential choice" of a profane existence. It is a choice which, I dare say, is existentially alien even for an atheistic Jew. The causal nexus between God's death and human responsibility is equally foreign to the Jew. Within Judaism, from the very beginning, it was God who called man to responsibility and entrusted the earth into his responsible safekeeping. Far from being able to "turn from the cloister to the world" as a result of God's death, it was God who never let the Jew turn to the cloister, but sent him into the world "to work it and to preserve it."[15] We may understand that it is possible for a man

11. Harvey Cox, *The Secular City* (New York: Macmillan, 1966), 71–72.

12. [This is a slightly altered form of a statement by Mircea Eliade (1907–86), an eminent Romanian-American scholar of religion. See Mircea Eliade, *The Sacred and the Profane* (New York: Harcourt, Brace, and World, 1959), 203.]

13. [Berkovits refers in a note to William Hamilton, "The Death of God Theologies Today," in Thomas J. J. Altizer and William Hamilton, *Radical Theology and the Death of God* (Indianapolis: Bobbs-Merrill, 1966), 36. This expression can be found in Dietrich Bonhoeffer's description of Martin Luther. See Dietrich Bonhoeffer, *The Cost of Discipleship* (New York: Macmillan, 1956), 51.]

14. [William Hamilton, "The New Optimism: From Prufrock to Ringo," in Altizer and Hamilton, *Radical Theology*, 165. William Hughes Hamilton III (1924–2012) was a leading proponent of "death of God" theology.]

15. [The reference here is to Genesis 2:15.]

to be optimistic about life and the world even without faith in God, but what kind of a distortion of the mind would require the death of God as the foundation of optimism? In Judaism, God is the only cause of optimism. . . .

Needless to say, the aspect of radical theology that comes closest to our specifically Jewish preoccupations is the absence of God. It is a problem of the post-Auschwitz generation. The El Mistater, the hiding God, is a Jewish concept; but the idea alone is far from being an answer to God's silence in the face of the agony of the concentration camps and the crematoria. Calling him the El Mistater, Isaiah says of God: "Verily thou art a God that hidest Thyself, God of Israel, Saviour."[16] In Christianity, because he is the savior, he cannot be a hiding God. But Isaiah calls the hiding God, Savior. We must know him even in his hiddenness. The El Mistater, in his very hiding, is Savior. Will our generation ever be able to behold in God's silence at Auschwitz the saving silence of the Redeemer of Israel? We are still far removed from an understanding of God's absence in our generation, in our history. And yet, what we make of his absence will ultimately determine the quality of our Judaism for generations to come, if not for all time.

In our search for the Redeemer in his very hiddenness, we shall have to weave into one great pattern of Jewish existence three decisive factors of our condition: the hurban, the destruction of European Jewry; the theological disarray within Christianity as revealed by radical theology; the rise of the state of Israel, the antithesis to the hurban. The moment in history at which we have almost lost our hold of this world completely, the moment at which the Jew had been almost completely eliminated from the City of Man, is also the moment at which the God of Christianity has come to grieve over the very same city from which he is being banished, as through the ages his followers were banishing the Jew. At this very moment in history, divine providence has placed in the hands of the Jew, in the form of the state of Israel, the secular city of man—for us to turn it into a City of God on this earth. Quite clearly, we have been called. How shall we, the post-Auschwitz generation, respond to the call of the—after all—not-so-silent God of Israel?

16. [Isaiah 45:15.]

German-born Erich Fromm (1900–1980) earned his PhD in sociology from the University of Heidelberg in 1922 and then trained as a psychoanalyst in Heidelberg. He came to the United States in 1934, becoming a prominent psychoanalyst who practiced and taught in a wide variety of frameworks in New York. Fromm was a cofounder of the William Allison White Institute and earned international fame for his writings in a vast array of disciplines. He spent his later years in Mexico and Switzerland.

Erich Fromm, *You Shall Be as Gods: A Radical Interpretation of the Old Testament and Its Tradition* (New York: Holt, Rinehart, and Winston, 1966), 225–29.

I have tried to show the development of the concept of God and man within the Old Testament and the post-biblical Jewish tradition. We have seen that it begins with an authoritarian God and an obedient man, but even in this authoritarian structure the seeds of freedom and independence are already to be found. From the very beginning God is to be obeyed precisely in order to prevent men from obeying idols. The worship of the one God is the negation of the worship of men and things.

The development of biblical and post-biblical ideas represents the growth of this seed. God, the authoritarian ruler, becomes God the constitutional monarch, who is himself bound by the principles he has announced. The anthropomorphically described God becomes a nameless God, and eventually a God of whom no essential attribute can be predicated. Man, the obedient servant, becomes the free man, who makes his own history, free from God's interference and guided only by the prophetic message, which he can either accept or reject.

As I have pointed out, however, there were limits to which man's freedom from God could be conceptualized: the same limits exist with regard to the possibility of discarding the very concept of God. They are natural to a religion which wishes to provide formulations of a unifying principle and symbol by which to "cement" its structure and hold its believers together. Hence, the Jewish religion could not take the last logical step, to give up "God" and to establish a concept of man as a being who is alone in the world, but who can feel at home in it if he achieves union with his fellow man and with nature.

I have tried to show that the God-concept is only "the finger that points to the moon."[17] This moon is not outside of ourselves but is the human reality behind the words: what we call the *religious attitude* is an x that is expressible only in poetic and visual symbols. This x experience has been articulated in various concepts which have varied in accordance with the social organization of a particular cultural period. In the Near East, x was expressed in the concept of a supreme tribal chief, or king, and thus "god" became the supreme concept of Judaism, Christianity, and Islam, which were rooted in the social structures of that area. In India, Buddhism could express x in different forms, so that no concept of God as a supreme ruler was necessary.

However, inasmuch as both believers and unbelievers strive for the same aim —the liberation and awakening of man—they both can appreciate, each in his own way, that love impels us to understand the other better than he understands himself. Thus, those who believe in God will think that the nonbelieving humanist is in error, as far his thought concepts are concerned, and vice versa. But both will know that they are united in their common goal, which can be discovered more from their actions than from their concepts. Above all, they will be united by their common fight against idolatry.

The Idolators, too, are to be found among both believers and nonbelievers. Such believers have made God into an idol, an omniscient, omnipotent power allied with those who have power on this earth. Similarly, there are unbelievers who do not accept God, but worship other idols (which are also those of many believers): the sovereign state, the flag, the race, material production and efficiency, political leaders, or themselves.

Those, however, who worship God in an unalienated fashion, and those who strive for the same goal in purely human terms, recognize that thought-concepts are secondary to the human reality behind the thought. . . .

Anyone, believer or not, who has experienced the value x as the supreme value and tries to realize it in his life, cannot help recognizing that most men in industrial society, in spite of their protestations, are not striving for this value. These are anxious, vacuous, and isolated consumers, bored with life and com-

17. [In some Buddhist traditions, the Buddha distinguished between the finger pointing to the moon and the moon itself. The finger in this parable refers to words and concepts, which can do no more than indicate ultimate reality.]

pensating for their chronic depression by compulsive consumption. Ever more attracted to things and gadgets than to life and growth, they are men whose aim is to *have* much and to *use* much, not to *be* much.

This whole book touches upon a question which has been given increasing attention in the last few years: Is God dead? The question should be divided in its two aspects: Is the *concept* of God dead or is the *experience* to which the concept points, and the supreme *value* which it expresses, dead?

In the first case one might formulate the question by asking: is Aristotle dead? This is because it is largely due to the Aristotelian influence that God as a thought-concept became so important and "theology" arose. As far as the God-concept is concerned, we must also ask whether we should continue to use a term which can be understood only in terms of its social-cultural roots: the Near Eastern cultures, with their authoritarian tribal chiefs and omnipotent kings; and later medieval feudalism and absolute monarchies. For the contemporary world, which is no longer guided by Aristotle's systematic thought and by the idea of kingship, the God-concept has lost its philosophical and its social basis.[18]

On the other hand, if what we mean to ask is whether the *experience* is dead, then instead of asking whether God is dead, we might better raise the question whether *man is dead*. This seems to be the central problem of man in twentieth-century industrial society. He is in danger of becoming a thing, of being more and more alienated, of losing sight of the real problems of human existence and of no longer being interested in the answers to these problems. If man continues in this direction, he will himself be dead, and the problem of God, as a concept or as a poetic symbol of the highest value, will not be a problem any more.

The central issue today is to recognize this danger and to strive for conditions which will help to bring man to life again. These conditions lie in the realm of fundamental changes in the socio-economic structure of industrialized society (both of capitalist and socialist societies) and of a renaissance of humanism that focuses on the reality of experienced values rather than on the reality of concepts and words. In the West, this renaissance of humanism is occurring today among adherents of Catholicism, Protestantism, and Judaism, as well as Marxist Socialism. It is a reaction to the two-toed threat which mankind faces today: that

18. The atheistic position prevalent in the nineteenth century suffers from the same bias as the theistic position, that of making the *concept* of God the main issue rather than the values which it symbolizes. Atheism was essentially a declaration of independence from the principle of the supreme ruler rather than an answer to the spiritual problem of man.

of nuclear extinction and that of the transformation of men into appendices of machines. If the spirit and hopes of the Prophets are to prevail, it will depend on the strength and vitality of this new humanism. For the nontheistic humanists a further question arises: What could take the place of religion in a world in which the concept of God may be dead but in which the experiential reality behind it must live?

Marcia Falk, "Notes on Composing New Blessings: Toward a Feminist-Jewish Reconstruction of Prayer"

Marcia Falk was born in 1946. A graduate of Brandeis University who received her PhD at Stanford University, Falk is a poet, liturgist, painter, and translator. She has taught in a wide variety of academic contexts, including Stanford and the Claremont Colleges. Falk is also a highly popular public figure and lecturer. Her deep engagement with English, Yiddish, and Hebrew poetry, as well as Jewish liturgy, has placed her at the heart of contemporary Jewish feminist discourse.

Marcia Falk, "Notes on Composing New Blessings: Toward a Feminist-Jewish Reconstruction of Prayer," *Reconstructionist* 53, no. 3 (1987): 10–12.

I was quite young—maybe four years old—the first time I was told that God was neither male nor female, that *he* had no body at all. *He* was beyond the limitations of gender. This was a bewildering concept that I *thought* I understood. But at the same time, I was being presented with an image implicit in the pronoun *he* and depicted in nouns such as *lord, father, master,* and *king.* Here was a verbal picture that was entirely genderful, entirely male, and this *picture* had far more impact than the *concept* of God's genderlessness.

How was this image impressed upon me? Mainly in two ways: through stories and through prayers. In Bible stories and in midrash, God was a character always referred to as *he,* no matter what God was doing. Of course, most of the time God was behaving much the way men did; but even when being motherly, or otherwise acting like a woman, God was always *he.* The implication was clear; *he* was big enough to play a feminine role on occasion.

In prayer, it was much the same: God may have had a few feminine characteristics, but he was *really* a male. And prayer was even more effective than story in impressing God's personality on me. Through story, God came dramatically alive, but through prayer, he became an intimate part of my life.

As a child praying, I never envisioned a female God; that was unthinkable. Which is to say, I did not *feel* my own likeness to God's image, even though I was taught that I was created in it. The image of God that was with me all through childhood and adolescence was never that of a woman, not even that of a half-man/half-woman, certainly not that of a neuter (what would an image of a neuter person be?), but exclusively that of a man. I would not have said, in so many words, "God is a man," because I knew that this was *conceptually* incorrect: Jews did not believe this. But I talked to him as though he were, as the Hebrew liturgy depicted him, which became the way *I* pictured him. God was an extremely knowledgeable, very intelligent old man—a genius, in fact. Of course, he was multilingual, but as he was particularly fond of being spoken to in Hebrew, I made a point of becoming conversant in his language. . . .

I struggled hard with prayer to try to effect a meaningful relationship with this omniscient, omnipotent Other. Regularly I rehearsed the performance language of the Hebrew liturgy, so that its images became first familiar, then automatic, and finally indelibly impressed on my tongue. Through this liturgy I learned that the real *other*, in all senses, was me: it was not just that God was God and I was only human; it was clear that maleness was primary and femaleness, secondary.

What I did not realize at the time was that, through my efforts to relate to God, I was also working out and practicing my relationship to authority *in the world*. At that stage of my life, I hardly wondered that rabbis were men, that rulers and people of great importance were men. Though not God, they were surely more like him than I, or any female, could ever be. The male God legitimated men's power.

And yet, there was much in the status quo that I did question at that stage, and the tradition itself encouraged me to do so—much as it taught me not just to read texts but to engage and debate with them. Indeed, although it posited a single absolute authority in God, Judaism also trained me to be suspicious of single-minded approaches to truth, and to appreciate the multiplicity of possibilities inherent in the interpretive process.

Most importantly perhaps, my earliest conception of justice came from traditional Jewish teachings, and the Jewish commitment to *pursue justice* inspired me deeply. So too today, this commitment continues to inspire and inform my work and my life, and to guide the way toward wholeness though the creation of a feminist Judaism. . . .

Recognizing the enormous power of God-talk to educate and shape our lives, feminist Jews in our time are taking back the power of naming. We have begun to address divinity in our own voices, using language that reflects our own experiences. We do this because we take theology seriously, and we want to affirm ourselves back into the place from which, we deeply intuit, we have been erased.

We have begun with relatively small amendments, such as introducing the pronoun *she* to refer to divinity. With this change, we are beginning to uproot the *he* that has been so deeply implanted in us—the all-pervasive *he* that blocks our attempts to read ourselves, in any satisfying way, into the theological relationship. We are choosing to redeem that forgotten half of the all-inclusive monotheistic divinity.

Yet when we do so, we are frequently accused of the deeply threatening heresy of paganism. From a purely rational viewpoint, the reaction is ridiculous. If God is not really male, why should it matter if we call God *she*? Clearly, it is not the inclusive One-God that is being threatened. The ultimacy of an exclusively male God has come into question, and his defenders are ready to attack.

This is a crucial point, for nothing less than monotheism, Judaism's original raison d'etre, is at stake. So let us think carefully: What is it that we are affirming with a monotheistic creed? I think that monotheism means that, with all our differences, I am more like you than unlike you; we share the same source, and one principle of justice must govern us equally. Monotheism means that if we are all created in the image of divinity, the images with which we point towards divinity must reflect us all.

But what *single* image can do this? All images are necessarily partial. *Man* is no less partial than *woman*, as clearly as *white* is no less partial than *black*. The authentic expression of an authentic monotheism, then, is not a singularity of image but an embracing *unity* of a *multiplicity of images*—as many as are needed to express and reflect the diversity of our individual lives. Indeed, much more than a feminine pronoun is needed; we must seek out a wide range of verbal imagery with which to convey our visions.

The search for theological imagery is a journey whose destinations are rarely apparent at the outset. As many feminists have discovered, it is not merely a matter of changing male images to seemingly equivalent female ones. The relatively simple (though still courageous) act of feminizing the male God has proved, to many of us, to be inadequate and often absurd. For a feminized patriarchal image is still patriarchal, though now in transvestite masquerade.

The process has been instructive, however, in clarifying our theological concerns. In transforming the king into a queen, for example, we realize that images of domination are not what we wish to embrace. We find instead that our search for what is authoritative leads us to explore more deeply what is just, and that the results of these explorations are not well represented by images of a monarch, either male or female.

And so we find we must create new images to convey our visions, and to do so we must be patient, for images will not be called into being by sheer acts of will alone. Rather, we learn what artists know well: that authentic images rise from our unconscious as gifts; that out of our living, from our whole, engaged selves, with the support of our communities, the images that serve us will emerge. We must trust the journey.

There are no shortcuts. The few female images already available in the tradition do not in themselves provide an adequate solution. The much-touted Shekhinah,[19] used to placate uppity Jewish women these days (as in, "The tradition *has* a feminine image of God, what more do you want?"), will not suffice.

The Shekhinah was not originally a female image; it did not become so until kabbalistic times. And when it becomes explicitly associated with the female, it did not empower women, especially not in kabbalistic thought, where male and female were hierarchically polarized.

Nor has the Shekhinah fared much better in our century. I, for one, cannot think of the Shekhinah without recalling her burning tears as they fell on the young poet Bialik's *Gemara* page.[20] In Bialik's poem, the Shekhinah was a pitiful mama bird with a broken wing, invoked to portray the frailty of Jewish tradition in Bialik's time.

Not that tears are not valid. Not that I don't want my images of divinity to include solitude and suffering. These are indeed important aspects of our experience that need expression in our theology. But should images of isolation and vulnerability alone be identified as the fundamental expression of God's "female side"? Do we wish to divide experience along these classically sexist lines?

Sad as it is, I cannot help but feel that, far from redeeming women, the image of the Shekhinah has until now supported the male-centered vision. In Jewish tradition, the Shekhinah has never been on an equal footing with the mighty *Kadosh Barukh Hu*, the "Holy-One-Blessed-Be-He," her creator, her master, her

19. [The word *Shekhinah* is a feminine noun from a root implying presence. From the Second Temple period it is used in a variety of contexts to refer to the divine presence, in expressions like "to be gathered under the wings of the Shekhinah," usually in reference to conversion to Judaism. In later Jewish esoteric literature this term comes to relate to the tenth divine emanation, and its feminine aspects are emphasized.]

20. [The reference here is to H. N. Bialik's 1902 Hebrew poem "Levadi," in which the image of the broken-winged Shekhinah is employed. She has been abandoned by all those who have left religion in favor of science and modernity, and her tears fall on the page of Talmud that Bialik, with all his ambivalence, still has open before him.]

groom, the ultimate reality of which she is only an emanation. And while I like the name itself—Shekhinah, from the Hebrew root meaning "to dwell"—I would like to see in-dwelling, or immanence, portrayed in ways that are not secondary to transcendence.

So too, I would like to see autonomous female images, not ones that imply the essential otherness of women. *In the name of monotheism*, for the sake of inclusive unity, I would like to see our God-talk articulate mutually supportive relationships between female and male, between immanence and transcendence, between our lives and the rest of life on the planet. In the end, it comes down to this: What I would like to see, I must help bring into being.[21]

21. [Falk, in 1996, fulfilled this commitment by composing and publishing a pathbreaking Jewish feminist liturgy, *The Book of Blessings*, with Beacon Press.]

Edward Greenstein was born in 1949. A graduate of the joint undergraduate Jewish Theological Seminary–Columbia University program, he received his doctorate from Columbia. Greenstein taught Bible at the Jewish Theological Seminary for twenty years until 1996, when he moved to Israel to take a position as Professor of Bible at Tel Aviv University. In 2006 Greenstein moved to Bar-Ilan University, where he currently holds the title of professor emeritus of Bible.

Edward L. Greenstein, "'To You Do I Call': A Critique of Impersonal Prayer,"
Reconstructionist 53, no.7 (1988): 13–16.

The God of the Torah subsumes all other gods. Lest we freeze God in our minds as any one of the false deities, a single persona, the Torah forbids us to fix God in any plastic image.... The siddur, however, has canonized a wide variety but finite number of verbal images of the God we worship. It is hardly news that, as in the Bible, virtually all images of God in the siddur are male.[22] Even relatively recent and progressive prayer books such as the present Reconstructionist edition[23] and the Conservative *Siddur Sim Shalom*[24] formulate the deity in exclusively masculine terms.

In a recent essay in these pages (December 1987), Marcia Falk has put her finger on the serious theological problems that stem from the masculine orientation of nearly all conventional liturgy. First, the exclusion or belittling of women in the prayer community. Men find male images that affirm them; women don't. As Judith Plaskow has put it: "The absence of female metaphors for God witnesses to and perpetuates the devaluation of femaleness in the Jewish tradition."[25]

22. See Ellen Umansky, "(Re)Imaging the Divine," *Response* 41–42 (Fall–Winter 1982): 111.

23. See Rebecca Trachtenberg Alpert, "The Reconstructionist Approach to Prayer: Some Questions and Answers," *Response* 41–42 (Fall–Winter 1982): 130.

24. See Paula E. Hyman, "Feminism in the Conservative Movement," in *The Seminary at 100*, edited by Nina Beth Cardin and David Wolf Silverman (New York: The Rabbinical Assembly and the Jewish Theological Seminary, 1987), 376.

25. Judith Plaskow, "God: Some Feminist Questions," *Sh'ma* 17.325 (9 January 1987): 39.

The second pernicious consequence of male-slanted God language in the siddur, even from a traditional perspective, is that it reinforces the idolatrous notion that not only is God sometimes male-like, but that God is always male. Such a result, as Falk explains, threatens the very essence of monotheism. It freezes the gender aspect of God. . . .

Many of us sympathetic both to monotheism and religious egalitarianism would, like Falk, want to correct the current liturgy. Few, however, have devised a way to do it. Arthur Green has proposed that we select from our Jewish sources feminine terms and images, such as the more immanent *Shekhinah* (Presence of God) or the more abstract *Elohut* (Divinity), that would enrich our traditional monotheism.[26] Both these concept-terms resonate in Jewish tradition. They are identifiably Jewish and theological, and that is what lends them authenticity within a Jewish liturgical context.

Falk has chosen a different path. She has sought to avoid gender-biased God language by discarding personal, anthropomorphic imagery altogether. She has replaced human-like projections of God with thing-like metaphors. Instead of blessing "the One who has bread come out of the land" she calls on us to "bless the source of life that brings forth bread from the earth." More tellingly, instead of acknowledging God as the source of our nourishment, as we do in *Birkat ha-Mazon*,[27] she invokes the inanimate land itself: "May we conserve the earth that it may sustain us *(vehi tekayemenu)*" [my emphasis].

Falk has soundly criticized an idolatrous monotheism, but she has endorsed in its place an impersonal pantheism. In struggling with a linguistic issue, albeit one with moral and theological ramifications, Falk has abandoned the monotheistic God. She has bypassed God and left the domain of theology altogether.

From what I have seen in print and from what she has shown me in handouts, Falk's *berakhot* (blessings) either address a feminine "source [water-spring] of life" or eschew any mention of deity. She talks about "Divinity," but she does not relate directly to it, as an I to a Thou. In Falk's *berakhot* we are called upon to bless "the source of life" or some other divine image. In none of her formulas is God actually addressed. Attempting to avoid the second person, which in Hebrew must denote either male or female, Falk relates us to an inanimate third person —an impersonal—reference.

26. Arthur Green, "Keeping Feminist Creativity Jewish," *Sh'ma* 16.305 (10 January 1986): 33–35.

27. [The traditional blessing after meals.]

Falk's compositions are at most invitations to prayer, preludes to prayer. They are simply not prayer. Prayer to be prayer must relate to God personally, in direct address. To pray in any meaningful sense one must say "You". . . .

But in rejecting God's maleness, Falk has rejected God's personness. To her God is not, or need not be, a Thou. As she has revealingly written: "Our right [is] not just to have our foremothers included in the prayers, but to have their images, *our* images, reflected in the God to whom (or *to which*) we pray."[28] Her God has become an It. Recalling the citation from Buber, the reduction of our relationship to God to a subhuman relationship demeans and diminishes God. In this respect, Falk's liturgy, in which God may be spoken about as an It, is in the literal sense of the phrase a *ḥillul shem ha-Shem* ("profanation of the name of God").

28. Falk, "Feminist Prayer," *Sh'ma* (9 January 1987), p. 38. My emphasis.

9

Sandra B. Lubarsky, "Reconstructing Divine Power"

Sandra Lubarsky (born 1954) is a graduate of Pomona College who earned her doctorate in process theology at the Claremont Graduate School. She taught for many years at Northern Arizona University and currently chairs the Department of Sustainable Development at Appalachian State University. Lubarsky has written on Jewish interreligious dialogue with other traditions and edited a major work on the implications of process theology for Jewish thought.

Sandra B. Lubarsky, "Reconstructing Divine Power: Post-Holocaust Jewish Theology, Feminism, and Process Philosophy," in *Women and Gender in Jewish Philosophy*, ed. Hava Tirosh-Samuelson (Bloomington and Indianapolis: Indiana University Press, 2004), 308–11.

How, then, does God act in a world that is constituted by beings with some degree of self-determination, in which heightened sensitivity and complexity carry the possibility of both increased good and evil and in which God, therefore, is metaphysically constrained? "God's role," Whitehead writes, "is not the combat of productive force with productive force. It lies in the patient operation of the overpowering rationality of his conceptual harmonization."[29] In a world in which all creatures have the two-fold powers of self-determination and efficient causation, God does not have either omnipotent or coercive power. But neither is God helpless. God has persuasive power over *all* things and, in fact, this kind of power is unlimited. *Persuasion is power,* but it is power exercised in response to the integrity of other beings. Its manifestation is felt, but is not necessarily physically visible. For it is a kind of power that relies on the openness of individuals and acts internally. To speak of power in this way presumes a world that is not conceived as mechanical, materialistic, or deterministic, that is a world in which power can only be external and coercive. Rather, it is to think of the world as home to real subjectivity and freedom; in this kind of world, power is not control over but the capacity to influence the decisions of another. If human beings

29. Alfred North Whitehead, *Process and Reality* [1929] (New York: Free Press, 1978), 346.

are in some way free and hence have some amount of power, then God works in a complicated world of relationships of power. And since process thinkers hold that it is not only human beings who have freedom and power, but that power and freedom are characteristics of the entire system of life, God is active in a world that is deeply complex. At every moment, God intervenes for good in the world, but at every moment God encounters the power that defines free and responsible creatures. Evil happens not because God allows it to happen, but because of the choices that are made by other free creatures who freely choose to ignore or oppose God's will.....

At the heart of Judaism is a divine-human partnership through which value and meaning become intimately known. The covenant is both a relationship of asymmetrical power in which God is in all ways understood as superior, and yet in which there exists a partnership. It is a relationship entered into by free subjects who regard each other as co-committed to an interpersonal relationship of trust, responsibility, and shared expectations. Within these parameters, what kind of power makes sense? Where there is both an extreme power differential and yet the requirement of mutuality, what kind of power is involved?

Clearly, coercive power violates covenantal mutuality. Though there is biblical affirmation of such power, there are important biblical, rabbinic, and kabbalistic renderings of divine power that point in a different direction, toward the quiet, hidden work of non-violent responsiveness. When the rabbis of the post–Second Temple period reshaped Judaism, they did so in response to the failure of their military strength. They created a Judaism that could survive without political power and they remade their image of God within this new context. The God who is in exile with the Jewish people is a God who rejoices in a different kind of mastery: the mastery of texts, of mitzvoth, and of prayer. . . .

Post-Holocaust Jews face a situation akin to that of the rabbis who survived the destruction of 70 C.E. Both process philosophy and feminist thought can contribute to that part of the rabbinic tradition which recognized the need for a reconstruction of divine power and human power, of the way God acts in the world and the way humans ought to act. What the rabbis came to understand —though they held this insight in tension with the tradition of dominating power—and what feminists and process thinkers have since affirmed—is that it is persuasive agency that empowers most fully. And the most powerful form of this kind of agency is love—love that encourages both the self-determination and the continuity of all beings. When God's power is conceived of as persuasive power, the language of love is given philosophical support. Bringing a process philosophical understanding of power and a feminist critique of patriarchal forms of power to bear on Jewish thought can lead to a more adequate way of imaging God's steadfast love in a post-Holocaust world.

Theological models of divine silence and invisibility continue to promote the very patterns of power they mean to condemn. Eliezer Berkovits and Irving Greenberg both oppose divine coercive omnipotence because it devalues human life. Yet divine silence in the form of passivity or hiddenness also devalues human life—as well as divine life—for God is denied significant participation in it. To exist and not to be recognized, to have one's power denied or trivialized, to be called to suffer but to lack the ability to prevent suffering: these are characteristics that have unjustly marked women's lives. Women have risen up against these conditions now recognized as the outcome of degrading human relationships. Heeding women's experience, what is to be gained by a model of divine powerlessness that promotes the very corruptions women have rejected?

Theological models of powerlessness are built on a patriarchal understanding of power. Feminist critiques have exposed such an understanding of power to be inadequate. All too often, such power leads to abuse. In response, feminist thinkers have proposed a re-conception of power as relational, non-competitive, and ideally, non-coercive. The feminist critique of power is supported by a process metaphysics in which power characterizes all of life. Feminist alternatives to patriarchal power and process claims about the structure of reality have much to contribute to Jewish theologians who are searching for alternative ways to understand God's power and activity in the world. They offer ways to conceive of God as powerful without being coercive and as active in the world without overwhelming human freedom. In so doing, these alternatives offer an image of God that may in fact be deserving of *imitatio dei*.[30]

---

30. [The imitation of God, a recurrent theme in ancient and medieval philosophy.]

10

Rebecca Alpert, "Location, Location, Location: Toward a Theology of Prepositions"

Rebecca Alpert (born 1950) received her PhD at Temple University, as well as rabbinical ordination from the Reconstructionist Rabbinical College. She has written major works on Jewish Reconstructionist thought as well as Jewish feminism. She served for many years as a professor in the departments of religion and women's studies at Temple.

Rebecca Alpert, "Location, Location, Location: Toward a Theology of Prepositions," in *Imagining the Jewish God*, ed. Leonard Kaplan and Ken Koltun-Fromm (Lanham: Lexington Books, 2016), 295–96.

The most sophisticated use of grammatical construction is the predicate theology of Harold Schulweis. Schulweis wants to take the implications of Mordecai Kaplan's naturalist theology one step further. Schulweis agrees with Kaplan that seeing God as an omniscient and omnipotent force in the universe or a personal God who rewards and punishes compromises God's goodness and cannot resolve the problem of evil. But Schulweis questions Kaplan's definition of God as the power that makes for salvation. Because that perspective views God as a subject (noun), he argues, it does not sufficiently deal with the problem of God as an actor in a post-Holocaust world, where the Power to make for salvation was absent, or as Buber suggests, in eclipse. A post-Holocaust theology, Schulweis argues, must abandon notions of God as a subject, even one as abstract as a Power or Force. Rather, we must turn the sentence around and put our energies into what he calls predicate theology: doing and being "godly." Making predicates the focus of our theology means rather than saying God is a Power, or God is Love, we should put our energies into acting lovingly and powerfully —"mercy, caring, peace, and justice are godly" (123). We also find godliness in "creativity, truth, compassion" (131).

As part of his description of how predicate theology works, Schulweis noted: "the key proposition in predicate theology is not 'in' or 'beyond' but 'with'" (139). This notion struck me as important: enough to form the basis of my own theological grammar. Perhaps the best way to understand theological concepts is not as nouns or pronouns, verbs or adjectives, subjects or predicates, but through which preposition was "key" to each theological understanding.[31]

Each theological approach is, like predicate theology, dependent on a unique preposition for its expression. Abstract metaphysical approaches to theology see God as "beyond" or "above," "outside" or "over." In a variation on that theme, the God of the deist comes "before." Those with more personal approaches to God as Friend (feminist theologian Judith Plaskow comes to mind here) imagine God as "near" or "close to" or "alongside." Immanentist theologians may also connect to God with prepositions like "in." The transnaturalist will find God "through." Or God may be "among" or "together with" us as Schulweis imagines, or as Buber suggests the connection "between" I and Thou. Personal theologies may also see God as operating "for" or "on behalf of" individuals, the Jewish people, humanity or the entire planet. In these perspectives, "to" and "from"—the relationship with God, matters. Each of these prepositions tells us more about how a theologian perceives God's work in the world than the tomes that have been written about Jewish theology.

Prepositional theology also leaves room for two other approaches not often considered. The Jewish secularist will be "without" God, and the atheist, "against" God. I consider these positions theological because they take a stance on where God is or is not found. These perspectives truly need to be taken into account, as at least half of those who currently identify as Jewish will find resonance with these views "of"/approaches "to" (or "away from") God. And being "against" God is a stance that was certainly taken by Abraham, Jonah, and later rebbes and teachers who knew arguing *against* what they saw as God's injustice was fundamental to being a Jew.

Why put so much value into prepositions? To paraphrase the Kotzker rabbi,[32] "God dwells where we let God in." Where people locate themselves in relationship to God is key to our understanding of how God is in the world, and more significant than what or how or who God is (or isn't). Prepositional theology shifts our focus of attention to how words connect, and gives us greater capacity to connect to others and ultimately to God, by whatever name you wish to call him or her or it. And while it's often said that the devil is in the details, to my mind it's in the details, like prepositions, where God truly dwells. . . .

31. Harold Schulweis, *Evil and the Morality of God* (Cincinnati: Hebrew Union College Press, 1983).

32. [Menachem Mendel of Kotzk (1787–1859), was a Polish Hasidic rabbi.]

Prepositional theology also appeals to me because I find it a comfortable way to understand transitions I have made during my lifetime. When I was young, imagining God as that which exists "between" everything really worked for me, and I still find Martin Buber a compelling teacher. And in my years as a card-carrying Reconstructionist, I found Kaplan's "through" and Schulweis's "with" to work well for me as I sought compassion and justice for the world alongside my fellow Jews. As someone who currently identifies as secular, seeing myself as being "without" God is a way for me to remain in the theological conversation. These days, I sometimes also find myself not only "without" but "against" particularly when the Israeli government and its supporters make me so angry that God has become my last resort conversation partner. In the end I lay claim to it all: a prepositional theology of with and without, through and between and sometimes against. I encourage you to figure out which prepositional theologies are right for you.

II | Revelation and Commandment

What happened at Sinai? How is the term *mitzvah,* usually translated as commandment, to be understood? In what sense can Jews as a people and Jews as individuals be understood to be commanded? What happens to Jewish ritual practice and observance in a profoundly voluntaristic setting? Traditional conceptions of revealed truths and binding laws present particular challenges in the American context, where truths are held to be self-evident and newcomers are greeted by the Statue of Liberty. To quote the title of a 1956 work by Ira Eisenstein, what are the contours of "Judaism Under Freedom"?

Mordecai Kaplan and Abraham Joshua Heschel both agreed that in the modern American setting, discourse about revelation had changed profoundly, but their understandings of the reasons for this change were starkly different. In Kaplan's view, "[t]he most difficult obstacle to be overcome in the reinterpretation of the Jewish tradition is no doubt the dogma that the Torah is supernaturally revealed. . . . In the light of modern research into the past and inquiry into religious practices and beliefs of civilizations other than our own, both ancient and modern, that assumption is no longer tenable."[1]

In a 1954 essay offering "A Preface to an Understanding of Revelation," Heschel rejected the notion that the most serious obstacle to understanding revelation derives from doubts based on modern research. Rather, he claimed, moderns have lost the capacity to experience God as an urgent presence. "The Bible is an answer to the supreme question: What does God demand of us? Yet the question has gone out of the world. . . . This is the status of the Bible in modern life: it is a great answer, but we do not know the question any more. Unless we recover the question, there is no hope of understanding the Bible."[2]

1. [Mordecai M. Kaplan, *The Future of the American Jew* (New York, Macmillan: 1949), 381.]
2. [Abraham Joshua Heschel, "A Preface to the Understanding of Revelation," in *Essays Presented to Leo Baeck on the Occasion of His Eightieth Birthday,* ed. N. Bentwich et al. (London: East and West Library, 1954), 29.]

If for Kaplan the premodern doctrine of revelation had to be reframed and reconstructed to accord with a modern outlook, Heschel drew what may appear to be the opposite conclusion. It is we who must be reframed, our consciousness reconstructed so that the essential nature of the human condition is recovered: "*I am commanded—therefore I am.*"[3]

Questions of revelation and commandment have been a preoccupation for American Jewish thinkers, as they have been for Jews in every locale and era. As we embark on this review of some American Jewish approaches to these themes, it is worth noting that many religious Jews in America subscribe to a view summarized well by Rabbi Menachem Schneerson, the seventh Rabbi of Lubavitch. He asserts that "[t]he revelation at Sinai marks a turning point in the spiritual history of the world. Before the Giving of the Torah, there was no possibility for union between the world's material substance and spiritual reality. With the Giving of the Torah, however, G-d nullified that original decree and said, 'The lower realms shall ascend to the higher realms and the higher realms shall descend to the lower. And I shall take the initiative.'" The two stages of this upending of the previous metaphysical order are divine descent, namely "the manifestation of G-dliness in the world," and then human ascent, or "the refinement of man and his surrounding environment and the transformation of man and his world into vessels for G-dliness. This process began with Moshe's ascent to Mount Sinai and has never ceased."[4]

While this belief or a version of it continues to exercise considerable influence, it has become necessary for many to examine the assumptions underpinning it. In 1966, the editors of *Commentary* magazine posed theological questions to Jewish thinkers of the day. The first of these relates to the central concerns of this chapter:

> In what sense do you believe the Torah to be divine revelation? Are all 613 commandments equally binding on the believing Jew? If not, how is he to decide which to observe? What status would you accord to ritual commandments lacking in ethical or doctrinal content (e.g., the prohibition against clothing made of linen and wool)?[5]

3. [Abraham Joshua Heschel, *Who Is Man?* (Stanford, CA: Stanford University Press, 1965), 111.]

4. [This distillation of his views from his *Likkutei Sichos* is adapted and translated in Menachem M. Schneerson, "From Sinai to Mashiach," accessed February 1, 2019, https://www.chabad.org/therebbe/article_cdo/aid/154221/jewish/From-Sinai-to-Mashiach.htm.]

5. ["A Symposium: The State of Jewish Belief," *Commentary* 42, no. 2 (August 1966), 73.

Here the question of Sinai is presented as a litmus test of Jewish belief.

Examples of the strategies outlined by Kaplan, Heschel, and Schneerson can be found in the twelve excerpts of Part Two.

In their responses to the 1966 *Commentary* symposium, Marvin Fox and Aharon Lichtenstein offer distinct analyses exemplifying a combination of Orthodox theology and philosophical sophistication. Lichtenstein makes use of terminology taken from the medieval Christian thinker Thomas Aquinas. Will Herberg offers a way of navigating between scholarly rigor and spiritual vigor in relating to the Bible, and Jakob J. Petuchowski presents the dilemma faced by the modern reader of Torah. In his classic essay, Joseph Soloveitchik portrays "Halakhic Man" as an ideal type for whom the commandment of a heteronomous God is the primary organizing principle of life.

The theological implications of what one believes to have happened at Sinai are discussed by Benjamin Sommer and Tamar Ross. While the former links the insights of biblical scholarship to approaches developed by modern Jewish philosophers, the latter discusses the implications of different conceptions of revelation, including what she terms "cumulativism," according to which divine revelation unfolds incrementally. Eugene Borowitz was the preeminent liberal theologian of the covenant, and we have included an excerpt from his most famous work on this subject. It is followed by contributions from two thinkers who are more conservatively inclined than Borowitz but are in dialogue with his thought, Susan Handelman and David Novak. Handelman's response is rooted in the world of postmodern discourse, while Novak's includes a poignant critique of liberal theology. In search of a new currency of halakhic authority, Rachel Adler employs the thinking of legal theorist Robert Cover (1943–86). Engaged in a similar quest, Mara Benjamin considers traditional notions of a commanding God in a new light, employing maternal imagery to question traditional hierarchical theological assumptions.

While it is not stated explicitly, this and the other questions sent to the thinkers appear to have been composed by Milton Himmelfarb. Thirty years later, the editors of the same journal turned to rabbis and intellectuals with an adapted set of questions. The latter version of this question read, "Do you believe the Torah to be divine revelation? Do you accept the binding nature of any, some, or all of the commandments?" See "What Do American Jews Believe?" *Commentary* 102, no. 2 (August 1996), 19.]

Marvin Fox (1922–96) was ordained as an Orthodox rabbi at the Hebrew Theological College (Skokie Yeshiva) in Chicago. A graduate of Northwestern University, Fox received his PhD in philosophy from the University of Chicago. An expert on Maimonides who wrote prolifically on medieval and modern philosophy, he taught for many years at the Ohio State University before moving to Brandeis University in 1974. There he served as Lown Professor of Jewish Philosophy and Chair of the Department of Near Eastern Languages and Judaic Studies.

Marvin Fox, *The Condition of Jewish Belief* (New York: Macmillan, 1966), 59–63.

It is essential to distinguish between the metaphysical aspects of revelation and the practical implications of revelation. With respect to both I believe in the traditional doctrine of *Torah min ha-shamayim*, the teaching that the Torah is divine. I also follow the tradition which allows great latitude in our theological understanding of the nature of revelation while insisting on rigorous adherence to fixed norms of behavior.

No one can reasonably claim to understand how God reveals Himself to man. The very idea of revelation leads us to paradoxes which defy rational explanation. We cannot make fully intelligible in the language of human experience how the eternal enters into the temporal world of man, or how the incorporeal is apprehended by corporeal beings. Yet we affirm in faith what we cannot explicate, for our very humanity is at stake. I believe, because I cannot afford not to believe. I believe, as a Jew, in the divinity of Torah, because without God's Torah I have lost the ground for making my own life intelligible and purposeful.

To believe because life demands is not peculiar to religious men. It is something that reasonable men do as a matter of course in other areas. For example, most men in Western society believe that there is some necessary relationship between reason and reality, though no decisive evidence can be offered for this conviction. They hold to it because if the world does not conform to human reason then it is unintelligible, and we find that an unbearable state of affairs. Rather than face the pain of an unintelligible world we affirm, as an act of faith, that it must be rationally ordered. We insist that whatever reason finds necessary must be the case in reality and whatever reason finds impossible can never be the case in reality. And we do so rightly, for with anything less our lives would become a hopeless chaos. The same holds true of the Jew who believes in the Torah as divine, even while acknowledging that he has and can have no decisive evidence. He believes because the order, structure, direction, and meaning of his life are at stake, because the alternative is personal and moral chaos. He believes because all that he finds precious hangs in the balance—the quality, substance, and texture of his own existence. His belief is not formulated as a set of dogmatic propositions. It is, rather, *emunah*, trust in God and in the tradition of the community of Israel. In that trust the believing Jew finds the ground of his own existence and opens himself to unique and exalted possibilities. In that trust he discovers that the truly human is a reflection of the divine, a discovery which has the power to transform and sanctify man and his world.

In affirming such a belief in revelation, I make no specific claim about the way in which revelation took place, except the traditional one that the biblical prophets are its only valid channel. Moses holds a unique place among these prophets and through him the Torah was transmitted to the community of Israel. Because prophecy transcends my own experience I cannot read the biblical descriptions of the prophetic vision in simple literal terms. Jewish tradition offers ample precedent for understanding the Torah in symbolic or metaphorical terms. The text, of course, must be studied perceptively and with meticulous care, but this is not to say that it is to be read in literal or fundamentalist fashion. One need only recall that *midrash* is a very early mode of understanding Torah in a nonliteral way, or that the first part of Maimonides' *Guide* is a caution against blind literalism. Even so recent an authority as the Nezib (Rabbi Naphtali Zvi Yehuda Berlin of Volozhin)[6] stresses that Torah must be read and understood as poetry.

In effect, this suggests a wide range of ways in which we might formulate our admittedly inadequate ideas of revelation. Presumably, a highly sophisticated philosopher or theologian will view the matter differently from an unlearned man of simple faith. What all affirm, if they stand in the normative tradition, is that God has addressed us through His prophets. I fully share this classical belief.

In noting the latitude and diversity of theological understanding, it was not my intention to suggest that there are no limits or boundaries. As a believing Jew, I conceive of revelation as including *Torah she-be'al peh*, the oral tradition. Here we find the valid Jewish guides to understanding the theological as well as

6. [Berlin (1816–93) was a giant of Lithuanian Jewish scholarship.]

the legal teachings of the Torah. The range of possible approaches to revelation is rooted in and defined by this oral Torah.

While allowing diversity of theological insight, I also follow the tradition in holding that all the commandments of the Torah are binding upon every Jew. To know what these commandments are we must again appeal to the oral tradition which continues to unfold through all the generations of Jewish history. The judgments and decisions of recognized and qualified Torah scholars have the binding force of law, for they are the very substance of Torah. Hence, I accept not only the 613 commandments of the written Torah, but equally the explication of those commandments through the oral Torah. In fact, we cannot know clearly what is intended by the commandments of the Torah except through the teaching of the oral tradition. Here, in contrast to the abstractions of theology, we have a clear and concrete pattern of practice. Of course, there are disputed questions concerning practice also, but for these there is a clear technique for decision. It is this unified pattern of religious behavior which binds us as Jews. Through the fulfillment of God's commandments we serve Him, express our love for Him, and achieve the ultimate purpose of Jewish existence—the sanctification of our lives.

The distinction which is suggested (in the first question) between ritual and ethical commandments is untenable for a believing Jew. The tradition, of course, recognizes that some commandments regulate intrahuman relations while others regulate man's relation to God, but the Torah gives us no ground for accepting the one and rejecting the other. The ethical commandments bind us because they are laws of the Torah. Precisely the same is true of the ritual commandments.

12

Aharon Lichtenstein, *The Condition of Jewish Belief*

Born in France, Aharon Lichtenstein (1933–2015) was raised in the United States, where he studied under Rabbi Yitzchok Hutner and Rabbi Joseph Soloveitchik, from whom he received rabbinical ordination. In parallel, he completed a PhD in English literature at Harvard University. Renowned as a Talmud scholar and philosopher, he moved to Israel in 1971, where he became Rosh Yeshiva at Yeshivat Har Etzion. Lichtenstein was a winner of the Israel Prize in Jewish Literature.

Aharon Lichtenstein, *The Condition of Jewish Belief* (New York: Macmillan, 1966), 132–34.

The Torah, both the written text and the oral law, constitutes divine revelation in three distinct senses. It was revealed *by* God, it reveals something *about* Him, and it reveals Him. First, the Torah comprises a specific narrative or normative *dictum*, an objective "given" invested with definite form and content, which was addressed by God to Israel as a whole or to its leader and representative, Moses. This datum consists of two elements:

(a) The *revelatum*, to use the Thomistic term, whose truths inherently lie beyond the range of human reason and which therefore had to be revealed if they were to be known at all: and

(b) The *revelabile*, whose truths—be they historical facts or the norms of morality or natural religion—could have been discovered by man in any event, and whose transcendental status therefore derives from the relatively extrinsic fact of their having been divinely expressed. The present character of both as revelation, however, is crucial. After the fact, both constitute God's living message to Israel.

Secondly, the Torah reveals something about God, and this in two ways: it presents direct statements about divine attributes; and, inasmuch as it is not merely a document delivered (*salve reverentia*) [with due deference] by God but composed by Him, it constitutes in its normative essence an expression of His will. As such, it affords us an indirect insight into what is otherwise wholly inscrutable. He who is hidden in His numinous "otherness"—*El mistater b'shafrir chivyon, ha-sechel ha-ne-elam mikol ra'ayon*[7]—or transcendent in His luminous majesty (Milton's "Dark with excessive bright thy skirts appear")—has chosen, *mutatis mutandis*, to condense His infinite will in the very act of its expression. Finite man is thus enabled, though ever so haltingly, to grasp it somewhat. Hence, as the *Tanya* emphasized,[8] the tremendous importance of the study of Torah for traditional Judaism. It is the one means of embracing and absorbing, as it were, God's presence as manifested through His revealed will. It becomes, therefore, not only an intellectual exercise but a religious experience.

But the revealed character of Torah does not exhaust itself in propositions imparted by God or concerning Him. It is realized, thirdly, as a revelation of the divine presence proper. Revelation is not only an objective *datum* or the process of its transmission, important as these may be. It is the occasion, exalting and humbling both, for a dialectical encounter with the living God. Revelation is not only a fixed text but, in relation to man, an electrifying I-and-Thou experience. Moreover, this experience is not confined to the initial moment of divine giving and human taking of a specific message. It is repeated recurrently through genuine response to God's message which ushers us into His presence. The rapture and the awe, the joy and the tremor of Sinai were not of a moment. They are of all time, engaging the Jew who truly opens himself to the divine message and God's call. "Every day let them [the words of the Torah] be in your eyes as if newly given."[9] The experience of revelation is repeated through response, be it study or action, to its content, and conversely, the awareness of its content is sharpened though an intensive sense of its experience.

To the committed Jew, this experience, at Sinai or at present, is not simply a momentarily rapturous encounter. It is enthralling in *both* senses of the word. It imposes binding obligation. The Torah, although it includes sizable narrative segments, is, in its quintessence, normative. . . .

Whether a particular commandment has "ethical or doctrinal content" is not the heart of the matter. The crucial point is that it *is* a commandment, that it elicits a response to the divine call. To put it more sharply, there always is "ethical

7. [Lichtenstein is quoting the first words of a sixteenth-century liturgical poem by Rabbi Avraham Maimon that may be translated as follows: "God, hiding in the beauty of concealment, intelligence beyond all conceptualization. . . ."]

8. [First published in 1797, the Tanya is an early work of Hasidic thought, written by Rabbi Shneur Zalman of Liadi (1745–1812), the founder of Chabad Hasidism.]

9. [Rashi to Deuteronomy 26:16.]

or doctrinal content." In the age-old controversy—dating from Plato's *Euthyphro*—as to whether things please God because they are good or they are good because they please Him, traditional Judaism has certainly held with Socrates that the divine will is not arbitrary but rational. As regards commandments, however, even if we ignore the intrinsic content, perhaps hidden from us, or a specific *mitzvah*, its merely being such has moral and religious import. It widens the scope of religious awareness. It inculcates that habit of acting in response to the divine will in all areas of endeavor. It develops a sense of the divine presence. It integrates all of human life into a normative and purposive existence. It enables the Jew to attain not only dignity but sanctity.

13

Will Herberg, *Judaism and Modern Man*

Arriving in the United States at the age of three, Will Herberg (1901–77) initially followed the atheist and socialist leanings of his Russian-Jewish parents. Following his encounter with the thought of the Protestant theologian Reinhold Niebuhr in the 1930s, Herberg became a leading Jewish theological voice in America for decades. He was the Religion Editor of the *National Review*.

Will Herberg, *Judaism and Modern Man: An Interpretation of Jewish Religion* (New York: Farrar, Straus, and Cudahy, 1951), 245–46.

It is hardly necessary to point out that fundamentalism today, while still widely affirmed, is thoroughly discredited with every critical mind. Much in the biblical writings, the bits of astronomical, geographical and biological information contained in them, for example—is obviously at odds with some of the best authenticated scientific knowledge of our time. The earth is not flat, the sun does not make its daily transit over it from one edge to the other,[10] and life on earth did not appear quite in the way described in Genesis. Neither the chronology nor the history recorded in the Scriptural works can be taken simply at its face value, although they have shown themselves in many ways better founded than scholarly opinion only recently was ready to grant. From another direction, the sacred writings themselves have been critically analyzed, and while much of the work of critical scholarship is by no means secure, it can no longer be seriously questioned that the Bible in its various parts is a highly composite work, reflecting a long and immensely complicated process of literary construction, redaction, and development. However it may be related to God, the Bible is obviously not simply a transcript from his dictation and therefore no seamless whole incapable of error. And to complete the case against fundamentalism, it has become increasingly clear that the rationalistic conception of revelation as the supernatural communication of infallible information is altogether out of line with the Bible itself and is not even in harmony with much of later tradition. Fundamentalism, in short, defends a view of revelation that not

10. [This is probably a reference to imagery in Psalm 19.]

only runs counter to substantial fact but is also of dubious religious power and significance.

As against the fundamentalist, the modernist accepts the findings of science and critical scholarship, but he so interprets these findings as to render revelation nothing but a figure of speech. The Scriptural writers, he concedes, were "inspired," but this means little more than saying that a Shakespeare or a Plato or a Buddha was inspired; the "inspiration" of the prophet is identified with the imagination of the poet and the illumination of the mystic or philosopher. As to the biblical writings themselves, they are, to the modernist, interesting compilations of myth, legend and folklore, in which are embedded a number of high ethical teachings. They are a kind of primitive literature, important for us culturally and pedagogically, no doubt, but hardly to be taken seriously as God's word. After all, we are reminded, has not criticism shown that even the Pentateuch is a patchwork of documents from different times, sources and historical settings—in other words, a compilation made by men rather than a single whole dictated by God?

Both modernism and fundamentalism agree on insisting that it must be either one or the other. If you question the fundamentalist premises, you must necessarily proceed to dissolve revelation into a meaningless phrase: and if you question the modernist conclusions, you must necessarily lapse into a benighted fundamentalism. Thus each protects itself by brandishing the scarecrow of the other. But we need not take this strategy too seriously. There is a third way, not "between" modernism and fundamentalism but beyond and distinct from both. Franz Rosenzweig and Martin Buber, among Jews, and H. Richard Niebuhr and Emil Brunner, among Christians, have shown how one may take Scripture with the utmost seriousness as the record of revelation while avoiding the pitfalls of fundamentalism. They have also shown how the findings of science and scholarship may be accepted at the same time that one affirms Scripture to be truly the vehicle of God's word. This third conception of revelation makes the attempt to be thoroughly biblical and thoroughly realistic at the same time, in the conviction that no conception can be the one without also being the other.

In this view, a shift in the very meaning of the term "revelation" is involved. Revelation is not the communication of infallible information, as the fundamentalists claim, nor is it the outpouring of "inspired" sages and poets, as the modernists conceive it. Revelation is the *self-disclosure of God in his dealings with the world*. Scripture is thus not itself revelation but a humanly mediated record of revelation. It is a story composed of many strands and fragments, each arising in its own time, place and circumstance, yet it is essentially one, for it is throughout the story of the encounter of God and man in the history of Israel. Scripture as revelation is not a compendium of recondite information or metaphysical propositions; it is quite literally *Heilsgeschichte*, redemptive history.

14 | Jakob J. Petuchowski, "Revelation and the Modern Jew"

A native of Berlin, Jakob Josef Petuchowski (1925–91) came to Hebrew Union College in Cincinnati in 1948. There he received both rabbinical ordination and his PhD. Petuchowski remained at Hebrew Union College–Jewish Institute of Religion for most of the rest of his life, as a professor of theology, liturgy, and Jewish-Christian studies. His publications were many, and he wrote broadly in the fields of theology, philosophy, and liturgy.

Jakob J. Petuchowski, "Revelation and the Modern Jew," *The Journal of Religion* 41, no.1 (January 1961): 33–37.

Of course, modern Jews are *modern* Jews. They cannot close their eyes to the findings of biblical criticism. They cannot act as if there were no such discipline as the study of comparative religion. They cannot ignore the scientific study of religious origins and evolution. And they cannot—in any *literal* sense—share the traditional belief that God revealed to Israel 248 positive commandments and 365 prohibitions. They cannot even believe that God reveals nice and ready-made theological systems. But they can believe—and some of them *do* believe—that God really reveals himself. . . .

The question of why does God give this ability to man—why, at certain moments in the course of history, does he raise happenings and events from the level of the routine and the ordinary to that of revelation—can only be answered by a reference to God's *love*. "For God so loved the world," says the Christian, "that He gave His only begotten son" (John 3:16). "With everlasting love hast Thou loved the House of Israel, Thy people," says the Jew in his daily evening service; "Torah and commandments, statutes and judgments hast Thou taught us."

Actually, as Franz Rosenzweig would have it, the divine love is the *only* content of revelation. Man, becoming conscious of this love of God, hears the divine command: "Thou shalt love the Lord thy God with all thy heart, with all thy soul, and with all thy might." Ordinarily, of course, love cannot be commanded. Only a lover, in a moment of aroused love, might, and does, demand of his beloved that she return his love, that she reciprocate the love shown to her. But that is precisely what the moment of revelation does imply. God shows his love and longs for man's love in return. All the rest is commentary and interpretation.

But as soon as man is able to reciprocate the love, as soon as man is able to hear the commandment, "Thou shalt love the Lord thy God," he cannot stop there. "If I truly love *one* person," writes Erich Fromm in *The Art of Loving*, "I love all persons, I love the world, I love life."[11] Man, aware of the love of God, tries to capture, to make concrete and permanent, this experience of love in terms which will ultimately influence and govern the affairs of all men. And so the experience of God's love for man results in yet *another* commandment: "Thou shalt love thy neighbor as thyself—I am the Lord."

These two great commandments, in turn, give rise to a host of other commandments—commandments of a ritual nature, in which man tries to relive the moment of revelation, and commandments of a moral and ethical nature, which aim at applying in practice, and in daily life, the commandment about loving one's neighbor.

Admittedly, these commandments are man's *interpretation* of the experience of revelation. And according as to how one values this "interpretation," he either will, or will not, find an inner relation to the legal and ceremonial tradition of the Jewish past. . . .

Here, of course, is the problem which the modern Jew has to face: On the one hand, he has to study the Hebrew Bible from a scientific perspective, reading it as the surviving remnants of ancient Hebrew literature. One the other hand, this literature is *also* the record of divine revelation. On the basis of the older view of revelation, the mechanical view which conceived of a *direct* divine origin of the text in hand, this problem would be insoluble. Or, it could be solved by cutting the Gordian knot—by rejecting either the belief in revelation or the modern scientific approach. In other words, the solution would be found in either an obscurantist fundamentalism or in a non-religious humanism. Happily, however, the modern Jew can escape this "either/or" straitjacket. . . .

The ancient rabbis already insisted that each Jew, in every generation, must regard himself as though he, too, had been liberated by God from Egyptian slavery. And they stressed the constant reference of the Scriptures to "this day," by

11. Erich Fromm, *The Art of Loving* (New York: Harper and Brothers, 1956), 46.

demanding that the Jew constantly *re-live* the experience of Sinai. It may, therefore, be suggested in all modesty and humility that, once modern Judaism has finally come to terms with the problems posed by revelation, it, too, will have been blessed by God with that felicitous union of "event" and "interpretation" which is the essence of revelation.

Scion of a remarkable Lithuanian rabbinic dynasty famed for its approach to Talmud, Joseph Ber Soloveitchik (1903–93) became one of America's most famous and influential figures, known simply as The Rav. Having arrived in the United States in 1932 after completing a PhD at the University of Berlin with a dissertation on the thought of Hermann Cohen, he served as the Rosh Yeshiva of the Rabbi Isaac Elchanan Theological Seminary at Yeshiva University for almost fifty years. His influence on American Orthodox Judaism was unsurpassed.

Joseph B. Soloveitchik, *Halakhic Man*, trans. Lawrence Kaplan (Philadelphia: Jewish Publication Society of America, 1983), 19–24.

When halakhic[12] man approaches reality, he comes with his Torah, given to him from Sinai, in hand. He orients himself to the world by means of fixed statutes and firm principles. An entire corpus of precepts and laws guides him along the path leading to existence. Halakhic man, well furnished with rules, judgments, and fundamental principles, draws near the world with an a priori relation. His approach begins with an ideal creation and concludes with a real one. To whom may he be compared? To a mathematician who fashions an ideal world and then uses it for the purpose of establishing a relationship between it and the real world, as was explained above. The essence of the Halakhah, which was received from God, consists in creating an ideal world and cognizing the relationship between that ideal world and our concrete environment in all its visible manifestations and underlying structures. There is no phenomenon, entity, or object in this concrete world which the a priori Halakhah does not approach with its ideal standard. When halakhic man comes across a spring bubbling quietly, he already possesses a fixed, a priori relationship with this real phenomenon: the complex of laws regarding the halakhic construct of a spring. The spring is fit for the immersion of a *zav* (a man with a discharge); it may serve

12. [The term "halakha" is derived from the word for walking. Referring to Jewish law, it denotes a systematic approach to the conduct of life in accordance with the dictates of Jewish law as interpreted through history.]

as *mei hatat* (waters of expiation); it purifies with flowing water; it does not require a fixed quantity of forty se'ahs; etc. [See Maimonides, *Laws of Immersion Pools*, 9:8.] When halakhic man approaches a real spring, he gazes at it and carefully examines its nature. He possesses, a priori, ideal principles and precepts which establish the character of the spring as a halakhic construct, and he uses the statutes for the purpose of determining normative law: does the real spring correspond to the requirements of the ideal Halakhah or not?

Halakhic man is not overly curious, and he is not particularly concerned with cognizing the spring as it is in itself. Rather, he desires to coordinate the a priori concept with the a posteriori phenomenon.

When halakhic man looks to the western horizon and sees the fading rays of the setting sun or to the eastern horizon and sees the first light of dawn and the glowing rays of the rising sun, he knows that this sunset or sunrise imposes upon him anew obligations and commandments. Dawn and sunrise obligate him to fulfill those commandments that are performed during the day: the recitation of the morning *Shema*, *tzitzit*, *tefillin*, the morning prayer, *Etrog*, *shofar*, *Hallel*, and the like.[13] They make the time fit for the carrying out of certain halakhic practices: Temple services, acceptance of testimony, conversion, *halitzah*,[14] etc. etc. Sunset imposes upon him those obligations and commandments that are performed during the night: the recitation of the evening *Shema*, *matzah*, the counting of the *omer*,[15] etc. The sunset on Sabbath and holiday eves sanctifies the day: the profane and the holy are dependent upon a natural cosmic phenomenon—the sun sinking below the horizon. It is not anything transcendent that creates holiness but rather the visible reality—the regular cycle of the natural order. Halakhic man examines the sunrise and sunset, the dawn and the appearance of the stars; he gazes into the horizon—Is the upper horizon pale and the same as the lower? —and looks at the sun's shadows—Has afternoon already arrived? When he

13. [The references here are to acts of piety incumbent upon the traditionally observant Jewish male. The first examples refer to the recitation of a collection of biblical verses beginning with Deuteronomy 6:4, the donning of fringes and phylacteries and the conduct of daily weekday prayer. The next examples include the citron, one of the four species which plays a special role in the festival of Sukkot, the ram's horn blown at the New Year, and the recitation of a collection of biblical psalms at pilgrim festivals and certain other festive occasions.]

14. [A ceremony releasing a brother from the duty to wed his deceased brother's wife.]

15. [Here the references are to unleavened bread eaten at Passover, and a forty-nine-day period of counting between Passover and Shavuot (Pentecost).]

goes out on a clear, moonlit night (until the deficiency of the moon is replenished) he makes a blessing upon it. He knows that it is the moon that determines the times of the months and this of all the Jewish seasons and festivals, and this determination must rely upon astronomical calculations. . . .

There is no real phenomenon to which halakhic man does not possess a fixed relationship from the outset and a clear, definitive, a priori orientation. He is interested in sociological creations: the state, society and the relationship of individuals within a communal context. The Halakhah encompasses laws of business, torts, neighbors, plaintiff and defendant, creditor and debtor, partners, agents, workers, artisans, bailees, etc. Family life—marriage, divorce, *halitzah*, *sotah*,[16] conjugal refusal (*mi'un*), the respective rights, obligations, and duties of a husband and a wife—is clarified and elucidated by it. War, the high court, courts and the penalties they impose—all are just a few of the multitude of halakhic subjects. The halakhist is involved with psychological problems—for example, sanity and insanity, the possibility or impossibility of a happy marriage, *miggo* [i.e., the principle that a party's plea gains credibility when a more advantageous plea is available], and assumptions as to the intention behind a specific act (*umdana*), the presumption that a particular individual is a liar or a sinner, the discretion of the judges, etc., etc. "The measure thereof is longer than the earth and broader than the sea" (Job 11:9).

Halakhah has a fixed a priori relationship to the whole of reality in all of its fine and detailed particulars. Halakhic man orients himself to the entire cosmos and tries to understand it by utilizing an ideal world which he bears in his halakhic consciousness. All halakhic concepts are a priori, and it is through them that halakhic man looks at the world. As we said above, his world view is similar to that of the mathematician: a priori and ideal. Both the mathematician and the halakhist gaze at the concrete world from an a priori, ideal standpoint and use a priori categories and concepts which determine from the outset their relationship to the qualitative phenomena they encounter. Both examine empirical reality from the vantage point of an ideal reality. There is one question which they raise: Does this real phenomenon correspond to their ideal construction?

And when many halakhic concepts do not correspond with the phenomena of the real world, halakhic man is not at all distressed. His deepest desire is not the realization of the Halakhah but rather the ideal construction which was given to him from Sinai, and this ideal construction exists forever.

16. [*Sotah* is a biblical ritual concerning a woman suspected of adultery.]

Benjamin Sommer (born 1964) graduated from Yale College, studied at the Hebrew University of Jerusalem, and received an MA from Brandeis as well as his PhD
in religion and biblical studies from the University of Chicago. Having served on
the faculty at Northwestern University, Sommer became Professor of Bible at the
Jewish Theological Seminary in 2008. His work straddles academic scholarship
and contemporary theological reflection.

Benjamin H. Sommer, *Revelation and Authority: Sinai in Jewish Scripture and
Tradition* (New Haven, CT: Yale University Press, 2015), 245–50.

In spite of their many differences, all the Pentateuchal sources agree that the
event at Sinai or Horeb was not merely revelation but lawgiving. While they
present varied lists of *Gesetze*, they speak with one voice in regard to *Gebot*.[17] This
point warrants emphasis, because one can imagine some readers jumping to an
unfounded conclusion based on the variety of views in the Pentateuch and in
postbiblical thought regarding revelation. One might infer from this plurality
of opinion that the boundaries of authentic Jewish thought are infinitely elastic.
Such an inference betrays our sources. What unites the maximalist and minimalist schools of interpretation . . . is greater than what divides them: they agree
that Israel must worship one God, no more and (this is the important point for
the modern Jew) no less; they concur that Israel must express its loyalty to God
by observing a binding covenantal law. Without these beliefs, no form of Judaism can claim to go back to Sinai or to be based on the Pentateuch, its sources,
or its successors.

But the differences between maximalist and minimalist interpretations of the
event at Sinai are consequential. For the maximalist, halakhic practice hinges on
the notion that specifics of the law either came directly from heaven or follow
from interpretations based on the precise wording of a text whose every letter,
vowel, and cantillation mark were penned by God. If the *Gesetze* themselves are

17. [These terms were most famously employed by Franz Rosenzweig, where *Gesetz*
refers to objective law and *Gebot* to personal commandment. See the Introduction, xix.]

the work of God or, through exegesis, only a single step removed from God, then the extent to which human authorities can change them will be limited. Insofar as one of the details of the system is that Jews are to follow the rulings of each generation's sages, the possibility of modest change within the system exists for maximalist sages. But they are likely to alter that system with great hesitancy. Furthermore, if I am sure that the details of the law I observe come from heaven, then I will believe my actions correspond precisely to the will of God. I may consequently develop an extraordinary spiritual confidence, which can easily devolve into arrogance. There is nothing quite so dangerous as human beings who think they know exactly what the deity wants—and nothing so lacking the humility that consciousness of our created status should engender. Empirical evidence abounds demonstrating the correlation between certainty regarding God's will, on the one hand, and arrogance, inflexibility, and intolerance, on the other.

The attitudes toward halakhic change and religious certainty that flow from the participatory theory of revelation will be entirely different. People who regard the *Gesetze* as Israel's attempt to translate the *Gebot* will feel obligated to carry out the *Gesetze* even as they are aware that it is possible that the translation occasionally errs. As a result, halakhic observance among minimalist interpreters should avoid the arrogance that can mar observance among some maximalists. And yet, here lurks a grave danger. The virtue of observance that is unsure of itself, taken to an extreme, leads to the sin of nonobservance. Empirical evidence for this assertion is, alas, as abundant as evidence of the dangers that result from theological certainty. The question of the law's malleability also appears in a new light when seen from within the participatory theory. If the *Gesetze* from the outset were part of Israel's response to divine *Gebot*, then it is entirely appropriate that the nation Israel and its sages today should strive to hear God's will more clearly and to alter details of the *Gesetze*—but only so long as the *Gebot* remains unaffected. This caveat is crucial, because greater willingness to alter *Gesetze* in the modern period correlates very closely with the loss of a sense of *Gebot*. Consequently, even though the participatory theology provides a theoretical underpinning for a binding but malleable halakhic system, it also forces us to confront the practical question of how to change the law, how much to change it, and how fast to change it. . . .

If Jews of all generations were present at Sinai, then Jews of all generations received the responsibility to participate in the response to revelation we call Torah. The authority that emanates from God at Sinai is offered to all those who witness the event. But the Catholic Israel that decides what is Torah does not include all Jews; it is limited to those Jews who observe the law. After all, the reason Catholic Israel or [18] כלל ישראל can change the law is that God gives it to Israel, and one has some right to alter one's own property. The fact that God gives, however, does not mean that all Israel has received. Only those Jews who accept the law take ownership in it; and the only way to accept the law is to observe the law. (This statement is tautological. One does not, for example, accept law by studying it, because if one merely studies it, it is not yet law; it is merely an academic exercise.) One can imagine very radical changes being introduced into the law by communities that observe it—but only by those communities. Authority, which God offers freely to Israel, belongs to a self-selecting subgroup. This observation has far-reaching ramifications for evaluating the legitimacy of halakhic changes proposed among contemporary Jewish communities.

The malleability of the law is appropriate, because we realize that our forebears' acts of translations were fallible. This principle, however, is a double-edged sword. Insofar as we, too, innovate, we, too, may err. Just as our ancestors and forebears in ancient Israel must have misunderstood God's will when they authorized the law requiring us to kill Amalekite babies in Exodus 17 and Deuteronomy 25, so, too, is it possible that we are sometimes mistaken as we attempt to apply God's command to our time. If we lack the humility to admit this, we ought not alter the *Gesetze*. We have the right to change the tradition that is joint property we share with God and with our forebears, but only if we do so in fear and trembling. The awesome responsibility of interpreting and applying God's command cannot be an exercise in shaping the tradition in our own image, in making it hew to our predilections. Thus, the minimalist tradition can provide a foundation for halakhic change, but the humility so essential to the minimalist approach also tempers the pace and depth of change. The covenant formed at Sinai is correlational, but it is not a contract between equals. Modern Jews eagerly embrace the idea of a dialogical covenant; we are comfortable with, indeed delighted by, the notion that we are God's partners. We have failed, however, to acknowledge the covenant's hierarchical side. Consequently, we cannot claim to have fully embraced the Sinai covenant, for in this covenant, there is a master

18. [*Kelal Yisrael*. The term Catholic Israel was coined by Solomon Schechter (1847–1915). Robert Gordis makes the same explicit point that Sommer does about reinterpreting Klal Yisrael in his *Judaism for the Modern Age* (New York: Farrar, Straus & Giroux, 1955), 175–180.]

and there are slaves, and as Leviticus 25:42 and 55 state clearly, the Jewish nation are the slaves. God did not tell Pharaoh, "Let my people go, because freedom is a good thing," but "Let my people go, so that they may serve Me" (Exodus 7.16, 7.26, 8.16, 9.1, 9.13, 10.3). Redemption from Egyptian slavery carries little value on its own in the Pentateuch, which does not find the notion of Israel's slavery inherently bothersome. The Pentateuch is concerned, rather, with the question of whom the slaves serve, and how.

If revelation is a dialogue, then I need to recall that in a dialogue, mine is not the only voice. Participating in any dialogue requires at times that one stop talking so that one can listen—how much the more so in a dialogue in which we are mere vassals! Part of our job in the Sinaitic dialogue is to be silent in God's presence in order to be open to God's voice. Further, we need to attend to the voices of the vassals who came before us. As we stand at Sinai, we remain in the presence of earlier members of Catholic Israel, whose voices in this dialogue continue to carry weight. The community of which we are part includes preceding generations, to whom we are responsible. For this reason, it is appropriate to allow older texts to moderate the pace of change.

Tamar Ross was born in the United States in 1938 and has lived in Israel since her twenties. She received her degrees, including her doctorate, from the Hebrew University of Jerusalem. Her teaching at Bar-Ilan University, at Midreshet Lindenbaum, and in a variety of academic and nonacademic settings, along with her writing, has earned her a prominent position in the discourse of Orthodox feminism both in Israel and in North America.

Tamar Ross, *Expanding the Palace of Torah: Orthodoxy and Feminism* (Hanover, NH: Brandeis University Press, 2004), 221–23.

A different type of objection to cumulativism comes from another quarter: Jewish traditionalists who are not enthusiastic about embracing a doctrine of accumulating revelations or "hearings" via the conduit of history. Preferring alternative theologies that do not submit history to such grandiose claims, they choose to rely on a rival tradition that is represented by Maimonides, who was interested in establishing a clear line of demarcation between texts representing revelation and the rabbinic interpretation of such texts.

As we have seen, the Tosafists[19] and their followers through the ages (including R. Kook[20]) seem to have been driven by the wish to convey their sense of rabbinic alignment with the divine will. They therefore speak of rabbinic interpretations as divinely inspired. In contrast, what seems to be at stake for Maimonides (and those who preferred to follow his tradition) is the need to protect the supremacy and inviolability of Mosaic law from the upheaval of further claims to prophetic inspiration. It was this interest that led Maimonides, in opposition to many predecessors in the Gaonic period,[21] to sharply distinguish between the role of the prophet who *reveals* God's word and the sage who *interprets* it; the role of prophecy and its appeal to charismatic authority is severely

19. [Medieval commentators on the Talmud.]

20. [Rabbi Abraham Isaac Kook (1865–1935) served as Chief Rabbi in pre-State Palestine, and is regarded as one of the fathers of religious Zionism.]

21. [Maimonides (1135–1204) was a giant of medieval Judaism. The gaonic period lasted roughly from the sixth to the eleventh centuries.]

circumscribed. Hence, prophetic powers play no role in the development of the Oral Law. This restriction appeals to some contemporary theologians who wish to emphasize the role of human autonomy in the interpretive process.

Such theologians would argue that because the potential for new interpretations is so well accepted in the traditional Jewish concept of Torah, one need not bind the resolution of current halakhic dilemmas to cumulativist claims of God's continuous revelation in history. Given that rabbinic tradition already recognizes the manifold interpretive possibilities of the revelation at Sinai, even a view that posits the finality of the Sinaitic revelation need not pose any obstacle in principle to the predicament of women today. On the contrary, it is precisely the belief in the completeness and perfection of that revelation that should serve as the founding principle of its continued relevance. This relevance is ensured by that work of the scholars of every generation who can and do uncover more of its original meaning without the benefit of any divine intervention. What they uncover is regarded as always having "been there"; new ideas are neither invented nor continuously revealed but discovered.

Such a view does not, of course, guarantee that future interpretation will take any particular direction. The absence of predefined limits to the Mosaic Torah and the resulting indeterminacy of its meaning should not be confused with skepticism about the possibility of meaning at all. It also should not be identified with a type of hermeneutic nihilism, asserting that anything can be taken to mean whatever we want so long as we want it enough. There are certain accepted interpretive procedures, so that not every direction can be developed with equal honesty. Nevertheless, given Judaism's powerful commitment to the belief in a righteous God whose Torah is just, it is both valid and appropriate that moral concerns play an important part in creating the needs for new interpretation and its formulation. If one adds this factor to the flexibility afforded by the notion of many levels of meaning in Torah, one might claim that any resolution to the feminist predicament (and to other instances of conflict between modernity and tradition) can be accommodated even within a Sinaitic framework, without resort to the concept of accumulating revelation.

If feminist morality is more than a passing fad, it is likely that the interpretive tradition will discover that some of the values expressed by the feminists are indeed those of the Torah and should be pursued accordingly. The fluidity of meaning that allows for this does not require that we understand that the Sinaitic revelation was incomplete. Other feminist values may be considered as opposing the values of the Torah and as such be rejected. Still other matters may remain in the realm of the permissible but not obligatory. Such a solution could be no less effective than claims to divine intervention in history in avoiding the theological pitfall of faulting the existing biblical text. Sufficient to this task should be an underlying assumption that the multiple meanings inherent in a divine message become apparent only through a protracted process of rabbinic interpretation.

In sum, even those who are reluctant to link the process of rabbinic interpretation to metaphysical claims of revelation can still maintain intellectual honesty regarding the various texts of the canon. Even when these appear to be reflections of particular (patriarchal) historical contexts, they need not sacrifice hope for a future accommodation of the Torah with feminist values. What is more, they need not resort to a contextual view of morality in order to resolve the question of God's justice. It might suffice them to explain the discrepancies between current practice and ancient religious sensibilities by pointing to the inability of ordinary human beings to absorb an ideal message already revealed to Moses in full. Alternatively, they may interpret such discrepancies in terms of the adaptation of perfect fixed principles to the vicissitudes of imperfect and changing situations.

These differing (though not mutually exclusive) interests lead to differing nuances and emphases on the mythic vocabulary of each approach. Cumulativists who prefer the notion of divine influence upon the course of interpretation would speak of a primordial Torah as the infinite divine message that history is out to reconstruct, by constantly stretching out the meaning of the primary but time-bound revelation at Sinai. The never-ending opportunities offered by history for fleshing out the Sinaitic revelation are designed gradually to increase the compatibility of that Written Torah with the original preverbal Torah that served as God's blueprint for the world. Those who prefer to regard the Sinaitic Torah as a one-time, complete, and perfect revelation in and of itself will shy away from rhetoric that accords further interpretations any revelatory status. According to them, the function of hermeneutics is to discover what is already there in potential, rather than to stretch it to mean anything new.

I can imagine that some readers will query the importance of this theological nitpicking. Indeed, it would be well to keep the stakes of this argument in perspective. When all is said and done, it is not a debate over the "facts of the matter." Rather, the argument revolves around which theological approach can best express and maintain faith and loyalty to a Judaism and *halakhah* that grants us some intimation of the Ultimate Being, the object of all religious belief. Nevertheless, I believe that, despite the fact that both positions outlined here confirm the dynamic possibilities of Torah, they do entail different sensibilities.

I personally find the doctrine of revelation through history more appealing theologically, for a variety of reasons. Viewing the Sinaitic Torah as merely the earthly reflection of a metaphysical Torah, which must be supplemented by history, avoids imposing the burden of infinite interpretive possibilities upon the former text alone. Any verbal message as such must be contextualized; its very commitment to language renders it time- and culture-bound. Therefore, I find it more convincing to load the potential for limitless interpretation exclusively upon a primordial, preverbal Torah. The primacy of the Torah of Sinai is still maintained in the understanding that it is precisely that revelation, together with the additional interpretations accruing to it over time, that provides us with the formula for reconstructing the earlier Torah to which all history leads.

The notion of an accumulating revelation also affords a view of God and the way He interacts with the world that I find more plausible. Relegating the notion of an infinite Torah to a metaphysical realm, beyond creation, avoids the necessity for grotesque anthropomorphism or other elements of the fantastic, allowing us to understand that transmission of God's word in a naturalistic manner (just as every miracle, once it occurs in the natural world, is subject to explanation by natural law). It even allows for the liberty of conceiving of the Torah of Moses in terms of a revelation that occurred over a period of time, via a process that is totally consonant with the findings of biblical criticism and archaeological discoveries (to the extent that these are scientifically verifiable and convincing). At the same time, we can still accept that process as God-given.

A final point is that belief in accumulating revelations grants religious significance to the events of history and the development of the human spirit. It also allows us to recognize that even when interpreting Torah "from the inside," the impact of outside forces on our definition of that view is never far behind. The ultimate decision as to what the Sinaitic Torah means is arrived at by a dialectic between inside and outside forces, with both subsumed under the larger interpretive goal: to achieve a holistic understanding of the divine will.

Eugene Borowitz (1924–2016) was the most influential Reform thinker to have emerged out of the American Reform movement in the twentieth century. A graduate of the Ohio State University and ordained rabbi at Hebrew Union College–Jewish Institute of Religion, Borowitz received doctoral degrees from both Columbia University Teachers' College and HUC-JIR. From 1962 until his death, he taught at the New York campus of HUC-JIR. Publishing in the areas of Jewish ethics and philosophy, he dealt extensively with covenant theology. Borowitz was also the founding editor of *Sh'ma* magazine.

Eugene B. Borowitz, *Renewing the Covenant* (Philadelphia: Jewish Publication Society, 1991), 288–93.

In contrast to contemporary privatistic notions of selfhood, the Jewish self, responding to God in Covenant, acknowledges its essential historicity and sociality. One did not begin the Covenant and one remains its conduit only as part of the ongoing people of Israel. Here, tradition and ethnicity round out the universal solidarity of humankind which this particularity grounds in its myth of the Noahide covenant. With heritage and folk essential to Jewishness, with the Jewish service of God directed to historic continuity lasting until messianic days, the Covenanted self knows that existence must be structured. Yet, as long as we honor each Jew's selfhood with a contextually delimited measure of autonomy, this need for communal forms cannot lead us back to law as a required, corporately determined regimen. Instead, we must think in terms of a *self-discipline* that, because of the sociality of the Jewish self, becomes communally focused and shaped. The result is a dialectical autonomy, a life of freedom-exercised-in-Covenant. It differs so from older non-Orthodox theories of folk discipline —Zionism or Kaplanian ethnicity—or personal freedom—Cohenian ethical monotheism or Buberian[22] relationship—that I wish to analyze in some detail its five major themes.

22. [The references here are to Hermann Cohen and to Martin Buber, mentioned in the Introduction (xxiv) as foundational European influences on American Jewish thought.]

First, the Jewish self lives personally and primarily in involvement with the one God of the universe. Whereas the biblical—rabbinic Jew was almost entirely theocentric, the contemporary Jewish self claims a more active role in the relationship with God. In the days of buoyant liberalism this self-assertion overreached to the point of diminishing God's active role, sometimes countenancing supplanting God with humanity writ large. Postmodernity begins with a more realistic view of our human capacities and a determination not to confuse the junior with the senior partner. . . .

Second, a Jewish relationship with God inextricably binds selfhood and ethnicity with its multiple ties of land, language, history, traditions, fate and faith. By this folk rootedness Covenantal Jewish identity negates the illusion that one can be loyal to humanity as a whole but not to any single people, and it rescues the messianic hope from being so abstract as to be inhuman. Ethnic particularity commits the Jewish self to the spirituality of sanctifying history through gritty social and political struggles. Internally as well, each Jew becomes implicated in this people's never-ending struggle to hallow grim social circumstances or the temptations of affluence and show itself another faithful Covenant generation. . . .

For all the inalienable ethnicity of the Jewish self, it surrenders nothing of its individual personhood. In a given matter, the Covenant people may be inattentive to its present duty to God, or in a given situation, an individual Jew of certain talents and limitations may find it Covenantally more responsible to go an individual way. Now Covenanted selfhood requires conscientious self-examination in the light of community standards to determine whether this dissent of the Jewish self is willfulness or an idiosyncratic sensitivity to God. . . .

Third, against the common self's concentration on immediacy, the Covenant renders the Jewish self radically historical. Our Jewish relationship with God did not begin with this generation and its working out in Jewish lives has been going on for millennia. Social circumstances and Jewish self-perception have changed greatly in this time yet the Jews we encounter in our old books sound very much like us. . . . For the Jewish self, then, Covenant means Covenant-with-prior-Jewish-generations.

Many modern thinkers deprecated the idea of such a spiritual continuity. They thought our vastly increased general knowledge made us more religiously advanced than our forebears and optimistically taught that each generation knew God's will better than the prior one, a notion they called progressive revelation. Postmodern thinkers, such as myself, reverse the hierarchy. On most critical religious issues, no one writing today can hope to command the respect the authors of the Bible rightly continue to elicit. Moreover, since their life of

Covenant was comparatively fresh, strong, and steadfast, where ours is often uncertain, weak, and faltering, we should substantially rely on their delineation of proper Covenantal existence. The biblical and rabbinic texts have every Jewish right to exert a higher criticism of the lives of each new generation of Jews, so classic Jewish learning must ground Jewish selfhood as firmly as does personal religious experience.

In one critical respect, however, we stand apart from previous generations: our conviction that we must exercise considerable self-determination. If some respect for individuality had not always characterized Jewish spirituality, we would be astonished at the luxuriant display of change and innovation we find in Jewish religious expression over the centuries. Our radically transformed social and intellectual situation elicits a corollary reinterpretation of Covenant obligation. In particular, our sense of linkage with God prompts us to identify spiritual maturity with the responsible exercise of agency. Hence, we find it necessary to take initiative in untraditional fashion in order to be true to what our Jewish self discovers in Covenant. Here, too, our sacred books make their authority felt by challenging us to ask whether our deviance has grown out of Covenantal faithfulness or trendy impulse.

Fourth, though the Jewish self lives the present out of the past, it necessarily orients itself to the future. All the generations of Jews who have ever been, including us, seek the culmination of the Covenant in the days of the Messiah. The glories of the Jewish past and the rewards of the Jewish present cannot nearly vindicate Israel's millennial service of God as will that era of universal peace, justice, love, and knowledge of God. A Jewishness satisfied merely to meet the needs of the present but not radically to project Covenantal existence into the far future betrays the hopes of the centuries of dedication that made our spirituality possible. The Jewish self, by contrast, will substantially gauge the Covenantal worthiness of acts by their contribution to our continuing redemptive process. For the Jewish self, then, Covenant means Covenant-with-Jews-yet-to-be, especially the Messiah. . . .

. . . Our Covenantal future-directedness may also compel us to break with an old, once valuable but now empty Jewish practice. For Jewish selfhood also requires us to assure the Jewish future by making our way to it through the presently appropriate Covenantal act. Even then, the awesome endurance of Jewish traditions will dialectically confront us with its question as to the staying power of the innovation we find so necessary.

Fifth, yet despite the others with whom it is so intimately intertwined—God and the

Jewish people, present, past and future—it is as a single soul in its full individuality that the Jewish self exists in Covenant. . . .

The self, free and self-determining, must then be given its independent due even though, as a Jewish self, its autonomy will be exercised in Covenantal context. At any given moment it is ultimately I who must determine what to make of God's demands and Israel's practice, tradition and aspiration as I, personally, seek to live the life of Torah in Covenantal faithfulness. For the Jewish self, then, Covenant means Covenant-with-one's-self. . . .

I have been describing more a spiritual goal than a present condition, my version of what Rosenzweig called our need to move from the periphery of Jewish living back to its center. By the standards of this ideal, fragmentariness and alienation characterize most Jewish lives today, our lives commonly reflect more the brokenness of humanhood in our civilization than any integrating Jewish vision. This diagnosis leads to a therapeutic goal: bringing Jews to the greater wholeness of Jewish selfhood, a reconstruction of Jewish life that begins with helping individual Jews find greater personal integration, one that ineluctably involves them in community as with God. This constitutes the obverse of Kaplan's emphasis on changing our pattern of Jewish community organization so as to foster a healthy Jewish life.

How might this ideal, so individualistically based, bring a critical mass of Jews to communal patterns of Covenantal observance? It cannot be created by a contemporary version of heteronomous law as long as we continue to accept the personal and spiritual validity of self-determination. But if Jews could confront their Judaism as Jewish selves and not as autonomous persons-in-general, I contend that they would find Jewish law and lore the single best source of guidance as to how they ought to live.

Susan Handelman was born in 1949. A graduate of Smith College, she received her MA and PhD in English from the State University of New York at Buffalo. Having served on the faculty of the Department of English at the University of Maryland for over twenty years, she moved to Israel in 2000, and she has been a professor at Bar-Ilan University since then. Specializing in the relationship between Jewish thought and literary theory, Handelman is an Orthodox Jew who has also translated and commented on the thought of the Lubavitcher Rebbe.

Susan Handelman, "'Crossing and Recrossing the Void': A Letter to Gene," in *Reviewing the Covenant: Eugene B. Borowitz and the Postmodern Renewal of Jewish Theology*, ed. Peter Ochs (Albany: State University of New York Press, 2000), 178–82.

I have chosen to be a *halakhic* Jew, and I believe that one of the key unmet tasks of postmodern Jewish thought is to overcome what I would call . . . a secularized theological antinomianism. That is partially a legacy from the German philosophers who also inspired the Jewish *haskalah* and modernist thought. Especially Kant, that great proponent of morality. Kant defined morality as duty observed out of inner conviction through reason and autonomy in contrast to duty observed due to externally commanded law (that is, through authority and heteronomy). In his schema, Judaism becomes an inferior religion of heteronomous law, rightly superseded by a higher Christian religion of inner freedom. Kantian autonomous reason, as Natan Rotenstreich once put it, is an equivalent or transformed version of Protestant grace or "inner illumination."

When I say that postmodern Jewish thought needs to recover the meaning of law in Judaism, I should insist on using the word *halakhah*, originating in the Hebrew root for "path, or walking." But I don't want to rehash worn old arguments between "Orthodox" and "Reform" Judaism—terms I am not comfortable with in any case. I want rather to emphasize here that *halakhah* cannot be understood in terms of modernist categories of "autonomy" and "heteronomy." As Emil Fackenheim once wrote in *Encounters Between Judaism and Modern Philosophy*,

Kant did not understand the nature of revealed morality in Judaism because it is outside the realm of both autonomous and heteronomous morality. Its source and life "lies precisely in the togetherness of a divine commanding Presence that never dissipates itself into irrelevance, and a human response that freely appropriates what it receives."[23]

Postmodernism can help move us beyond the sterile antinomy of autonomy/heteronomy. For one thing, the autonomy/heteronomy dualism presupposes an independent isolated self. A notion which is heavily criticized in postmodern thought. For another, it is a mistake to identify the obligation, the "must" of a *mitzvah* with the "must" of rational propositions and deductive logic. Rosenzweig and Levinas well understood the need for this "third term" beyond the heteronomy/autonomy dualism. The paradigm for their construction of the self is the biblical cry of *hineni*, *"Here I am."* These are the words with which Abraham responds to God before the *Akedah*.[24] And with which Moses responds at the burning bush, and which the prophets use when they are called by God. Rosenzweig writes that when God calls out to Abraham in direct address, in all his particularity, then Abraham answers, "all unkicked, all spread-apart, all ready, all-soul: 'Here I am.' Here is the I, the individual human I, as yet wholly receptive, as yet only unlocked, only empty, without content, without nature, pure readiness, pure obedience, all ears."[25]

Or let me quote Peter Pitzele, who eloquently describes what is so difficult for us moderns to understand about Abraham's "obedience": "History has given obedience a bad name; too many docile lambs led to the slaughter; too many obedient functionaries murdering the lambs. Whenever we hear talk of obedience, we are likely to feel ambivalence and fear. And a personal revulsion curdles the word as well. . . . Obedience is a giving over of one's personal power; it is a loss of control." But there is another kind of obedience, Pitzele notes:

The word *obey* in English comes from the Latin word meaning "to listen, to hear." Abram *listens* to the call to leave his native land. And his father's house. He obeys. He experiences the call as something coming from a God who is felt to be Other and outside him. But this God is also inside him. Deep speaks

23. [Emil L. Fackenheim, *Encounters between Judaism and Modern Philosophy*, (Philadelphia: Jewish Publication Society of America, 1973), 44.]

24. [The tale of the binding of Isaac in Genesis 22.]

25. Franz Rosenzweig, *The Star of Redemption*, 2nd ed. (1930), trans. William Hallo (Notre Dame, IN: Notre Dame University Press, 1985), 176.

to deep. . . . Abram is not being obedient to some external dictate, to some chain of command. On the contrary, he breaks with customary conventions. . . . What Abram obeys flashes upon him like a beacon, points a way, then disappears. . . . On each step of his journey he must renew his commitment to his task, for his obedience is voluntary, not compelled.[26]

So often you[27] reiterate that central to your project is the need to protect our integrity in the face of the God who commands. But this is what the interpretive tradition of Oral Torah has always done. The Talmud already voices your concerns about an external compulsion which invalidates the revelation at Sinai in the famous passage in *Shabbat* 88a. I want to quote at some length from the Talmud here, for as much as I cherish the personal moments in *Renewing the Covenant*, I also sorely miss in it the embodied texture of classical Jewish discourse —the cacophonous yet melodic weave of voices from different eras and times in the commentaries and super-commentaries, the dialogic voices of Talmud and *midrash*.

The biblical text tells us that the Israelites stood *b'tachtit ha har*—translated idiomatically "at the foot of the mountain," but having a more literal sense of "at the underside." Here the Talmud comments:

> Rav Avdimi bar Hama bar Hasa said: this teaches us that the Holy One Blessed be He turned the mountain over on them like a cask and said; "If you accept the Torah, all is well; if not, here will be your grave." Rav Aha bar Jacob said: "Based on this, a major complaint can be lodged against the Torah." Rava said: "Nevertheless they reaccepted it willingly in the days of Ahasuerus, for it is written, "the Jews [*kimu v'kiblu,*] confirmed and accepted." They confirmed what they had accepted previously.[28]

Rashi explains the nature of this complaint: "for if they were brought to judgment about why they had not fulfilled what they had accepted upon themselves, they could answer that they were compelled by force to accept it." In other words, it was not of their own free will. Nevertheless, they reaccepted it a thousand years later in their exile in the Persian Kingdom of Ahasuerus—"from," says Rashi, "the love of the miracle that was done for them."

26. Peter Pitzele, *Our Fathers' Wells: A Personal Encounter With the Myth of Genesis* (New York: Harper San Francisco, 1995), 90–91.

27. [These words are directed to Eugene Borowitz.]

28. [Babylonian Talmud Shabbat 88a.]

In other words, what the book of Esther is referring to in verse 9:27 ("the Jews confirmed and accepted upon them and upon all their seed . . . to observe these two days of Purim") is not just the Jews' confirmation and acceptance of Mordecai's instructions about how to commemorate their miraculous rescue. On a deeper level, they confirmed and accepted what had previously been "forced" upon them a thousand years earlier at Sinai; only *now* they did it out of free will. In "The Temptation of Temptation," Levinas' commentary on this passage, he understands that this *midrash* on the relation of Sinai and Purim as indicating a "third way" beyond the dualistic alternative freedom/violence or autonomy/heteronomy. It signifies that there is a certain "non-freedom" prior to freedom, one which makes freedom possible—a prior saying of *Na'aseh Ve-Nishma* "we will do and we will hear/obey/understand," a prior calling to responsibility which is what in fact constructs the self. The self is defined by saying *hineni*, "Here I am for you." Moreover, Levinas notes, the thousand years of history between Sinai and the Persian exile were filled with the difficult consequences and suffering resulting *from* that first acceptance of the Torah. In reaccepting it at Purim, we do so in full cognizance of its price. In this light, I also find Rashi's comment even more poignant: the motivation for reaccepting the Torah was from "love of the miracle." Acceptance out of love, and in a time of threatened mass annihilation. For Purim is, in its own way, a holiday made for a postmodern sensibility: a holiday of masks, inversions, comic mockery, concealment of God whose name is never even mentioned in the *Megillah*. For the rabbis to make out of this a second Sinai is an act of hermeneutical genius and profound theology.

This is the continuing task of any Jewish theology, of course, to continue Sinai. The great climactic scene at Sinai filled with thunder, lightning, and the Voice from heaven, is followed in the biblical narrative by a seeming let down: the minutiae of law regarding goring oxen, Hebrew bondsmen, and so forth. Then come the long, seemingly tedious narratives of the building of the *mishkan*, the Tabernacle, descriptions of its boards and nails, the dress of the high priests; and then we proceed on into the book of *VaYikra* (Leviticus) and its elaborate descriptions of the sacrificial system. These are the parts I usually skip when I teach "The Bible as Literature" to my mostly non-Jewish undergraduates. But perhaps this is a mistake. For these are also the parts that are so distinctly Jewish, ways in which the elevated abstractions are brought into the concrete world. This is what *halakhah* is: Second Sinai, the continuations of the voice of God echoing through the voice of human interpretation, and the extension of the revelation into the seemingly most mundane aspects of human life.

For revelation cannot remain an awesome inchoate Presence. It needs to be concretized and brought into the realm of the everyday. A student of mine once made a startling comment about the prosaic ending of the book of Job. After the voice from the Whirlwind, the text returns to a strange, prose episode which matter-of-factly recounts that God restored to Job double what he had lost; Job became wealthy, Job remarried, had many sons and daughters, lived to a ripe old age and "died, old and full of days." My students are often offended by this ending. After God has taken everything away and tormented Job unfairly and then made a thundering speech from the Whirlwind, what is this, they ask indignantly? Some kind of attempt at recompense? How could that ever make up for all his suffering? But this one student said: No. One cannot continue to exist on the level of the Voice from the whirlwind. One has to come back into daily life. Remember the Voice, be transformed by it, but come back to living day-to-day in the prosaic rounds of family life. A more "orthodox" way of saying all this would be to characterize it as the "Will of God." The divine will must manifest itself and be reflected in the minutiae of daily life. Where else should it manifest itself? Where else do we make a *mishkan*, a holy dwelling for God, if not in those areas of life most central to human finite existence: food, dwelling, clothes, sex, economics?

Our Jewish postmodern world is a post-*shoah*, post-whirlwind world as well. And the hermeneutic theories of postmodernism have helped us gain a new appreciation of the radicality of rabbinic ways of reading and rereading. These insights fortify me on my own path of *teshuva*.[29] But it is not just in the realm of *aggadah* that humans are partners with God; that partnership has always been part of the traditional *halakhic* imperative. That is the whole notion of the Oral Torah. It is a caricature to describe the classical notion of *"Torah Mi Sinai"* as something handed down by a dictatorial God who takes away autonomy.

29. [A classic rabbinic term for repentance.]

David Novak, "Is the Covenant a Bilateral Relationship?"

David Novak (born 1941) is Professor of Religion and Philosophy at the University of Toronto and formerly taught at the University of Virginia. He received his undergraduate education at the University of Chicago, rabbinical ordination at the Jewish Theological Seminary, and his doctorate in philosophy at Georgetown University. His areas of expertise include Jewish ethics, social philosophy, the concept of election, and Jewish-Christian relations, and he has published extensively in all these areas.

David Novak, "Is the Covenant a Bilateral Relationship? A Response to Eugene Borowitz's *Renewing the Covenant*," in Ochs, *Reviewing the Covenant*, 85–87.

The difference between a phenomenology of personal relationship and an ontology of creation as the best explanation of the reality of the Jewish Covenant with God is the philosophical core of the theological differences between Professor Borowitz and myself. (In an age when intellectual discourse in general and Jewish intellectual discourse in particular is so often debased, I do not take for granted the privilege of having a thinker like Eugene Borowitz with whom to have such an exalted disagreement—hopefully, one for the sake of God.)

Our fundamental difference is whether the Covenant requires a God who actually speaks. Without a God who speaks I do not see how we can have a durable bridge from revelation to communal norms qua *mitzvoth* (namely, the commandments *of* God), and not just universal ethical imperatives as in Hermann Cohen's theology, or ethnic folkways or religiously significant sancta as in Mordecai Kaplan's theology. For Cohen's ethical imperatives are grounded in the autonomy of the self (following Kant as he does), and Kaplan's folkways and sancta are grounded in the heteronomy of the group (following Durkheim as he does). Indeed, in both contractual and interpersonal relationships as models of the Covenant, the theological problem is the equality of the partners, and that follows from the fact that the relationship itself requires that both parties speak to each other. But does the liberal theology that assumes that God's word is *bespoken* by humans not actually place humans at a decided advantage over

God? Is it not even more theologically problematic than the former two models, autonomy and heteronomy, for just that reason?

If only the human partner is able to speak the reality of the Covenant in the name of God, then how is that to be distinguished from autonomous or heteronomous *projection* of essentially human will onto an idealized God? Is this not the great critique of religions of revelation conducted by Feuerbach, Marx, Freud, and their respective followers? Of course, these enemies of revelation would attribute revelation and its norms to projection irrespective of how theologians constitute it. Nevertheless, when theologians constitute revelation in a way more consistent with biblical and rabbinic teaching, both of which continually affirm the God who speaks his commandments, they have not seen in it a meaning that cannot answer the charge of projection. Therefore, the debate with the enemies of revelation is not only about its truth (which cannot be settled until the "end of days") but about its meaning as well. Meaning is always more accessible than truth; being immediately public it can be authenticated here and now. To lose the battle over meaning leaves nothing left to be won by the final revelation of truth. Since truth and normativity are so intimately linked in Judaism, this leads to what can only be termed the crisis of authority in the liberal, religious, Jewish community, of which Borowitz is in the mind of many the leading theorist.

It is not that the liberal, religious, Jewish community is devoid of *halakhah*, for *halakhah* simply means "law," and no human community can exist without law of some kind or other. But this community seems to have law only in the area of interhuman relationships—what the tradition calls the "realm *bein adam le-havero*." The best example of this is the virtually unanimous consensus in this community on the issue of gender equality as a moral norm. But in the relationship between God and humans—what the tradition calls the "realm *bein adam le-maqom*"—there seems to be virtual antinomianism, if not anarchy, whether the issue be the observance of the Sabbath, the content of the liturgy, the status of mixed marriages, or even the identity of members of the Covenant.

Why is this the case? I think it is the case because a nonverbal revelation at the core of the religious reality, not having a God who speaks, must revert to either the voice of an individual human being (namely, *auto*-nomy) or the voice of a community (namely, *hetero*-nomy). Considering the general preference for autonomy by contemporary liberals, especially evidenced by the prominence of highly individualistic "rights-talk" in our current political and social discourse, it is little wonder that contemporary Jewish liberals, even religious ones, look to liberalism, not classical Judaism, for their normative model. In the liberal community, made up as it is by autonomous selves, religion as the relationship between a human person and *his* or *her* God is essentially a matter of individual preference. Only what is strictly interhuman is a matter of social concern here. Law can never be anything so individual, operating as it does by generalizing categories.

What is needed to get us out of this theological impasse is a constitution of the classical Jewish doctrines of election and verbal revelation. This need not back us into a position of fundamentalist literalism, which has enjoyed such a resurgence of late in certain traditionalist circles, Jewish and otherwise, as part of a concerted attempt to repeal modernity in the name of a pre-modern utopia. Clearly, classical texts which record revelation have a history of communal transmission and cannot be understood apart from it. At this point in time, it cannot be understood without a judicious incorporation of the methods and findings of modern critical-historical scholarship. Nevertheless, this requires the far more profound theological task of a philosophically cogent constitution of the classical Jewish doctrine of verbal revelation. Only a theological project of that magnitude can insure us that the incorporation of these modern methods and findings be truly incorporated *into* Judaism and not vice versa. Without such a constitution, I cannot see how there can be any real covenantal community between God and Israel, which is true to the reality of God and the nature of human creatures. And without it, I cannot see how any truly binding norms can emerge from this understanding of the Covenant.

Rachel Adler was born in Chicago in 1943. She is a leading figure in Jewish feminist thought and theology. While Adler lived for many years as an Orthodox Jew, she later was ordained as a Reform rabbi after earning her doctorate in religion at the University of Southern California. Adler serves as Professor of Modern Jewish Thought on the Los Angeles campus of Hebrew Union College–Jewish Institute of Religion.

Rachel Adler, *Engendering Judaism: An Inclusive Theology and Ethics* (Boston: Beacon Press, 1998), 34–36.

The presumption liberal halakhists share is that modern halakhah must be a version of traditional halakhah adapted for a modern context by bringing formalist or positivist legal strategies to bear upon traditional texts. Decision making would remain in the hands of a rabbinical elite whose prescriptions are to be handed down to hypothetically obedient communities. The goal of liberal halakhah is to repair inadequacies of classical halakhah exposed by modernity while leaving the system basically intact.

Liberal halakhah believes itself to be modern because it is reactive to classical halakhah; to be truly progressive, however, a halakhah would have to be *proactive*. The place to begin is not with the principles we need to preserve or the content we may need to adapt but with what we mean by halakhah altogether. An understanding of law that lends itself to such a project can be found in the work of an American legal theorist, Robert Cover. Using Cover's understanding of what is meant by law, it is possible to explain how the feminist project qualifies as a lawmaking enterprise. Cover's account of the constitutions and transformation of legal meanings could provide sufficient common ground to enable representatives of classical and liberal versions of halakhah and their feminist critics to enter into conversation. It offers a basis upon which feminist hermeneutics, praxis, and commitments can make defensible claims to authenticity.

Law is not reducible to formal lawmaking, Cover maintains, because it is generated by a *nomos*, a universe of meanings, values, and rules, embedded in stories. A *nomos* is not a body of data to master and adapt, but a world to inhabit.

Knowing how to live in a nomic world means being able to envision the possibilities implicit in its stories and norms and being willing to live some of them out in practice.

Cover characterizes the genesis and the maintenance of law as to distinct elements in legal development. He calls these the *paidaic* or world-creating mode and the *imperial* or world-maintaining mode. Paidaic activity effects *jurisgenesis*, the creation of a *nomos*, a universe of meaning, out of a shared body of precepts and narratives that individuals in community commit themselves to learn and interpret. This generative mode is unstable and impermanent, but without its creative and revitalizing force, societies could not sustain the sense of meaning and shared purpose essential to communal survival.

The paidaic mode can create worlds, but it cannot maintain them. Inevitably, the single unified vision that all social actors share in a paidaic period splinters into multiple nomic worlds holding different interpretations. To coordinate and maintain these diverse worlds within a coexistent whole, there is a need to enforce standard social practices among them. The imperial mode universalizes the norms created by jurisgenesis and empowers institutions to reinforce them by coercion, if necessary. However, institutionalization and coercion are not the only means by which the imperial mode maintains the stability of law. Because the imperial world view does not strive for unanimity, but harmonious coordination of its different parts, it can admit as an adaptive mechanism some tolerance for pluralism, a value foreign to the paidaic ethos. Cover imagines these two legal moments, the paidaic and the imperial, coexisting in dynamic equilibrium.

Our modern problem with halakhah is reflected in the failure of this equilibrium, in the unmediated gap between the impoverished imperial world we inhabit and the richer and more vital worlds that could be. It is into this "paidaic vacuum" that Skotsl and her mission vanished.[30] By means of feminist jurisgenesis, we can bridge that gap and regenerate a *nomos*, a world of legal meaning in which the stories, dreams, and revelations of Jewish women and men are fully and complexly integrated.

Cover offers the image of the bridge to express the dynamism of the meaning-making component that both constitutes and propels law. Law-as-bridge is a

---

30. [Early in the chapter from which this excerpt is taken, Adler recounts a Yiddish folktale in which a representative of women seeking to protest to God the exclusion of women sits atop a pile of women, all perched on each other's shoulders. When the other women tumble down, she is nowhere to be found.]

tension system strung between "reality," our present world of norms and be-havioral responses to norms, and "alternity," the other normative worlds we may choose to imagine. In other words, the bridge is what connects mainte-nance-law to jurisgenerative potentiality. Law is neither reality nor alternity but what bridges the gap between them: "the committed social behavior which constitutes the way a group of people will attempt to get from here to there."[31] Ultimately, law is maintained or remade not by orthodoxies or visions but by commitments of communities either to obey the law as it stands or to resist and reject it in order to live out some alternative legal vision.

Cover's image of the bridge built of committed praxis grounded in story re-inforces the necessity of halakhah, for only by means of halakhah can Judaism embody its sacred stories and values in communal praxis. At the same time, Cover's bridge image makes it possible to think freshly about halakhah, because it counters precisely those features that progressive Jews, and progressive femi-nists in particular, find repressive in halakhah's traditional formulations. It is dy-namic rather than static, visionary rather than conservative, open to the outside rather than closed, arising communally, cooperatively, covenantally, rather than being externally imposed and passively obeyed. The metaphor of the bridge also expresses what it is like to inhabit a modern *nomos*. Bridges are generally open rather than enclosed. They span gaps and connect disparate entities, functions that reflect the needs of open, democratic societies populated by diverse groups of highly individuated modern selves. . . .

Because the Torah is no longer in heaven, mistakes cannot be rectified by building a tower from history into eternity. Instead, we must discover within ourselves the competence and good faith through which to repair and renew the Torah within time. We must *extend* Torah as we extend ourselves by reaching ahead. The aptest metaphor for that constructive task is that of the bridge we build from the present to possible futures.

31. Robert Cover, "The Folktales of Justice: Tales of Jurisdiction," *Capital University Law Review* 14 (1985): 181.

Born in 1972, Mara Benjamin is a graduate of Hampshire College who received her doctorate from Stanford University. She taught for a number of years at the Lutheran St. Olaf's College in Minnesota and is currently Chair of the Department of Jewish Studies at Mount Holyoke College. Benjamin writes extensively on topics in modern Jewish thought, feminism, and gender.

Mara H. Benjamin, *The Obligated Self: Maternal Subjectivity and Jewish Thought* (Bloomington: Indiana University Press, 2018), 11–14.

As Jews entered the crucible of modernity, they increasingly faced social and political conditions within which rabbinic concepts of obligation could not be sustained. Enlightenment thinkers, and the emergent European nation-states that aspired to Enlightenment ideals, condemned the heteronomous obligation that had long organized Jewish communal practice and individual piety. Enlightenment thinkers rebelled against "obligation" in the expansive sense of being bound to the world and to others. The new civil sphere would now expect demonstrations of Jewish loyalty and the relinquishment of competing communal loci of obligatory action, from ritual (such as the many practices that demarcated Jewish religious identity) to competing social and civil obligations (such as educational systems that reinforced Jewish languages and social formations) and political obligations (the *kahal* that had the power to sanction transgression). The mitzvot, especially those that were the most "visible," increasingly offered proof of Jews' inadmissibility for emancipation and integration into the liberal, quasi-secular, nation-state.

Most Jews in modernizing European societies—the Netherlands, France, the German states—enthusiastically supported religious reform, eagerly throwing off forms of obligation that hindered their participation in the wider civil society, and, when permitted, embracing new configurations of Jewish identity. Most Jews redefined their identity in voluntaristic, faith-based terms that downplayed and recast the heteronomous nature of Jewish obligation.

But the condition of obligation did not simply disappear from Jewish thought. Rather, modernity necessitated a narrower sphere in which obligation might be legitimately construed. Most Jewish thinkers, while not entirely jettisoning the mitzvot, dramatically transformed their meaning and reference point. In the modern Jewish imagination, obligation would be confined to the intimate, intersubjective realm. The sphere of obligation was to be primarily realized within dyadic encounters between an individual and the "neighbor."

Jewish thinkers in the twentieth century responded to the challenge of a shifted intellectual, political, and social landscape by rendering obligation not as the status imposed by a commanding God on the Jewish people, but rather as the result of encounters between two subjects in everyday human relationships. The intersubjective dyad became an oasis, a realm untouchable by the liberal critique of religion and its role in the public sphere. Instead of justifying the mitzvot, the performance of which became increasingly problematic in the modern nation-state, these thinkers conceived of humans as existentially, but not practically, obligated to the other.

This restriction of obligation to the intersubjective sphere testifies both to theological creativity and, simultaneously, to the impoverishment of the scope of obligation in the modern period. The emergence of the modern liberal nation-state seemingly required the disruption if not dismantling of Jewish obligation's traditional ritual, civil, social, political, and economic reference points. What remained was the dyadic encounter with another individual, a realm protected from the social and political critiques that continued to vex practitioners of the mitzvot.

In an intellectual and political environment hostile to traditional Jewish life, Jewish religious philosophers landed on an ingenious strategy for retaining but transforming the significance of obligation. The cost of this approach, however, was a fully realized concept of the individual to whom the self is obligated. Most influential Jewish thinkers conceived of the intersubjective encounter, and therefore of the individuals who participate in it, in decidedly abstract terms. The "other" they envisioned has no specific social location or set of needs. It is difficult, on the basis of these thinkers' writings, to imagine how such meetings occur in the course of ordinary life, and how duration of relationship, social proximity, and differences of power might affect them. An insistent tendency toward abstraction enabled these thinkers to argue for the universality of dyadic encounter and obligation.

A turn to concrete manifestations of obligation, by contrast, reveals the possibilities and limits of the relocation of obligation to this privatized sphere of engagement. Adults' embodied, daily experiences of obligation vis-à-vis their children offer a path forward. Taking maternal experience as a starting point, obligation can become an alternative to both the privatized notion of obligation and the tendency toward abstraction we find in so much twentieth-century modern Jewish thought. And contrary to the construction of agency merely in terms of liberal, rational choice, a feminist examination of maternal subjectivity suggests that agency dialectically informs obligation and vice versa.

The theological implications of this pursuit are admittedly startling: if the rabbinic notion of obligation comes into felt experience most viscerally in caring for young children, then God is not an overlord but a vulnerable, dependent being who needs virtually constant attention. This concept inverts the biblical metaphorical economy, in which God is parent, not infant, and the rabbinic sources that speak of God as king and as father, not as subject or son. But since these are metaphors, one in which God is imagined as a baby invites us to name the condition of being obligated to God as being compelled and beguiled, shackled and infatuated, all at once. The care for an infant perfectly captures the pairing of command and love at the heart of rabbinic thought. If God is not only loving parent but demanding baby, we may find within ourselves the resolve to meet the demand.

III | Spirituality

"Much like religion or experience, spirituality is bedeviled not by a lack of definitions but by an almost endless proliferation of them."[1] In recent decades the
term spirituality has undergone "a major discursive shift,"[2] and today Jewish
spirituality relates to many aspects of experience, including how a person in-
habits their body in sickness and health; how a person eats, learns, and loves;
how to find meaning in the annual cycle and the life cycle; how best to function within a fragile ecosystem and a fractious political system, both glob-
ally and locally; how to relate to the sources of Judaism while being open to
wisdom culled from diverse sources; and perhaps above all, how to live "[l]ife
in the presence of God."[3]

Some see "Jewish spirituality" as an alien intrusion on the true spirit of Judaism. Rabbi Aharon Kotler (1891–1962), for example, is quoted as warning
students at his Yeshiva against being tempted to study in secular and impious
institutions for the sake of learning a profession:

> This association is all the more unavoidable and pernicious in the College
> setting where they weigh Toras Hashem [the Divine Torah] and its values
> with their human intelligence which is . . . muddled with the race after ma-
> terialism and pleasure-seeking to the point of Avodah Zorah mamish [pal-
> pable idolatry]. It's their "spirituality"![4]

This blistering attack suggests that what passes for "spirituality" is in fact
gross materialism, mired in ignorance and error, and is to be both denigrated
and rebuffed. For Rav Aharon, one of the greatest figures of Lithuanian and later

---

1. [Courtney Bender, *The New Metaphysicals: Spirituality and the American Religious Imagination*, (Chicago: University of Chicago Press, 2010), 5.]

2. [Boaz Huss, "Spirituality: The Emergence of a New Cultural Category and Its Challenge to the Religious and the Secular," *Journal of Contemporary Religion* 29, no. 1 (2014): 49.]

3. [Arthur Green, "Introduction" in *Jewish Spirituality: From the Bible through the Middle
Ages* (New York: Crossroad, 1986), xiii.]

4. [In Yitzchok Dershowitz, *The Legacy of Maran Rav Aharon Kotler*, (Jerusalem: Feldheim,
2005), 157.]

American ultra-orthodoxy, spirituality is a code word for vacuity and idolatry combined. This stern rejection has interesting echoes in non-Orthodox American Jewish thought, as illustrated by the thinkers Will Herberg and Arnold Jacob Wolf, the second of whom is featured in this chapter. Both of them were light years removed from Kotler. Nonetheless, they too contrasted religious authenticity with what they deemed to be "ersatz narcissism."

Attempts to dismiss, downplay, or defuse spirituality are themselves a reflection of the extent to which it has become an active part of American Judaism. In a section of his 1955 masterwork *God in Search of Man* entitled "Spirituality Is Not the Way," Abraham Joshua Heschel (1907–72) argued that "[t]he world needs more than the secret holiness of individual inwardness. . . . God asks for the heart because He needs the lives. It is by lives that the world will be redeemed, by lives that beat in concordance with God. . . ."[5] Heschel, who was to become a major inspiration for many later exponents of Jewish spirituality, was concerned lest obsession with inwardness come at the expense of mitzvoth understood in their widest sense—ritual and activism, tradition and redemption. But rather than dismiss the spiritual quest, he was keen to expose the roots of spirituality embedded firmly within historic Judaism. These roots had been too long ignored, and were now ripe for exploration.

Two anthologies published within the space of a few years exemplify the growth of this trend. In the mid-1980s Arthur Green edited a two-volume collection of essays on Jewish spirituality throughout history. The books were the Jewish contribution to a series on world spirituality that claimed to provide "An Encyclopedic History of the Religious Quest." Green, both a scholar and practitioner of spiritual innovation, as well as a teacher of rabbis, was ideally placed to act as a convener of the Jewish part of this broader conversation. In 1992, Ellen Umansky (born 1950) and Dianne Ashton (born 1949) published a sourcebook anthologizing *Four Centuries of Jewish Women's Spirituality*.[6] Both of these projects of Jewish scholarship can be seen as part of a movement toward uncovering the sources of spirituality within tradition. Developments such as the rise of the Havurah movement[7] and the later growth of what has become

5. [Abraham Joshua Heschel, *God in Search of Man* (New York: Farrar, Straus, and Cudahy, 1955), 296.]

6. [Ellen M. Umansky and Dianne Ashton, eds., *Four Centuries of Jewish Women's Spirituality* (Boston: Beacon Press, 1992).]

7. [In the course of the 1960s, a number of men and women who went on to play a central role in Jewish religious life in America were involved in the creation of intense

known as neo-Hasidism[8] represent one of the most influential developments in American Jewish thought and practice. In each case, American Jews in the postwar era brought a sense of creative dissatisfaction and spiritual search to the attitudes and institutions of the Jewish community and created significant change. New or renewed areas of discourse within Jewish life involving prayer, meditation, counseling, therapy, wellness, eating, sex, community development, and much else have emerged in recent decades.

Unsurprisingly, a number of Jews have focused their interest outside or beyond Jewish parameters. It is noteworthy that a serious reader on *American Spiritualities* contains writings by a number of individuals of Jewish origin, but none of those included in the present anthology are mentioned.[9] Rather, the editor has included contributions from Tamar Frankiel (born 1946), an Orthodox scholar of religions; the counterculture icon and social activist Jerry Rubin (1938–94), writing about est; an excerpt from the memoir of Emma Goldman (1869–1940); and Starhawk (born 1951), a leading exponent of neopagan, goddess, and Wiccan spirituality, born in Saint Paul, Minnesota, into a Jewish family. American Jewish searchers have traveled far from normative Jewish life in their quests for meaning. While some have returned to enrich Judaism from within, others have not.

In Part Three, we highlight ten American Jewish voices. Skepticism about the preoccupation with Jewish spirituality is expressed in the words of Arnold Jacob Wolf, who fears it may deflect from serious engagement with the world. From a different perspective, Joseph Soloveitchik rejects a spirituality unmoored in traditional practice. While the former believes that political engagement offers a more genuine spiritual fulfillment that in any case is morally preferable, the latter argues for the fulfillment to be found in a life of halakhic conformity. The section from Abraham Joshua Heschel's *The Sabbath* is indicative of Heschel's foundational influence on the rise of a language of spirituality in America, a language that is furthered and deepened in the

---

alternative, experiential Jewish environments. See Susannah Heschel, "Changing Forms of Jewish Spirituality," *Proceedings of Rabbinical Assembly* XLII (1980): 146–58; Michael Strassfeld, *A Book of Life: Embracing Judaism as a Spiritual Practice* (New York: Schocken, 2002).]

8. [Shaul Magid distinguishes between neo-Hasidism and what he terms "paradigm shift" Judaism. See Shaul Magid, "Between Paradigm Shift Judaism and Neo-Hasidism," *Tikkun* 30, no. 1 (2015): 11–15, 58–62.]

9. [Catherine Albanese, *American Spiritualities: A Reader* (Bloomington: Indiana University Press, 2001).]

neo-Hasidic thinking of his student Arthur Green, and that is applied in the kabbalistic reflections of Daniel Matt. The two excerpts from Green show him as both a scholar and a practitioner of the field, while Matt brings to bear his expertise in the literature of the Zohar in his discussion of the creation of the world. Aspects of what might be termed a manifesto for Jewish renewal are to be found in the words of Zalman Schachter-Shalomi and Marcia Prager. The former incorporates terminology from Jewish liturgy and elsewhere to outline his vision for a new Yavneh. If the original Yavneh was the town to which the rabbis fled following the destruction of the Second Temple, the new Yavneh is in construction as Jewish thought and practice meet the consciousness of a new age. Prager picks up on the image of a Judaism in need of renewal after the demise of the old paradigm. Nancy Flam and Arthur Waskow provide specific examples of the spread of Jewish spiritual consciousness into a range of fields, healing in Flam's case, and food ethics in Waskow's. A coda is provided in the words of Sheila Weinberg, as she quotes the poetry of Judy Chicago.

A recurrent theme in this anthology, namely the interaction between scholarship and creativity in American Judaism, is clearly evident in the area of spirituality. A number of the writers here, and others whom we might have included, have been engaged both in the scholarly understanding of Jewish spirituality, and in the promotion of an approach to Jewish life in which spirituality is not an object of research but rather a living quest. It could be argued that this is one of the ways in which American Judaism has found its particular mode of expression.

One of the myriad definitions of spirituality is provided by Lawrence Hoffman, who styles it "a catchall phrase for organized religion's loyal opposition during historical moments of religious ferment and regeneration called awakenings."[10] While for some Jewish spirituality is an essential part of the revitalization of the Judaism of the millennia, others see it as a harbinger of a new millennium, as a new axis full of promise and risk, crowded with the challenges of a warming planet and a melting economic and political order, and yet replete with the promise of greater consciousness. Not all proponents of this new emphasis on Jewish spirituality reject traditional Orthodoxy, as

10. [Lawrence A. Hoffman, "Ethnicity, Religion, and Spirituality in Postwar Jewish America," in Between Jewish Tradition and Modernity, ed. Michael A. Meyer and David N. Meyers (Detroit: Wayne State University Press, 2014), 258.]

the writings of Aryeh Kaplan (1934–83) demonstrate.[11] The doubts expressed by Rabbi Kotler and others may continue, but they are now often accompanied by an acceptance that American Jews from many backgrounds and affiliations are searching for a spiritually resonant Judaism.

At the start of the period covered in the present volume, Jewish spirituality as a distinct area of inquiry hardly existed. Some eighty years later, Amazon lists eight thousand book titles connected to it. Whether this fact is greeted with enthusiasm or a sense of misgiving, it cannot be denied that Jewish spirituality is a central preoccupation of contemporary Jewish life in America.

11. [See, for example, Aryeh Kaplan, *Jewish Meditation: A Practical Guide* (New York: Schocken, 1985).]

Arnold Jacob Wolf (1924–2008) was a Reform rabbi ordained at Hebrew Union College in Cincinnati. He served congregations in Chicago for most of his career, though he was also Hillel Director at Yale University during the 1970s, where he worked together with William Sloan Coffin as a social activist. Together with his HUC classmates Steven Schwarzschild and Eugene Borowitz, he was part of an intellectual group of liberal thinkers offering a critique both of Classical Reform and of new trends in spirituality.

Arnold Jacob Wolf, "Against Spirituality," *Judaism* 50, no. 3 (2001): 363–64.

Jews and Judaism are deeply committed to bonds of loyalty and social connectedness. We are, after all, a religious people, a civilization, if you prefer, with historical roots that unite us and make us responsible for one another. To lose this social capital is to undermine our religious life with all its gifts.

Jewish Boomers created the short-lived havurah movement with consequences that still enrich our community life. But many of our now aging Jewish families are absenting themselves from congregational and communal life, preferring the private joys of domesticity and the rewards of demanding professional life to sharing the tasks and rewards of commitment to Jewish and human needs and tasks. Many of them would say, "I am not religious but I am spiritual." That, in my view, translates into eschewing group traditions and obligations, choosing instead to find Judaism within the narcissistic self. God is discovered not in a people's search, but in introspection, meditation, and, above all, "spirituality." That kind of spirituality, or "Jewish renewal," found everywhere today, can be the enemy, not the ally, of social capital.

If one examines the catalog of Jewish Lights, the most successful and prolific Jewish publisher today (with the possible exception of the neo-*frum* ArtScroll), one finds "spirituality" by far the most pervasive concern. Forty-seven of the new catalog's seventy-nine pages fall under that rubric. Representative book titles include:

Criminal Kabbalah
The Jewish Lights Spirituality Handbook

Moonbeams
Six Jewish Spiritual Paths
One God Clapping: The Spiritual Life of a Zen Rabbi

There are also, of course, books on holidays, but far more on meditation. There are almost no books at all on ethical or political issues, but a great many on healing and recovery, that is to say on personal self-improvement. Something profound is missing, and I believe it is precisely the communal, the historical, the great Jewish legacy of collective social responsibility.

Another testimony to the inundation of personal spirituality is the ninth international *Aleph Kallah*, held in DeKalb, Illinois, from July 2–8. Perhaps the best of the many Jewish spirituality centers, *Aleph* is not unaware of community needs that are social and political. But most of its energy is focused on topics like these:

The Art of Spiritual Ripening
Illuminating Your Life Choices with the Light of Your Soul
Movement as a Spiritual Path
The Boundaries of the Soul: Depth Psychology and Jewish Mystical
    Practice
Freeing the Soul
Turning G:dsparks into Ritual Dance
Returning to Oneself
Dancing Kabbalah: Releasing the Sparks Within
Purifying the Heart
Kabbalistic Drumming
Entering the Tree of Life: Engaging with the Sephirot as our Personal Map of
    Consciousness

These courses emphasize inner search and personal struggle for spirituality. But authentic Jewish methodology is more intellectual, more obedient than self-realizing, more about what is between human beings than within. Under the shadow of the dark religious genius, Reb Zalman,[12] and led by rabbis ordained by him, this renewal, alternative Judaism is inviting but, perhaps, dangerous. Kabbalah should not be approached lightly or prematurely, perhaps not at all in a week-long kallah. Boomers need more than inner peace to link themselves

12. [The reference is to Zalman Schachter-Shalomi, an excerpt of whose work appears in this volume.]

to a great, if often unwelcoming, Jewish *polis*. Most of all, a transcendent God is the limit to any immanent deity, to the "God" within. We cannot find ourselves alone. We need each other and each other's otherness; we need God's supreme and distant Self.

For a biographical sketch, see Part Two, p. 55.

Joseph B. Soloveitchik, *Halakhic Man* (Philadelphia: Jewish Publication Society of America, 1983), 57–60, 82–84.

A subjective religiosity cannot endure. And all those tendencies to transform the religious act into pure subjectivity negate all corporeality and all sensation in religious life and admit man into a pure and abstract world, where there is neither eating nor drinking, but religious individuals sitting with crowns on their heads and enjoying their own inner experiences, their own tempestuous, heaven-storming spirits, their own hidden longings and mysterious yearnings —will in the end prove null and void. The stychic[13] power of religion that seizes hold of man, that subjects and dominates him, is in force only when the religion is a concrete religion, a religion of the life of the senses, in which there is sight, smell, and touch, a religion which a man of flesh and blood can feel with all of his senses, sinews, and organs, with his entire being, a sensuous religion which conative[14] man will encounter, in a very palpable way, wherever he may go. A subjective religiosity comprised of spiritual moods, of emotions and affections, of outlooks and desires, will never be blessed with success.

Is halakhic man devoid of the splendor of that raging and tempestuous sacred, religious experience that so typifies the ecstatic *homo religiosus*?[15] Can he attain such peaks of enthusiasm that he will cry out in rapture: "How manifold are Thy works, O Lord! In wisdom hast Thou made them all" (Ps. 104:24). Is it possible for halakhic man to achieve such emotional exaltation that all his thoughts and senses ache and pine for the living God?

Halakhic man is worthy and fit to devote himself to a majestic religious ex-

13. [This word can be used to mean: objective, dynamic, natural, uncontrollable.]

14. [Striving for purposeful fulfillment.]

15. [The religious person. Soloveitchik here displays the influence that scholars such as Joachim Wach, Rudolf Otto, and Mircea Eliade, who popularized this term among students of religion, had upon him.]

perience in all its uniqueness, with all its delicate shades and hues. However, for him such a powerful, exalted experience only follows upon cognition, only occurs after he has acquired knowledge of the a priori, ideal Halakhah and its reflected image in the real world.

From the midst of the order and lawfulness we hear a new song, the song of the creature to the Creator, the song of the cosmos to its Maker. Not only the qualitative light, perceptible to the senses, with its wealth of hues and shades, its whirl of colors, sings to the Holy One, blessed be He; so do the quantitative light waves as well, the fruit of man's cognitive knowledge. Not only the qualitative world bursts forth in song, but so does the quantitative world. From the very midst of the laws there arises a cosmos more splendid than all the works of Leonardo da Vinci and Michelangelo. Perhaps these experiences of cognitive man are lacking in the emotional dynamic and turbulent passion of aesthetic man; perhaps these experiences are devoid of flashy and externally impressive bursts of ecstasy or stychic enthusiasm. However, they are possessed of a profound depth and a clear penetrating vision. They do not flourish and then wither away like experiences that are only based upon a vague, obscure moment of psychic upheaval. Such an experience is not some fleeting, unstable phenomenon that ebbs and flows, but is fixed and determined, possessed of a clear and firmly established countenance of its own. So is it also with halakhic man. His religious experience is mature and ripe when he cognizes the world through the prism of the Halakhah.

25 | Abraham Joshua Heschel, *The Sabbath*

For a biographical sketch, see Part One, p. 9.

Abraham Joshua Heschel, *The Sabbath: Its Meaning for Modern Man*
(New York: Farrar, Straus, and Giroux, 1951), 97–100.

To the common mind the essence of time is evanescence, temporality. The truth, however, is that the fact of evanescence flashes upon our minds when poring over things of space. It is the world of space that communicates to us the sense for temporality. Time, that which is beyond and independent of space, is everlasting; it is the world of space which is perishing. Things perish within time; time itself does not change. We should not speak of the flow or passage of time but of the flow or passage of space through time. It is not time that dies; it is the human body which dies in time. Temporality is an attribute of the world of space, of things of space. Time which is beyond space is beyond the division in past, present and future.

Monuments of stone are destined to disappear; days of spirit never pass away. . . .

Technical civilization, we have said, is man's triumph over space. Yet time remains impervious. We can overcome distance but can neither recapture the past nor dig out the future. Man transcends space, and time transcends man.

Time is man's greatest challenge. We all take part in a procession through its realm which never comes to an end but are unable to gain a foothold in it. Its reality is apart and away from us. Space is exposed to our will; we may shape and change the things in space as we please. Time, however, is beyond our reach, beyond our power. It is both near and far, intrinsic to all experience and transcending all experience. It belongs exclusively to God.

Time, then, is *otherness*, a mystery that hovers above all categories. It is as if time and the mind were a world apart. Yet, it is only within time that there is fellowship and *togetherness* of all beings.

Every one of us occupies a portion of space. He takes it up exclusively. The portion of space which my body occupies is taken up by myself in exclusion of anyone else. Yet, no one possesses time. There is no moment which I possess exclusively. This very moment belongs to all living men as it belongs to me. We share time, we own space. Through my ownership of space, I am a rival of all other beings; through my living in time, I am a contemporary of all other beings. We pass through time, we occupy space. We easily succumb to the illusion that the world of space is for our sake, for man's sake. In regard to time, we are immune to such an illusion.

Immense is the distance that lies between God and a thing. For a thing is that which has separate or individual existence as distinct from the totality of beings. To see a thing is to see something which is detached and isolated. A thing is, furthermore, something which is and can become the possession of man. Time does not permit an instant to be in and for itself. Time is either all or nothing. It cannot be divided except in our minds. It remains beyond our grasp. It is almost holy.

Time is the process of creation, and things of space are results of creation. When looking at space we see the products of creation: when intuiting time we hear the process of creation. Things of space exhibit a deceptive independence. They show off a veneer of limited permanence. Things created conceal the Creator. It is the dimension of time wherein man meets God. Wherein man becomes aware that every instant is an act of creation, a Beginning, opening up new roads for ultimate realizations. Time is the presence of God in the world of space, and it is within time that we are able to sense the unity of all beings.

Creation, we are taught, is not an act that happened once upon a time, once and for ever. The act of bringing the world into existence is a continuous process. God called the world into being, and that call goes on. There is this present moment because God is present. Every instant is an act of creation. A moment is not a terminal but a flash, a signal of Beginning. Time is perpetual innovation, a synonym for continuous creation. Time is God's gift to the world of space.

A world without time would be a world without God, a world existing in and by itself, without renewal, without a Creator. A world without time would be a world detached from God, a thing in itself, reality without realization. A world in time is a world going on through God; realization of an infinite design; not a thing in itself but a thing for God.

To witness the perpetual marvel of the world's coming into being is to sense the presence of the Giver in the given, to realize that the source of time is eternity, that the secret of being is the eternal within time.

We cannot solve the problem of time through the conquest of space, through either pyramids or fame. We can only solve the problem of time through sanctification of time. To men alone time is elusive; to men with God time is eternity in disguise.

Creation is the language of God, Time is His song, and things of space the consonants in the song. To sanctify time is to sing the vowels in unison with Him.

This is the task of men: to conquer space and sanctify time.

We must conquer space in order to sanctify time. All week long we are called upon to sanctify life through employing things of space. On the Sabbath it is given us to share in the holiness that is in the heart of time. Even when the soul is seared, even when no prayer can come out of our tightened throats, the clean, silent rest of the Sabbath leads us to a realm of endless peace, or to the beginning of an awareness of what eternity means. There are few ideas in the world of thought which contain so much spiritual power as the idea of the Sabbath. Aeons hence, when of many of our cherished theories only shreds will remain, that cosmic tapestry will continue to shine.

Eternity utters a day.

Born in 1941, Arthur Green has made a remarkable contribution to American Judaism as a rabbi, a scholar, and a neo-Hasidic theologian. He received his BA and PhD from Brandeis University and was ordained as a rabbi at the Jewish Theological Seminary of America. From his days in the chavurah movement in the 1960s, Green has played a central role both in the secular academy and in rabbinical seminaries, having served as a professor at both the University of Pennsylvania and Brandeis, as well as serving as President of the Reconstructionist Rabbinical College and founding Dean of the Rabbinical School at Hebrew College in Boston. Green is currently the Rector of the Rabbinical School of Hebrew College and remains a prolific scholar and theologian.

a. Arthur Green, "Introduction" in *Jewish Spirituality: From the Bible through the Middle Ages* (New York: Crossroad, 1986), xiii–xv.

b. Arthur Green, *Seek My Face, Speak My Name: A Contemporary Jewish Theology* (Northvale, NJ: Jason Aaronson, 1992), 11–13.

A.

Seeking the face of God, striving to live in His presence and to fashion the life of holiness appropriate to God's presence—these have ever been the core of that religious civilization known to the world as Judaism, the collective religious expression of the people Israel. Such a statement of supreme value—aside from questions of how precisely it is to be defined and how achieved—could win the assent of biblical priest and prophet, of Pharisee and Essene sectarian, of Hellenistic contemplative and law-centered rabbi, of philosopher, Kabbalist, *Hasid*, and even of moderns who seek to walk in their footsteps.

Life in the presence of God—or the cultivation of a life in the ordinary world bearing the holiness once associated with sacred space and time, with Temple and with holy days—is perhaps as close as one can come to a definition of "spirituality" that is native to the Jewish tradition and indeed faithful to its Semitic roots. Within this definition there is room for an array of varied types, each of which gives different weight to one aspect or another of the spiritual life. For some the evocation of God's presence includes an "ascent" to a higher realm and implies knowledge other than that vouchsafed to most mortals. Others content themselves with "preparing the table of the Lord" or, alternatively, seek to discover "the tabernacle within the heart" and allow the *shekhinah* (Presence) to find a dwelling there. The ultimate vision may be one of a highly anthropomorphic Deity seated on His throne, an utterly abstract sense of mystical absorption with the presence, the imminent arrival of messiah, or simply that of a life lived in the fulfilment of God's will. What all these have in common is a commitment to the life of holiness, a faith in the power of Israel's ancient code to embody that holiness, and a knowledge that such a life fulfils God's intent in creation and in the election, however understood, of His "kingdom of priests," the people Israel. This consensus had lasted until modern times when we find, as we shall see, Jews in search of the spiritual life who can no longer accept its premises as classically outlined by Judaism.

The definition of Jewish spirituality offered here has rather little to do, it will be noticed, with the term "spirituality" itself, for there *is* a precise Hebrew equivalent, *ruhanniyut*. The reader sensitive to the nuances of Hebrew speech will recognize this word as a latecomer to the ancient Hebrew tongue. It is an artifice of the medieval translators that was created first to express philosophical and scientific concepts that were Hellenic in origin. It was taken over only later by Kabbalists and pietists to describe a religious ideal that by then indeed was a thorough amalgam of the spiritual legacies of Israel and Greece. Spirituality in the Western sense, inevitably opposed in some degree to "corporeality" or "worldliness" (all apologies to the contrary notwithstanding), is unknown to the religious world view of ancient Israel; it is rather a late element, though an important one, among those factors that make up the religious legacy of medieval and later Jewry. Defining spirituality as the cultivation and appreciation of the "inward" religious life, we find both assent and demurral in the sources of Judaism. Surely the Psalmist was a master of inwardness, and the early rabbis knew well to speak of "the service within the heart" and the values of silence and solitude. There are latter-day Hasidic treatises focused almost entirely on the cultivation of *ruhanniyyut* and *penimiyyut* ("inwardness"). At the same time, concern is aroused lest the inner be praised at the expense of the outer. The rabbi, the spiritual descendant of both priest and prophet in this matter, will perforce rise to defend the externals. If inwardness implies a depreciation of the outer and dismisses religious behaviour (in the moral as well as the ritual realm) as mere ceremonies or trappings, the rabbi will find this a notion hard to tolerate. Religion, as far as the rabbi is concerned, is the living word of God, ever evolving through interpretation, a word that concerns itself with proper behaviour in every domain of life at least as much as it does with matters of the heart.

Aware of these reservations, and wary generally of applying to a particular tradition terms and categories that are alien to it ("mysticism" too is a category that does not exist within classical Jewish sources), we nevertheless permit ourselves to speak of Jewish spirituality, defining it as we have: Israel's striving for life in the presence of God.

B.

God Above, God Within

The particular ancient Near Eastern culture out of which the Jewish people and our religion emerged was one that worshipped sky gods. Especially after the Bible eliminated polytheism with its pantheon of gods and concentrated all the deities and their powers into one, the primary residence of God *in the heavens* was firmly established. From its very earliest origins, Jewish (hence also Christian, Islamic, and general Western) conceptions of God were tied to this *vertical metaphor* for the God-world relationship. "Where does God live?" the child is asked. "Up there," is the answer expected of the 3-year-old, with a finger pointed toward the heavens. True, we also hope that he or she will sweep a hand around and say "Everywhere!" and eventually (though probably quite a few years later) point inward to the heart as well. But the first answer expected is that which reconfirms for yet another generation the myth of verticality, the root-metaphor of our Western understanding of the relationship between God and world.

As much as we outgrow such thinking in our strivings for mature religion, the image of "God above" never quite leaves us. It is reinforced every time we read a Psalm about God who "dwells in heaven," every time we tell a story about Moses "going up to heaven" to receive the Torah, every time we encounter a text that speaks of spiritual growth as a series of "steps" up the cosmic "ladder." Even our mystical literature is much influenced by this deep-seated way of thinking: the visionary "ascends" through the seven heavens before seeing the throne of God's glory: the contemplative binds rung to rung to reach ever greater "heights" of understanding.

But suppose for the moment that we allowed ourselves to be freed from this upper world–lower world way of thinking. Dare we imagine a Judaism less than fully wedded to this single metaphor? Some of our greatest philosophers and mystics surely understood that this way of seeing things could well be replaced by one that spoke in terms of "inner" and "outer," rather than "upper" and "lower." Let us think of the journey to God as a journey inward, where the goal is an ultimately deep level within the self rather than the top of a mountain or a ride in the clouds. The Torah tells us that our ancestors were diggers of wells. Let us try to reach for the understanding that flowed as water from the depths of Abraham's well, rather, for the moment, than the one that came down carved in stone from the top of Moses' mountain. This journey inward would be one that peels off layer after layer of externals, striving ever for the inward truth, rather than one that consists of climbing rung after rung, reaching ever higher and higher. Spiritual growth, in this metaphor, is a matter of uncovering new *depths* rather than attaining new *heights*. Perhaps we could even try to think of Torah itself as having been given at the deepest level of inner encounter, rather than from the top of the mountain, the mountain serving as *a vertical metaphor for an inward event.*

Have we lost our Jewish souls in the course of this exercise? I think not. In fact, we may encounter a certain renewal of vigour in our spiritual language as we work on reading it in this other—and by no means entirely new—way. I am not suggesting that all vertical metaphors be eradicated from Jewish sources. This could not be done without destroying all the beauty and ancient charm that makes the language of Judaism so attractive and valuable in the first place. The metaphor needs to be preserved, but it needs to be placed in perspective. Our attempt to replace the upper with the inner as a focus of devotion helps us to see what a central place that single vertical metaphor has in our lives, in the forming of our psyches as well as our people's religious civilization.

Prayer, our sages surely knew, is an inward act. "The Compassionate One wants the heart," the Talmud teaches.[16] The locus of activity in human reaching for God is primarily inward, a turning of heart and mind that is attested by, but never fully subsumed within, outward deeds. The Bible's elaborate descriptions of the Tabernacle are read by Jewish authors of many later generations as outward symbols of inward states of devotion and grace, as Israel is told to "make a Tabernacle that I may dwell *within* them."[17]

This inwardness is not only that of the person, but the shared inner self of the human heart, the human community, and the world around us. Inwardness means that the One is to be found within all beings. We find God by a turning in to ourselves, to be sure, but also in the inner experiences that we share with others. The inner sight that we develop in such moments then leads us to an ability to see the inwardness of all creatures, to come to know them as the many faces of the One.

16. [Sanhedrin 106b.]
17. [Exodus 25:8.]

Daniel Matt was born in 1951. He received both his BA and PhD degrees from Brandeis University and was Professor of Jewish Spirituality at the Graduate Theological Union in Berkeley from 1979 to 2000. Matt has also taught at Stanford University and the Hebrew University of Jerusalem. A prolific scholar of Kabbalah and Jewish mysticism, his English translation of the Zohar, published by Stanford University Press, has made that work accessible to a new generation of readers.

Daniel C. Matt, *God and the Big Bang: Discovering Harmony between Science and Spirituality* (Woodstock, VT: Jewish Lights, 1996), 109–14.

Maybe God spoke only the first command, or only the first word. There is a later, mystical view that goes even further: Only the very first letter of the Ten Commandments was spoken by God. And what is the first letter? The *alef* of *Anokhi*, "I am." An *alef* without a vowel has no sound. It simply represents a glottal stop, a position taken by the larynx in preparation for speech.

A silent *alef* indicates the beyond. It frames a window onto the infinite realms of possibility. A kabbalist would appreciate the German mathematician Georg Cantor's decision to symbolize various types of infinity with the *alef*. The *alef* is the uncarved block, preceding the shape of the words, the verbal formulations of Torah. It represents pure potential, with no specific content spelled out. The Written Torah, the Five Books of Moses, is already a commentary on the *alef*, a series of glosses inscribed in its boundless margins.

The silent, pregnant *alef* resonates with another mystical insight. The Talmud teaches that the Torah was originally written with "black fire on white fire." According to one kabbalist, this implies that the white space between the letters is the essential Torah. The letters and words represent merely one interpretation of the white expanse.

The *alef* of revelation cannot be pronounced, yet it finds expression moment by moment. Its ineffable oneness can be rendered only in fragments, only by being translated into the duality of language, where each word symbolizes a separate thing. Revelation turns into Torah, into this and that, do's and don'ts, countless questions and answers across the generations. The *alef* generates Torah, which characteristically begins with the *bet* of *Bereshit* ("In the beginning"), letter number two. In the words of the Psalms, "One, God has spoken; two have I heard." *Ahat dibber Elohim, shetayim zu shama'ti.* Similarly, the multiplicity we experience in the world derives from a primordial unity fractured by the breaking of the vessels, a symmetry broken in the big bang.

The *alef* is the essence that cannot be grasped, an indication that essence cannot be packaged. The Written Torah—written in the margins of the *alef*, written to interpret essence—has been mistaken for essence. Accustomed to this interpretation, can we interpret the raw power of Primordial Torah? One particular reading of the divine mind has guided us for millennia and still has a hold on us. Through midrash, we have stretched the Written Torah, applied and contemporized it, personalized it: we have, in effect, interpreted the interpretation. But can we return to the source of it all? Can we uncover the unadorned *alef* and perceive the timbre of revelation: the sound of sheer silence, *qol demamah daqah?* . . .[18]

Silence is essential. We cannot hear something new if we are babbling away or carrying on a constant internal monologue. By quieting the mind, by emptying ourselves of preconceptions, we create a space for the *alef* to spell itself out in new ways. Why was the Torah given in the desert? Because "one cannot acquire wisdom or Torah unless one makes oneself like an ownerless desert."[19]

To enter the desert, to *become* the desert, we must surrender our images. The vast wilderness mocks our mental habits, and its stark grandeur inspires the *I* to renounce the claim to who it thinks it is, to see through itself—if only for a moment.

Even if the self becomes transparent, the next moment of revelation is mediated to each person differently. The message is not standardized, but designed for the individual. . . .

We may realize that the energy coursing through us is the same energy that pervades all life, but we often think, act, and speak in banal ways. Revelation provides awareness, not a detailed plan. To listen to the *alef* is to pause and to intuit our connection to something beyond self. We do not know where the *alef* will lead us. Perhaps our next thought will be selfish, depressing, or violent. The *alef* is open-minded, and we are capricious, so uncertainty dominates. Yet, as we

18. [1 Kings 19:12.]
19. [*Bamidbar Rabbah* 1:7.]

remind ourselves of our link to everything that exists, we challenge ourselves to channel the energy more effectively and harmoniously.

Having encountered the *alef*, we see Torah in a new light. No text can render the experience of revelation, but Torah focuses on what comes *after* revelation, how to live when we come down from the mountain. We need ethical guidelines, and Torah is a never-ending experiment in formulating them. Having exposed ourselves to the *alef*, we can now read some of the white spaces behind the letters of the Torah. Some of what we know from the Written Torah will need revision. Guidelines are not absolute. They change in the light of other wisdom, other renderings of the *alef*, such as philosophy, ethics, and the non-Jewish religions of the world. "Who is wise?" asks the Mishnah. "One who learns from every human being."[20]

20. [Pirkei Avot 4:1.]

Zalman Schachter-Shalomi (1924–2014) was born in Poland and raised in Vienna. He came to the United States in 1941 and was ordained by the Chabad movement. He also received a DHL in the psychology of religion from Hebrew Union College and served as Hillel Director at the University of Manitoba and Professor of Religion at Temple University. In the late 1950s, together with Shlomo Carlebach, he was active in promoting meditative practices; in the course of the 1960s, he moved away from the Chabad movement. In 1968, he helped establish Havurat Shalom in Somerville, Massachusetts, and in subsequent years he played a foundational role in what became known as the Jewish Renewal movement.

Zalman Schachter-Shalomi, *Paradigm Shift: From the Jewish Renewal Teaching of Reb Zalman Schachter-Shalomi*, ed. Ellen Singer (Northvale, NJ: Jason Aaronson, 1993), 277–81.

YAVNEH II

YHVH Melekh![21]

Paradigm shift, epoch change, New Age, Sinai Event, the RAINBOW—these are all part of seeing ourselves as Jews and planetary citizens. We realize as such that the way we need to do this is not merely by acting as individuals—reflecting and deciding. We know that we can't continue business-as-usual and survive. Change is essential, and we want to make the changes that are demanded by the aggregated process occurring in this new environment, our global village.

YHVH Malakh![22]

This has happened to us before now. When the Second Temple was destroyed, and with it our sacred technology, we were so disoriented we no longer knew how to JEW in the new circumstances. Except for Rabban Yohanan ben Zakkai and the few disciples in his *yeshivah* at Yavneh,[23] the only group that undertook to

---

21. [God reigns.]

22. [God has reigned.]

23. [The reference here is to the establishment of a center of Jewish learning in the immediate aftermath of the destruction of the Second Temple in 70 CE.]

handle the shift then were the new messianists, followers of the Nazarene and his scribes. Their move was discontinuous. Thank God that the few at Yavneh had the vision, the guts, and the know-how to lead the rest by following their insight into "*Et laasot laYHVH—heferu Toratekha!*" ("It is a moment in which we must act for God—by shifting Thy Torah."[24]) Thus they ensured continuity.

YHVH Yimlokh![25]

Prayer replaced sacrifice; Sabbath candles and blessings over food replaced worship at the Temple. The changes begun 250 years earlier by the *Anshei Knesset HaGedolah*[26] heightened the schism between the Sadducees (followers of Zaddok, founder of the high-priestly family, prior to the Maccabees) and the New Agers of that time, the Pharisees.

The Holy power was once vested in Moses, a single individual (paralleling the practice of the time, which was monarchy, governance by a single, absolute ruler). Following him and the later prophets, the rabbis too saw the power reside in the forum (paralleling the Senate in Rome). It was a broadening of the power base. In our day the power base shifts again to the total and egalitarian *havurah* of the committed, paralleling our civil representation.

When the Temple was destroyed, a number of shifts occurred. The Holy in the biblical period had been in *space*, a traveling *mishkan*,[27] on *bamot*, that is, high places or altars (*altus*—high in Latin). Later, after a dimension of *time*.

The Holy had been in the world of *action*. From the biblical perspective there was little need or requirement for making verbal statements to accompany sacrifice. After the destruction of the Temple, the rabbis moved the Holy into the world of the *word*—and with it created an entire technology of word *magic*, projecting it on the universe and God. Instead of seeing the Source of creation and revelation in heaven, we came to see it as immanent in us: "*Lo bashamayim*"[28] —but shared only by all the ordained.

Our view of God moved from the deistic projection of the totally transcendent God, who involves Himself in our history and "comes down" on Mount

24. [This rabbinic reading of Psalms 119:126 in Mishnah Berachot 9:5 is employed to sanction innovation.]

25. [God will reign.]

26. [The men of the Great Assembly, referred to in rabbinic literature as active in the period of the Second Temple.]

27. [A tabernacle.]

28. [Deuteronomy 30:12: Not in the Heavens.]

Sinai, to One "who becomes manifest" (as the *Targum* renders it): "just as the soul fills the body so does the Blessed Holy One fill the world." She is now seen as the *anima mundi*.

There were many aspects to the Yavneh shift . . . the most important point is that now, 40 years after the Holocaust, Hiroshima, and the establishment of the State of Israel, we are in a position similar to that of Yavneh—though later in the spiral of history.

Le'Olam Va'Ed![29]

The paradigm shift is not only a function of the history of the Jews. It has in a most palpable way become the shift for the entire planet. It was the same in the past. But then, though the whole planet was affected by the shifts, we didn't see them as more than a Jewish issue. Today that's no longer true.

Every reality map is affected when a paradigm shift occurs. The people who go through them are compelled to remap their most cherished grids, to redefine their central realities. All life is touched.

Adon Kol Toladot![30]

Mind moves of such vast proportions aren't made in leisure. They're birthed under irresistible duress by difficult and heavy contractions. We called them the *hevlei mashiach*.[31] We knew in the past and know today that such birth both propels and mirrors momentous change. Luria[32] saw such birthing in *yetziyat Mitzrayim*.[33] But the values and the constructs of past eons can't sustain our present lives. Like a fetus that must become a child in a new and seemingly impossible environment, we are similarly being birthed into a new and difficult time.

For those of us whose minds were blown in the sixties, who had to learn to ground their new visions in the emerging technologies and consciousness, it has become clear that the move is from sacred space and time to the sacredness inherent in *persons*.

Olam, which gave way to *shanah*, now gives way to *nefesh*.[34] The worship and

29. [For ever and ever.]
30. [Lord of all generations.]
31. [The birth pangs of the Messiah.]
32. [Rabbi Isaac Luria (1534–72), the leading figure of the kabbalistic revival in Safed.]
33. [The exodus from Egypt.]
34. [These three terms, which can be translated as "space," "time," and "soul," are central concepts in the Jewish esoteric tradition.]

service of God, *avodah*, once mainly bounded by action and speech, is now evolving toward consciousness and thought. The locus of revelation and law is moving from the masculine rabbinic elite to a male-female base of shared power. The planet is not seen as a dead chunk of matter but a cherished organism that demands to be nurtured as our life-sustaining mother.

Tradition in the Service of the Present!
TORAT HAYIM![35]

Withal, the Holy tradition isn't something to be overthrown but instead understood as the womb that begat our present. It is nonetheless impossible to remain in it and even less possible to return to it.

There is a new attitude toward women and children, and animals too—witness the increasing turn to vegetarianism; and we also see an emerging change of attitude toward the religious strivings of others who are evolving with us, whom in the past we labelled *goyim* and cultivated no more relationship with than was absolutely necessary.

Many who seek God today look for some needed spiritual vitamins in the liturgical and theological medicine chests of others. . . .

Dialogue Communication!

In the dialogue with social scientists and people-helpers, we have seen cardinal aspects of Torah renewed for us, particularly by the contributions of psychologists. When we read some of the transpersonal psychologists, our Kabbalah opens in new, process-directed ways. What we understood as angelic entities in the past we begin to see as functions and processes operative in our lives.

A new dimension of vision became accessible to all when women, with the lessening of oppression that restricted their communication, began to teach us in the white letters of the Torah the inner that men have missed.

The pace of global destruction goads us to become a *Mamlekhet Kohanim veGoy Kadosh*, "a Kingdom of Priests and Holy nation," as part of the organism of the *Adam Kadmon*, God's vision of global humanity. The atoning and Holy-making (sacrifice) functions of what inheres in us as part of providential endowment needs the interaction with other parts of that *Adam Kadmon*.[36] These are our elemental *Hayot Hakodesh*—beings of sacred life—of the ecological and

---

35. [A Torah of life.]
36. [Primordial Adam.]

holistic *Merkabah*,[37] the rest of humanity, the animal, vegetable, and mineral kingdoms.

Not Only Are We God's Partners—God Is Our Partner, Too!

We are not alone in this enterprise. What we have in the past called *ruach ha-kodesh*, the spirit of the Holy that we considered the gift of special individuals, that HOLY SPIRIT is now active and can be experienced in our midst. It is part of our social process as we study Torah and meditate in ways that seek to emulate group telepathy.

The Bat Kol![38]

The act of faith required to take the next step is really small. It's only one step of extrapolation from our present self-awareness. We intuit that there are aggregates still higher than our consciousness entering into our process, guiding and helping in ways we can at present reach only through the gates of our imagination.

The process of our renewal pervades everything: politics, economics, philosophy, physics, relationships, generations, and genders, Jew-Goy, Israeli-Palestinian, producer-consumer—all these and too many more to mention are being changed and metamorphosed. The developments are happening in ways that inform us so that we can cooperate in a conscious and ecstatic birth.

Some of us have dreamed the dream together and want to make it more explicit to ourselves and our colleagues. We want to plant our fantastic *neshamah*[39] potential into one synergy of *kavvanah*[40] to enlarge our intuition and to focus it for greater clarity.

So we reasoned that if we could meet, communicate, share, and allow to emerge what we hope for, then our process would fulfil one of the purposes of the pilgrimage Holy days, the *mitzvah* of *hakhel*,[41] to gather in holy spacetime with holy persons.

---

37. [The terminology employed in this sentence—angels, the chariot—are taken from the Jewish esoteric tradition.]

38. [In rabbinic literature, God's voice issues forth by means of the Bat Kol, the divine echo.]

39. [Soul.]

40. [Intention.]

41. [The commandment to gather for the purpose of hearing the law is found in Deuteronomy 31:9–13.]

This is happening in many places and situations. When we look at the brochures of summer offerings by organizations and movements parallel to us, we're amazed at how massively the Holy *Shekhinah* is agitating the birthing efforts.

We reach out to others who are regenerating as we are and hope to be included in their rebirthing. Still, what is special to us in our tradition is what we will celebrate and share most.

How awesome is this time! It must be that this is the process of God!—an opening of heaven (a paraphrase of Genesis 28:17).

A graduate of the Reconstructionist Rabbinical College who also received personal ordination from Rabbi Zalman Schachter-Shalomi, Marcia Prager (born 1951) has become a leading figure in the Jewish renewal movement. She currently serves as rabbi of the P'nai Or Religious Fellowship in Philadelphia and directs ordination programs at ALEPH: Alliance for Jewish Renewal. She writes and teaches on prayer, spirituality, and related topics.

Marcia Prager, *The Path of Blessing: Experiencing the Energy and Abundance of the Divine* (New York: Bell Tower, 1998), 162–67.

The rabbis who reconstructed Jewish life after the destruction of the *Beyt Ha'Mikdash*, the Second Temple, were the midwives of a paradigm shift which initiated halakhic Judaism, a Judaism based on Torah and *mitzvot* as interpreted by rabbinic authority. Halakhic Jews assume unquestioningly the eternal validity of that chain of command and assign authority for its evolution only to rabbis trained in Jewish law, historically an exclusively male elite. Non-halakhic Jews have abandoned the premise that the full package of traditional Jewish practice is binding, and participate in flexibly interpreted Jewish customs. Thus for most Jews outside the Orthodox minority, *halakha* is no longer the context of their lives.

History is change. Out of nomadic biblical Judaism evolved the complex sacred practice of the Temple, itself transformed in turn into halakhic Judaism by the revolutionary vision of the rabbis. Then medieval feudalism gave way to modernity in a vast economic and conceptual upheaval replacing land-based agrarian economies and their rigid social hierarchies with capitalism, the democratic "social contract," and unprecedented social growth. The success of each paradigm fostered the growth of the very phenomena that both built upon and replaced it.

History is now moving us toward the next shift—not, I hope, toward a minimalist and purely personal "non-halakhic" Judaism but toward a "post-halakhic" Judaism deeply rooted in the contributions of the rabbinic paradigm but "reformatted" to take Jewish wisdom, spiritual insight, and committed practice into the next age.

We are as a human community moving (however fitfully) into an era that will reshape the whole human story. Out of the ashes of the most terrible man-made destructions human history has known, a new view of the earth and our role in its evolution is emerging. Old forms, old "reality maps," however tenacious, are slowly giving way in the face of unprecedented forces of change.

The planet shrinks as global communications and computer technologies link individuals and cultures in patterns of interconnection unimaginable a few short years ago. Science, which once strove to demystify nature, now points us again to the fundamental mystery of all existence. Feminism encourages women's voices toward full participation in the human community, supporting global movements to bring women full human rights and honor women's wisdom. A radically new ecological awareness comprehends the inherent connectedness of all the fragile ecosystems of our planet. Human-potential movements expand our capacities for growth and illuminate new horizons for human aspirations. An egalitarian, humanistic consciousness spreads, rejecting all forms of abusive power and celebrating the intrinsic worth of each human being. Space exploration pushes our minds to imagine and embrace our planetary citizenship. In both a perilous and a tremendously exciting time of human history, a new metamorphosis begins.

Jewish renewal is a response to the desire to tap ancient wisdom in the service of the future. We are creating an authentic and inspired Jewish life-style, which applies Jewish spiritual teaching to the array of new concerns facing the human community. We embrace a vision of renewal that updates and restores the Jewish mystical tradition to centrality, and brings the richness of Jewish meditation back into the mainstream of Jewish spiritual practice. Hasidic teaching brings us a rich legacy of insight into the psychospiritual dimension of prayer and a path of joyous celebration fostering enriched personal and communal spiritual religious practice. We affirm that legacy and employ it to nurture the spiritual journey of each unique person and honor the truths expressed in all faith traditions.

Once the Kotzker Rebbe[42] posed the same question to his students that my husband asked the children in the *sukkah*: "Where is God?" The children all pointed toward the sky. At an adult spiritual retreat some participants pointed at their hearts, others pointed in a circle all around them. The Kotzker Rebbe's answer was a simple one: "God is where we let God in."

42. [Menachem Mendel of Kotzk (1787–1859).]

In the very first question in Torah God calls out to the earthling, "Where are you?" We let God in when we turn to face God and find God turning to face us calling, "Where are you?" Like Avraham and generations of others, we call out *Hineni*, "Here I am." Here I am, ready and prepared. Here, I am present and open. I wear no mask. I am free of pretense. Here I am with all that I can offer, which is my life. What is it You would have me do?

At such a moment we again enter the covenant; we are lovers, accountable not only for our intentions but for our actions. Awareness without action is like a love unconsummated. At those moments when we and God turn to face each other in fully mutual "I-Thou-ness," we grasp our role as finite beings with Godly work to do. We are partners with God in perfecting Creation or even, as one radical commentary suggests, as partners in the fulfillment and perfection of God. We pray that our actions will be an extension of the light of God, a channel for divine intention, true and faithful to the mutuality of our desire.

When I call out my *brakha*[43] to the Source of life, I open myself again to the Wholeness. I am recognized and loved. In the intimacy of connection I feel not only an embrace but also a demand, an enveloping and unfolding imperative to act in alignment with the Whole. The Power that opens to me wants not only my praise but also my effort. Each *mitzvah* opens me up again to that authentic within-and-without voice calling me to hope, love, praise, and act.

We are human beings whose souls are a spark of the living God whose name is I AM. We are also human "doings" whose work is to reflect the divine character of that spark. Where is God? Living with us in holy relationship, flowing through us in holy intention, fulfilled in the covenant binding us to holy action.

43. [Blessing.]

Nancy Flam was born in 1960. Ordained by Hebrew Union College–Jewish Institute of Religion, she has played a pivotal role in a number of institutions at the forefront of American Jewish spirituality. She was a cofounder both of the National Center of Jewish Healing and of the Institute for Jewish Spirituality.

Nancy Flam, "Healing the Spirit: A Jewish Approach," *Cross Currents* 46, no. 4 (1996–97): 488–90, 495.

Over the past several years, the American Jewish community has shown a growing interest in healing of the spirit by using the tools of Jewish tradition and community. A focus on healing is allowing Jews to explore the life of the spirit in a new way. This is because healing and spirituality are linked; indeed, healing implies spirituality. Spirituality is our sense of God's presence in our lives. There are many ways that presence may be felt: through connected human relationship, through prayer or meditation, through study and reflection. When we bring any of these resources which enhance our spirituality to the places of pain in our lives, then we call that healing. As we go about our complex lives, it is hard to find an entry point for general spiritual exploration. But at a time of illness, pain, or loss, our yearning for God's presence is often more acute than usual. Indeed, in the midst of tragedy many of us Jews find ourselves suddenly needing to explore or re-explore our Judaism. When great adversity rips us open and lays us bare, as life's trappings fall away and we set about the task of reconstructing our lives, we search our religious tradition for insight, comfort, guidance, and perspective. My work over the past five years with Jews who are ill has taught me how illness often serves as a springboard for profound spiritual exploration.

I think of one woman in particular. When we first met she said, "I've been diagnosed with ovarian cancer. As a child, my brothers both got Jewish educations and fancy bar mitzvahs, but, as a girl, I got nothing. I've been a secular Jew all my life; I rejected the tradition because it rejected me. But now I'm very sick and I want to know what I'm rejecting; maybe Judaism has something to offer me." Over the course of the following three years, this bright, passionate attorney joined a women's Torah study group, began attending healing services, and even joined a synagogue, much to her surprise. Six months before her death, she and her grown daughter celebrated their joint bat mitzvah by being called up to the Torah. For this woman, prayer, study, ritual, and holy relationship became the focus of her life; she could finally develop her spirituality at a time when it was clear her body would not be healed.

I think, too, of the man with prostate cancer who came back to Judaism after his diagnosis, searching the tradition for strength to deal with surgery, treatment, and loss. Through daily prayer, study, and deeds of loving kindness, he cultivated a profound sense of his own life's blessings. Although many people, understandably, would not share his feelings, he would not have traded his cancer for anything; it had provided him an opportunity to change his life in profoundly positive ways.

Exploration of the Jewish tradition's healing resources has become an acceptable, accessible way for those who are ill—and even for those who are not—to consider or reconsider the spiritual resources of Judaism. There are two reasons why such exploration has grown in recent years. First of all, we live in an age of postethnic Judaism; it is not enough simply to belong to the tribe. The death and rebirth mythology of the Holocaust and the establishment of the state of Israel, so powerful for the years after the war and into the seventies, no longer holds for American Jews; we cannot base our everyday Jewish lives on the Shoah and the events that take place in the Holy Land. Profoundly important as they are, they are not the stuff of daily religious living. Secondly, as the drive for communal survival is less pressing, Jews are freer to contemplate their individual lives as meaningful. To contrast to a pre-modern tradition which produced a liturgy written in the first person plural, American Jews find themselves in the midst of a postmodern culture which prizes autonomy and the experience of the individual. For both these reasons, many American Jews yearn for a specifically religious Jewish identification which values the inner life of the individual. American Jewry finds itself needing to create a new Jewish identity, religiously and not ethnically based. We are looking for new pivots, anchors, symbols, and meanings. Progressive American Jews are in need of a defining religious mythology.

One mythic structure that has caught the progressive Jewish imagination is that of Lurianic Kabbalah, that is, of Jewish mysticism: the idea that when the world was created, there was a fissure which allowed for evil, that at this time of great cosmic breakdown when sparks of holiness spilled out among the shards of existence, it became the task of humanity to redeem those sparks through deeds, to do acts of repair (tikun). Reform Jews in particular have adopted that view and vocabulary in our understanding of tikun olam, the repair of the world, doing acts of social justice that make our world more perfect, more redeemed. But there is another kind of tikun, one equally as important, and that is tikun hanefesh, the repair of the individual soul, the healing and perfecting of the person.

This framework of brokenness and repair is powerful. Within this framework, Jews understand that our work is both to do social justice, and to create healing and wholeness within. When Jews come to synagogue, it has always been clear that we come as part of a community, but now we also want to come as individuals, with particular gifts and particular needs. We want to matter. And we want to feel that each of us is welcome in our entirety: not only what is pleasant in our lives, but also what is difficult and painful. If "real life" is to happen in the synagogue, then we need to bring our "real selves." If true community is to take place in the synagogue, then we need to bring our true natures. Only then can our yearning for a sense of wholeness and for integration be achieved as Jews. This means that both the joys of b'nai mitzvah and the pains of divorce and addiction belong in the synagogue. This means that both the joys of marriage and the pains of illness, disability, and loneliness belong in the synagogue. Although most people are ashamed of being vulnerable, fallible, weak, and dependent, these are ineluctable features of our lives. . . .

American Jewry's recent interest in spiritual healing is a fascinating, hopeful, and complex development. It is my understanding that Jewish healing has begun to surface in American Jewish life because it recognizes and accepts human weakness and vulnerability. It has begun to surface because it helps Jews focus upon and nourish our spiritual sensibilities. As an overarching religious sense of brokenness and repair frames many contemporary Jews' experience of the holy, the Jewish healing resources of human relationship, spiritual development, and theological reflection help balm the wounded soul. Jewish healing focuses attention on God's relationship to our personal experience. For many American Jews yearning for a deepened spiritual life, the language, practice, and community of Jewish healing marks the beginning of a deeply personal religious renewal.

Born in 1933, Arthur Ocean Waskow remains one of Jewish Renewal's most influential leaders after more than fifty years. A graduate of Johns Hopkins University who received his doctorate in American history from the University of Wisconsin in 1963, Waskow soon thereafter began to combine his interests in political activism and spiritual quest. He received rabbinical ordination from a private interdenominational *bet din* headed by Rabbi Zalman Schachter-Shalomi and founded the Shalom Center, which he still heads, in 1983. He has been a prolific author and social activist.

Arthur Waskow, *Down-to-Earth Judaism: Food, Money, Sex, and the Rest of Life* (New York: William Morrow, 1995), 118–20.

The triumph of Modernity profoundly affected the eating habits of the Jewish people. While part of the community adhered to the tradition of kosher food, the majority of Jews in the world abandoned the rules in their flight from ghettoized Jewish communities, and in their identification with secularism and "universalism" and the potential of modern technology (in producing food as well as many other things).

In our own generation, however, this triumph of Modernity has become a trauma. In order to produce more food and other "consumables," the human race has subjected the earth to pollution and destruction. And the whole earth is striking back by threatening atmospheric decay, desertification, drought, flood, famine, the extinction of species. On the one hand, the whole notion that food must be treated as sacred has almost vanished. And on the other hand, the whole notion of treating the earth as sacred through rhythmic sabbatical rest for earth and earthlings has almost vanished.

The crisis of the Biblical Eden appears in our own day with more sharpness than ever before. For Eden is an archetype: Its crisis was, is, that we become fully knowledgeable humans only in the process of splitting ourselves off from the earth, eating from the earth in a split-off way. The tragedy is that we are in truth both split off from the earth and not split off from it. We are the one species that is able to rise "above" the earth, see it as a whole, and therefore choose to act as if we were not really embedded within it. Since as biological beings we are in fact still embedded in the earth's biology, when we act as if we are "beyond" earth, we ourselves are still shattered.

Today the breadth and depth of our knowledge is so great that we have acted with even greater power to separate ourselves than in the agricultural or industrial revolutions. The result is that we and the earth stand in much greater danger than ever before—the danger that we may be forever exiled from the one great earthly garden.

During the last three hundred years we have learned how to consume some of the fruits of Planet Earth, fruits of the Tree of the Knowledge of Opposites and Distinctions, which were hidden away throughout our history: fossil fuels, and nuclear energy. The result of this consumption has been both enormous wealth and a new kind of war with the earth. We have eaten so carelessly that we have poisoned the earth, and she is responding by poisoning us.

It is not clear that the planetary biosphere can long survive the careless treatment we are giving it. So we have made the gift of food from the earth more problematic than ever.

Technology has also transformed the medium of the relationship between earth and human earthling. Originally, food was the great connection. There were others—clothing, housing, wood for energy—but food made up the largest and most potent aspect of what we received from the earth.

That is no longer so. Much of the human race has created an economy in which many other products of the earth that are consumed by humans may outweigh food—in market values, if not in survival importance. What implications does this pose for Jewish practice?

At the same time that Modernity has deeply affected the relationship between human beings and the earth, it has eaten away at the close-knit communities that had populated the earth. Breaking down the ghetto walls has given Jews new freedoms, new equalities; it has also left them bereft of dependable and loving relationships and a sense of meaning in life and death that stem from living in coherent communities.

Out of these discoveries have come new desires and new searches. In the arena of food and eating, some Jews have concluded that pure individualism leads to the death of ethics and community, and that accepting communal standards for what to eat might make sense. For many, the ethical issues stem from a belief that all peoples eat from all the earth, and that a specific Jewish peoplehood does not express such broad concerns.

They may welcome communal discussions about vegetarianism, macrobiotic diets, or boycotts of foods grown by oppressed workers, but feel much less comfortable in choosing a distinctively Jewish diet.

Or they may feel unhappy with *kashrut*, not only because it divides Jews from others but because its own patterns are so much in the form of "This you *must* and this you must *not*." For Jews who resist the external imposition of black-and-white distinctions upon their lives, this may seem one of the most unpleasant characteristics of *kashrut*.

In the last several years, some have been trying to reshape Jewish values so they might affirm and protect the wholeness of the earth precisely by affirming and strengthening Jewish life. They have been attempting to reconnect the idea of *kashrut* with some broader values and obligations toward the earth that stem from Jewish tradition. They have drawn upon those underlying ethical concerns for the earth and its creatures that some have said were encoded in traditional *kashrut*.

On the other hand some Jews who have been exploring new meaning in *kashrut* have started to look beyond the traditional definitions. From this deeper exploration, "eco-kosher" has become more than a word. It has begun to take on reality in the world.

Sheila Weinberg, "Images of God: Closeness and Power"

Sheila Peltz Weinberg was born in 1946. She is a graduate of the Reconstructionist Rabbinical College and worked both in congregations and on campus in a rabbinical capacity. She created the Jewish Mindfulness Teacher Training Program.

Sheila Weinberg, "Images of God: Closeness and Power," in *The Divine Mosaic: Women's Images of the Sacred Other*, ed. Theresa King (Saint Paul, MN: Yes International, 1994), 86–87.

The God of liberation is the God of redemption. The capacity to imagine unity is itself a divine gift enabling us to chart a course toward wholeness. Exile and return are united in the eternal home that we carry with us. One name for God is Makom, place. The place of unity within. The stillness always present in the dance. The balance point between inhale and exhale.

Unity, redemption, and hope are known in liberating moments of creative insight in art. Unity, redemption, and hope are known in passionate sexual union when boundaries evaporate in bliss. I also glimpse the trace of the divine shadow when I expand beyond the limits of my imagination, in moments of empathy and compassion, when the wolf lies down with the lamb.

Judy Chicago has written a wonderful poem/prayer[44] that captures the profound hope that I identify with the divine. Images of creation and liberation fuse in a promise of oneness and peace.

And then all that has divided us will merge
And then compassion will be wedded to power
And then softness will come to a world that is harsh and unkind
And then both men and women will be gentle
And then both men and women will be strong
And then no person will be subject to another's will
And then all will be rich and free and varied
And the greed of some will give way to the needs of the many

44. "Merger Poem," 1979.

And then all will share equally in the earth's abundance
And then all will care for the sick and the weak and the old
And then all will nourish the young
And then all will cherish life's creatures
And then all will live in harmony with each other and the Earth
And then everywhere will be called Eden once again.

As I look back upon my life from the momentary calm of the rock's shelter, what do I see? I see signs of a presence, footprints in the sand, glimpses of a back, a face, a hand, a moment of risking liberation, a moment of embracing creation. There were times in my life when I was ready to say yes or no in a strong enough voice to make a new boundary. This is how I understand the God of liberation. There were other moments when the truth of my own belonging burst through into the light of awareness. This is how I understand the God of creation.

These accumulated moments pass through times of change, fear, loss, uncertainty, and pain. They teach me that I am worthy and responsible. My actions matter. I am part of something greater than myself. I am not alone and am not lost.

IV | Hermeneutics and Politics

"In the beginning there is interpretation. The necessity of commentary thus constitutes the very texture of existence from the vantage point of the Jew."[1] This statement by Elliot Wolfson places interpretation at the very heart of the Jewish experience. Perhaps this age-old predilection is reflected or triggered by the lack of indicative vowels within the original Hebrew alphabet. Words appear in their latent, unvocalized form, and it is up to the individual reader or the community of interpretation to decide which of a range of possible readings ought to be employed. To read is to ascribe meaning rather than simply to decode.

A long tradition presages the modern Jewish engagement with interpretation. Jews have played a disproportionately central role not only in biblical hermeneutics, but in language and literature more generally. For example, George Steiner, a major Jewish intellectual of our times, has asserted that with the exception of Saussure, "the master-players in the critique of language, in philosophic and formal linguistics have been Jews or of Jewish origins."[2] Steiner was not making a claim for some innate superiority, but rather an assertion of the profound connection between Jews and interpretation, a connection which has continued through the upheavals of modernity.

If American Jewish thought inherited a rich tradition of hermeneutical theory and practice, the same could hardly be said for political thought. Jews have only known short periods of sovereignty in the course of their long history. Modernity has heralded what Emil Fackenheim provocatively termed the Jewish Return into History, a new engagement with concepts of political power and agency. Political philosophers schooled in America such as

1. [Elliot R. Wolfson, "From Sealed Book to Open Text: Time, Memory, and Narrativity in Kabbalistic Hermeneutics," in *Interpreting Judaism in a Postmodern Age*, ed. Steven Kepnes (New York: New York University Press, 1996), 145–46.]

2. [George Steiner, *Grammars of Creation* (New Haven, CT: Yale University Press, 2001), 281.]

Daniel Elazar and Michael Walzer, in conjunction with Israeli colleagues, have sought to recover a tradition of Jewish political thought which has previously been largely ignored. And while much attention has understandably been directed toward the experiment in Jewish sovereignty unfolding in the State of Israel, an American Jewish political sensibility characterized by a strong sense of belonging and commitment has also come into being.

As a bridge between these two themes of hermeneutics and politics, we offer readings on a theme common to both of them: pluralism. Approaches to plurality and diversity are central both to the interpretive act and to the development of a political philosophy. Pluralism speaks to the question of dialogue between Judaism and other faith traditions; the boundaries of acceptable disagreement within traditional Jewish discourse; and the creation of political structures flexible enough to encompass diverse philosophies and lifestyles.

In recent decades, religious and ethnic groups in America have come together to explore commonalities and differences, and as a result a literature and theology of interreligious encounter has been taking shape. Jewish involvement in this theory of intergroup encounter exists alongside a debate about the conditions for intra-Jewish discourse.[3] Pluralism as an interpretive strategy and a political imperative has been a hallmark of much of the American Jewish experience.

To be sure, not every Jew in America embraces pluralism with enthusiasm, and we have included some voices of demurral in this chapter, some of which resonate with the debate raging between liberals and conservatives in the political sphere. Traditionalists and iconoclasts, neoconservatives and ultraprogressives, these and others have given American Jewish thought on hermeneutics and politics its particular hue.

Constructions of a possible American Jewish politics remain diverse. Starting Part Four with a discussion of the interpretation of texts, moving to the interpretation of plurality, we conclude with sharply differing interpretations

3. [For example, see Abraham Joshua Heschel et al., *No Religion Is an Island: Abraham Joshua Heschel and Interreligious Dialogue* (Maryknoll, NY: Orbis, 1991); Irving Greenberg, *For the Sake of Heaven and Earth: The New Encounter between Judaism and Christianity* (Philadelphia: Jewish Publication Society, 2004); David Novak, *Talking with Christians: Musings of a Jewish Theologian* (Grand Rapids, MI: Eerdmans, 2005); Peter Ochs, *Another Reformation: Postliberal Christianity and the Jews* (Grand Rapids, MI: Baker Academic, 2011); and Tikva Frymer-Kensky et al., eds., *Christianity in Jewish Terms* (Boulder, CO: Westview Press, 2000).]

of the political and the contemporary. In each of the selections we see American Jewish thinkers in search of a distinctly Jewish vocabulary. We open with three excerpts relating explicitly to hermeneutical considerations. Michael Fishbane offers a contemporary interpretation of classical Jewish modes of interpretation, Steven Kepnes outlines the core principles of an approach he and others have called Jewish textual reasoning, and Jose Faur presents a distinction between semiological and metaphysical modes of interpretation. David Hartman's thoughts on pluralism provide a bridge between these first excerpts and the subsequent selections, which relate to aspects of Jewish thought in the political realm. The first of these, by Leo Strauss, challenges the conceptual underpinnings of pluralism as it sets out a distinction between Athens and Jerusalem. Hannah Arendt's classic distinction between the Jew as pariah and as *parvenu* provides the basis for a discussion of the modern Jewish condition. Michael Walzer, an acute analyst of the Jewish political tradition, relates to an aspect of that tradition's biblical roots. Mitchell Cohen and Jill Jacobs offer insights on the prospect of an American Jewish politics, while the closing excerpt presents the voice of an outlier and controversialist, Meir Kahane. He speaks with venom and irony about what he sees as a frontal collision between the values of America and the timeless values of Judaism. In these ten readings our aim is to conjure up something of the rich discourse in which North American Judaism is engaged—about text and pluralism, conservatism and progressivism, the power of interpretation and the interpretation of power.

Michael Fishbane (born 1943) is one of American Judaism's most influential scholars. He received his doctorate from Brandeis University and taught there in the
Department of Near Eastern and Judaic Studies for many years. Since 1990, Fishbane has been Professor of Jewish Studies at the Divinity School at the University
of Chicago, and his research has focused on biblical hermeneutics.

Michael Fishbane, *Sacred Attunement: A Jewish Theology* (Chicago: University
of Chicago Press, 2008), 104–7.

In the preceding discussion,[4] we observed how different types of reading
practices can sponsor different types of sensibility, which serve different ways
of living thoughtfully in the world, and can also cultivate different types of theological attention and attitude. Reading may therefore be a site of reflection, and
its processes can contribute to one's life-process. I would thus suggest that each
one of the four modes of interpretation is a kind of rite of passage, whereby a
reader is inducted into different types of understanding of the ways that we make
meaning in life—in the natural world all around us, for the purpose of practical affairs, and also in the world of moral values and spiritual apprehensions.
These may variously interact and affect one another; or they may be kept apart
as distinct sensibilities. There is no one pattern. Each person, at different moments of life, can activate and integrate these modes in different ways. Still and
all, one always stands on the ground of the *peshat*. The ancient rabbinic sages put
it this way: "Scripture never loses its plain sense." For them, this dictum meant
that, when all is said and done, one always comes back to the base line. For us it
means that we always walk on the earth, and must first hone primary skills for
understanding the basic sense of words and things in our natural environment.

4. [This excerpt is taken from a chapter entitled "A Jewish Hermeneutical Theology,"
in which Fishbane employs classical Jewish categories of interpretation in a modern
theological context. The Hebrew word PaRDeS (orchard) is used as an acronym for four
levels of textual interpretation in ascending order of abstraction: *peshat* relates to the plain
meaning, *derash* to rabbinic expansions and innovations, *remez* to hints and implicit connections, and *sod* to esoteric truths.]

But this is not the whole of life; our initial understandings are quickly taken up by other matters, since we also live with moral values and spiritual concerns. These latter fold back into the everyday world and infuse it. Not bound by the exclusive importance of any one mode of reading and thinking, or by fixed hierarchies of value, we may live with the awareness of a more complex simultaneity of meanings. How these are activated or discerned is part of the larger rite of passage that constitutes our lives on earth.

Here is one possible way of understanding these matters in a theological context.

First and foremost there is always the *peshat*, our world of common sense. It is always there as the foundational level of religious consciousness. In this realm we name people and things, act and talk, and share a public realm. This is the sphere in which the self is embodied and joins with other persons, where we eat and suffer and die, and where we love and struggle. This is the world of good and evils, in which the covenant is forged and expanded, or changed and revised. It is also the realm where interpretations are proposed and realized, or rejected and scrutinized. All our words and acts in this world of common sense reveal new aspects of it, even as they may conceal others from view. We need one another to keep the fullness of speech and perspective alike for the sake of flourishing human life. In such ways we honor God; for by our actions the vastness of divine vitalities is humanized, and the world is no mere natural or neutral realm, but is revealed, part by part, over the course of human civilization, as a creation. It is not always a creation, for the features of this realm can be obscured by habitude and disregard, or distorted by mean-spiritedness or evil. But it *can* be the context for a creation. By focusing on the everyday, the *peshat* fosters a mindfulness of the details of life, and thus treats with sacred trust and deed the humanly perceived fullness of God's illimitable effectivity.

What does the *derash* dimension add? Just this: it opens our minds to the constructed natures of our common world of language and value, and to the possibilities that may reshape our common world with new thoughts and purpose. This is the domain of the Oral Torah, which keeps our minds and perspectives fresh, and challenges all routine and idolatry. The mindfulness of *derash* is the mindfulness of the play of language and its creative possibilities, and also the realization that we are the custodians of language as well as its priests. Language constitutes both the gifts offered and received, and the offerings whose substance is always transmuted in the world of persons and values. To cultivate a theological mind infused by the qualities of *derash* is to cultivate an ongoing mindfulness of our responsibilities for how the living God is realized and named in the common world. Here then is a delicate simultaneity: the *derash* guards against the stultification of the *peshat*, while the *peshat* grounds the *derash* in the common world; the *derash* is a prophetic voice decrying fundamentalistic reductions, while the *peshat* keeps counsel with the basic truth that circumstances require choices about values and meaning. In the fullest sense, the *derash* helps God remain God in our world by keeping the vastness of possibilities alive through the Oral Torah; but just as vitally, the *peshat* of the common world reminds us that we must always act in the here and now, and that this is the domain where Divinity may become actual and humanly real. Both factors must be held in mind; both are truths of a living theology.

And what more might the mode of *remez* contribute? It may keep us attuned to the flash of possibility, suggested in some way or another, *and* to the fact that all hints are rooted in human discernment and judgment. As such they may be helpful or not, wise or just plain folly. We build networks of sense out of hints at all levels of our perception, for there is no mere matter of fact. Who is to say if there is really something there beneath the surface, or whether we are just bumbling along thinking that we have discerned a deeper meaning? The phenomenon of *remez* should cultivate an attitude of humility before the so-called clues and allusions we proclaim as we make decisions about people and events and writings, as well as the larger "meaning of things." Even the hints we gather in tradition may get our minds stuck, as Job came to realize in the course of his life. One must therefore always proceed with caution, and a readiness for reconsideration. New hints may compel an overhaul of one's thinking, or put some things in abeyance. There is no easy way. The miracle is that we actually do build our world out of hints, and find ways to let them dilate and join with other allusions, and thus create patterns for our thinking and judgment. The flicker or flash of insight may smash an idol of thought or belief that has hardened in our hearts. On such occasions, *remez* serves God and truth.

Ultimately, the three levels just considered participate in the *torah kelulah*,[5] and give it a human voice. Consciousness of this superordinate dimension is the work of *sod*. It opens the domain of mystery, and of possibilities beyond imagination. But it must be brought to mind and kept in mindfulness. The kind of complex religious consciousness that I have adumbrated here, cultivated by four

---

5. [Earlier in the book, Fishbane translates this term as "the Torah of All-in-All," and employs it to refer to God's primordial Torah, encompassing all future potentialities.]

(separate and interactive) levels of scriptural interpretation, would stand in the common world amid its needs and obligations, ever mindful of the divine depths below and beyond. Such an orientation may also develop a mindfulness infused with humility and care before the fragility of life fashioned out of the whirlwind. Each point of consciousness is a holy shining through the darkness of our unknowing, the thick cloud through which God is revealed to our mortal minds.

Born in 1952, Steven Kepnes is a Professor of Jewish Studies at Colgate University. He received his doctorate from the University of Chicago and has been actively involved in a group of postcritical readers of Jewish tradition. From 2010 to 2013, Kepnes was coeditor of *The Journal of Textual Reasoning*.

Steven Kepnes, *The Future of Jewish Theology* (Chichester, UK: Wiley-Blackwell, 2013), 184–87.

Taking seriously the postmodern turn to language and texts and the variety of new models for religion as a series of metaphors and models, a group of Jewish philosophers including Peter Ochs, Robert Gibbs, Yudit Greenberg, Laurie Zoloth, and I, attempted to find a way to bring Jewish thinkers together to do Jewish philosophy differently from the ways in which the classic Ethical Monotheists did it. This led in 1992 to the founding of the postmodern Jewish philosophy group. In the year 2000 at the Jewish Theological Seminary, the Society of Textual Reasoning was founded along with an internet journal. We changed our name from "Postmodern Jewish philosophy" to "Textual Reasoning" because we felt that philosophical postmodernism had taken rather a nihilistic turn in which it was only concerned with deconstructing Western philosophy. Postmodernism, we believed, supplied too few ways to retrieve meaning and truth in religious texts and we sought to do precisely that.

We desired to use the new theories of language, signs, texts, and interpretation to develop new forms of Jewish thought and theology that would be more successful than the purely cognitive forms of medieval philosophy and some of the rationalist Jewish modernists. We also sought to take advantage of developments in Jewish philosophy that occurred after the development of modern Ethical Monotheism.

From Buber we took seriously the notion of dialogue, that Jewish thought must not be developed by the isolated autonomous self locked away in his or her library cubbyhole, but must be based on conversation and discussion. From Franz Rosenzweig, Textual Reasoning took the notion of "speechthinking." . . . Speechthinking, for Rosenzweig, means that real Jewish thought takes the form of oral discussion and argument and is not a matter of the individual contemplation of eternal ideas. Genuine thinking occurs in language, in time, and between interlocutors. This means that real Jewish thinking is, as the rabbis call it, "oral torah." From the pragmatist philosopher C. S. Pierce, we took the sense that Jewish thinking must have a dimension of creative trial and error and hypothesis-making, what Pierce called "abduction" (to distinguish between induction and deduction as the traditional modes of logic). Jewish thinking for Textual Reasoning then is a process, it is the thinking of the seminar, the Beit Midrash. Jewish Textual Reasoning is social reasoning of the group and not the thought of the isolated individual. There is a place for individual thought and there is also a place for writing (as the Talmud was eventually written down), but that comes after communal study. Thus, written philosophy and theology by Jewish textual reasoners should take the form of notes on a dialogue. Theology is then schematization of acts of communal speechthinking. So Jewish thought and theology is then dynamic and temporal and not static, set, eternal. And this perhaps mimics the very dynamic nature of our relation with God.

From Cohen[6] and the Ethical Monotheists we took the directive to turn our study toward important moral issues in the Jewish community and in the broader world. Thus underlying every session of Textual Reasoning there should be a compelling moral or theological issue that plagues Judaism and the world. Our unique method of addressing the issue is to search in and through Jewish texts so that we can be aided by the wisdom and ethical strategies of the Jewish tradition.

In the move to Textual Reasoning, we decided to base ourselves more on principles of biblical and rabbinic thought instead of Western philosophy. As I have tried to show, biblical thought is more reliant on metaphoric than philosophic forms of thinking. And rabbinic thought is at once exegetical, dialogic, argumentative, and pragmatic. That is, rabbinic thought is based on interpretation of Torah and Mishnah, and it functions through a communal process of dialogue which is both synchronic, in the moment, and diachronic, existing in the history of rabbinic interpretation over time.

The move to Textual Reasoning requires a commitment to do Jewish thinking in a new way with four methodological principles in mind: 1. Jewish Textual Reasoning should begin by placing a Jewish text at the center and not a philosophical concept or argument. This means that Jewish thought becomes

6. [The reference here is to Hermann Cohen.]

exegetical or hermeneutical thinking. 2. Textual Reasoning should attempt to do Jewish thinking as much as possible, in *chavurot* or small groups. Here, the model is taken from rabbinic forms of thinking in which group oral dialogue takes a central role. 3. Textual Reasoning should allow for argument and difference in interpretation and not have to move too quickly toward consensus and agreement. When agreement is reached it should result from a process of discussion and be considered provisional, hypothetical, and appropriate as a solution for a current problem rather than a statement of eternal truth. 4. Textual Reasoning should have at the beginning and at its horizon a contemporary ethical or theological issue that concerns the Jewish community and/or the larger world. This continues the ethical focus of modern Ethical Monotheism while adopting the models of exegetical and pragmatic ethics from rabbinic theology and modern pragmatism.

These four principles should make it clear that Jewish Textual Reasoning is at once traditional and contemporary, textual and philosophical, collective and pragmatic. As a form of traditional theology, it begins with "Torah" in the widest sense of the term as sacred Jewish texts. Here, Textual Reasoning accepts the rabbinic canon, which begins with the Tanakh and Midrash and includes the Mishnah and Gemara or the Talmud both Palestinian and Babylonian. Jewish Textual Reasoning however, is contemporary in that it encourages its participants to bring their own contemporary science, art, and concerns to the act of group study. Jewish Textual Reasoning endeavors to be new and open to Jewish thought through the role of contemporary interpreters who approach an older text with contemporary eyes and concerns.

Jose Faur was born in 1934 in Buenos Aires, Argentina, into a Syrian Jewish family. Arriving in the United States in his late teens, he studied at the yeshiva in Lakewood, New Jersey, founded by Rabbi Aaron Kotler. Faur received a secular education, including his doctorate, at the University of Barcelona, and his rabbinical ordination from Hakham Suleiman Haggai Abadi in Jerusalem. From 1967 to 1985, he taught Talmud and rabbinics at the Jewish Theological Seminary. In the 1990s, he moved to Israel, where he taught Talmud at Bar-Ilan University. Faur published scores of articles and books in his fields of study.

Jose Faur, *Golden Doves with Silver Dots: Semiotics and Textuality in Rabbinic Tradition* (Bloomington: Indiana University Press, 1986), 23–29.

In contradistinction to the Greek thinkers who conceived of the Universe in metaphysical terms, the Hebrews viewed it as a semiological system. For the Hebrews, not only was Creation realized through speech; it actually *is* the speech of God. It must be noted that in Hebrew, God's "word" (*dabar, 'imra*) is a dynamic, creative force. The *dabar* of the Lord "is as a fire . . . and like a hammer that smashes the rock" (Jer. 23:29). The Universe was effected by His word. With his *dabar* "the Heavens were made" (Psalms 33:6). The blessing before consuming non-vegetal foods states "that everything was with His *dabar*." Similarly, in the blessing on the occasion of the New Moon, it is said "that with His speech [*ma'amaro*] He created the firmaments, and with the spirit of His mouth everything that they contain." In the first blessings before the evening *Shema'*, it is said "that with His *dabar*, [He] brings on the evening with wisdom, opens the [heavenly] gates with understanding, alters the moments and changes the times, and arranges the stars in the firmaments according to His will. . . ."

There are no *a priori* grounds to determine whether the Universe is to be apprehended as a metaphysical or a semiological system; it is a matter of choice; which will determine the validity of one system over the other. Here a metaphor may be helpful. Suppose that an object exhibiting some marks reaches this planet—it could be examined ontologically or semiologically. The marks may be considered fortuitous, like astrological configurations, the lines on the palm of the hand, or the stripes of a tiger. In this case the marks would be void of any signification. Any message that one may "decode" must be considered as pure fabrication. The only way to understand it would be through scientific analysis. Conversely, the marks may be perceived as signs, such as writing or mathematics. In this case, the scientific analysis is irrelevant to the message, just as the material on which a letter was inscribed and the ink and the instrument with which it was written are not relevant to decoding its meaning.

The most important difference between a semiological and a metaphysical entity is that the former signifies, whereas the latter *is*. An ontological entity, like the Universe of classical mechanics, must be value-free: the "explanations" are mere interpolations which actually interfere with the primary presence of an ontic-ontological being. For the people of the Book, however, physical phenomena are significant: "writing" is intrinsic to nature. . . .

Semiological knowledge is interpretive and subjective. 'Emet, the Hebrew term for "truth," implies "trust," "faith" (as does its English equivalent). It is context-bound. 'Emet cannot be grasped in the abstract. Outside a specific context it is meaningless. R. Isaac 'Arama, commenting on the verse "and your truth [extends] until the firmaments" (Ps. 57:11; 108:5), noted that 'emet is valid only within the context of the created Universe: outside the real world it is not significant.

A semiological entity must be thoroughly transparent. A condition of semiology is that, ultimately, significance must permeate the sign. Once the value of a sign is determined and the message decoded, the sign vanishes. From the point of view of semiology, the opacity of any given entity is a state prior to interpretation, not an absolute condition. Before being decoded an entity is opaque. "Reading," which is the decoding of an encoded message, means that significance has thoroughly permeated the script and rendered it transparent. Therefore, "opacity" is synonymous with "undecoded." . . . Significance is the function of interpretation. The Hebrew term for interpretation, *peter (pitaron)/pesher*, implies the notion of compromise. Interpretation involves the integration of various elements. In Hebrew, it also means "lukewarm." In a sense, "interpretation" may be conceived as blending different elements, as when mixing hot and cold water. Thus "to interpret" is to integrate two or more signs and make a "compromise" which contains them all but is identical with none of them, just as lukewarm water is neither hot nor cold. . . .

Particularly after Plato, the Greek *aletheia* is "truth" in itself; it is context-free, and therefore universally valid: it "un-veils" and "discovers" the evident. This truth is static and absolute: like Euclidean geometry it transcends all contexts. Ideally, this type of knowledge ought to be thoroughly descriptive and objective. Therefore the truth is essentially tautological. The formula A = A' expresses the ultimate goal of this type of knowledge. . . .

The distinction between "context-bound" and "context-free" types of truth may best be understood in light of the two-process mechanism of the brain described by Karl Pribram.[7] On the basis of neurological considerations, Pribram distinguished two classes of communicative acts. One is "context-free." Its meaning is not predicated on any context. "A rose is a rose regardless of whether it appears in a garden, on a dinner table, or in the garbage pail." Another class of communicative acts "derive their meaning from their past use and from the current state of the organism using them." Their meaning is predicated upon the specific context in which they appear. Within the limits of our purpose it is important to note that "context-free" meaning is a function of abstraction. They "derive meaning by selective attention to aspects of the Image they signify." Their concern is the "objective," "real" world. Invariably, they intend some part of the World-Out-There. The "context-bound" meaning is the effect of a subjective operation. More specifically, they "derive meaning by establishing a context within which interest and feeling become organized." In contrast to the other class which is concerned with the spatial, concrete world, the "context-bound" refers to "occurrences in the domain of the organism's World-Within." This type of process is both internal and subjective. The "context-bound" serves to express "what the organism has registered from its experience and its valuation of that experience—what he is interested in, what he cares about. Caring largely consists of being sensitive and responsive to changes occurring in the communicative context."

The opposition of "context-free" and "context-bound" types of truth results in two different models for the organization of thought and human experience. An opaque object, perceived as context-free in the World-Out-There, must be grasped visually. Opacity not only establishes the ground for ontological reality but it also determines the means by which such a reality can be apprehended: opacity is the function of visual thinking and spatial organization. The context-bound type of truth perceived in the World-Within is grasped either syntagmatically, by relating it to the context at hand, or paradigmatically, by relating it to an

7. Cf. Karl Pribram, *Languages of the Brain* (Englewood Cliffs, New Jersey: Prentice-Hall, 1971). [All quotations in this paragraph are from this work.]

ideal model.[8] The processing of such data is best modeled in terms of temporal organization and successive synthesis. The Greeks and Hebrews developed their respective cultures and way of thinking in terms of each of these models.

8. [Faur is using a distinction first made by the Swiss linguist and semiotician Ferdinand de Saussure (1857–1913). In its original context, the distinction is between parts of a sentence that all appear together, and rely on each other for the sentence to make sense (syntagmatic), as opposed to elements that are connected by meaning but replace each other (paradigmatic.) If I say, "the car is green," then the relation between all the words in that sentence is syntagmatic. Together, they form a sentence. If I now say "the car is pink," then the relation between "green" and "pink" is paradigmatic. They are linked because they both describe colors, and I have to decide which of them I am going to use. Faur seems to be arguing that Jewish interpretation is fundamentally contextual, concerned with dynamic unfolding in a particular situation. The Hebrews, then, look for truth syntagmatically, framing it in a specific context, while the Greek search for truth is more abstract and therefore paradigmatic.]

David Hartman (1931–2013) was a graduate of Yeshiva College who received his rabbinical ordination at the Rabbi Isaac Elchanan Theological Seminary of Yeshiva University. He earned his doctorate in philosophy at Fordham University. Hartman served as a rabbi in his native New York and in Montreal before moving to Israel in 1971, where he became Professor of Jewish Thought at the Hebrew University of Jerusalem. He was also the founding president of the Shalom Hartman Institute, and through the work of the Institute, he continued to exert considerable influence on many denominations of Jewish life in North America long after his move to Israel.

David Hartman, "Judaism as an Interpretive Tradition," in David Hartman, *A Heart of Many Rooms: Celebrating the Many Voices within Judaism* (Woodstock, VT: Jewish Lights, 1999), 21–23, 34–36.

There is a beautiful metaphor in the Tosefta[9] that describes the kind of religious sensibility the Talmud tried to nurture: "Make yourself a heart of many rooms and bring into it the words of the House of Shammai and the words of the House of Hillel, the words of those who declare unclean and the words of those who declare clean" (*Sotah* 7:12). In other words, become a person in whom different opinions can reside together in the very depths of your soul. Become a religious person who can live with ambiguity, who can feel religious conviction and passion without the need for simplicity and absolute certainty.

In this type of interpretive tradition, awareness of the validity of contrary positions enhances, rather than diminishes, the vitality and enthusiasm of religious commitment. So while the law may be decided according to the views of one teacher or school of thought, alternative views are not discarded as if falsified but are retained and studied and may even become law at some later date. The Mishnah or the Talmud may determine the official law by choosing among opposing views on the basis of accepted mechanisms of decision making, but

9. [The Tosefta is a collection of rabbinic traditions with a parallel structure to that of the Mishnah, and roughly contemporaneous with it.]

they never eliminate the rich variety of opinions or diminish the creativity of the moral imagination that is able to make sense of alternative positions.

Perhaps it is owing to the specific nature of legal reasoning, which recognizes the need for and the validity of decision-making procedures to resolve disagreements (in contrast to science or philosophy, where majority rule or any other extrarational mode of determining truth is an absurdity), that the participants in a talmudic debate do not present their views as evident and necessary, i.e., as the only valid truths. It is with this in mind that the Tosefta says "make yourself a heart of many rooms" so that your heart can contain a variety of conflicting opinions.

This, then, is the distinctive legacy of the talmudic interpretive tradition: an understanding of revelation in which God loves you when you discover ambiguity in His word. He loves you for finding forty-nine ways to make this pure and forty-nine ways to make it impure. Revelation is not always "pure and simple" but may be rough and complex.

Since you may find yourselves arguing interminably, you may decide the law according to such principles as majority rule. But even if God, the Law Giver, were to intervene in a legal debate among scholars and were to reveal that this interpretation was correct or that legal formulation should become law, the rabbis would object and say: "Sorry, God. You may not interrupt and terminate discussions among students of Torah. If our minds appreciate and conceive of the ambiguity of the human situations in which your word must be implemented, you may not interfere to change our minds. Torah is not in heaven."

In other words, the religious personality this system tries to produce is able to interpret situations in multiple ways and to offer cogent arguments for opposite positions and points of view. This orientation reflects a particular kind of religious humility. What has often been portrayed as legalism and pilpulism (casuistry) is a superficial misrepresentation of the deep joy in study and fascination with the rich complexity of the Torah.

The test of excellence of the Torah scholar was the ability to read and analyze a talmudic text, to explain and defend both sides of a disagreement by offering imaginative and compelling reasons for both positions. The student's interest in and competence at reproducing both argument and counterargument convincingly were often rooted in a genuine appreciation of the moral and intellectual complexity of the subject matter.

I would even say that there was a distinctive sense of humor that typified the classical Jewish tradition: a sense of humor—and therefore of humility—about your certainties, about what you believed "could not be otherwise." In all my years of study with Rabbi Joseph B. Soloveitchik, I never once heard him call someone a heretic or dismiss a soundly argued opinion as illegitimate. You argued, you discussed, you disagreed with intensity, but you understood that you were defending a human point of view, not the final word of God. And even then (according to the midrash), we would not hesitate to reprimand God for exceeding the limits of divine authority in the domain of halakhic debate. Revelation gives you the word of God, but the interpretive strategies for implementing that word are "not in heaven." ...

The crux of the religious worldview I am discussing can be summarized as follows: I find joy in serving God in this incomplete, fragmentary world with my limited and fragmentary mind. The only God I know is the God mediated in the everyday rhythms of the temporal world. While I would surely accept the gift of divine grace if God were to choose to redeem history, this, however, is not the operative hope that informs my religious life.

My reality is essentially temporal and limited; I make religious choices and decisions without the benefit of perceiving life *sub specie aeternitatis*.[10] I leave messianism and eschatology to God and try to get on with life as an incomplete, finite human being building a religious life without knowledge of whether there is a secret divine scheme for history.

The acceptance of finitude and limitation and the absence of metaphysical certainties do not entail a weakening of conviction and passion. Love can grow out of partial understanding and an appreciation of the knowledge that our convictions and beliefs are inherently limited and incomplete.

Although I live in a world where disagreement is widespread and acute, I do not admit to a lack of strong convictions. The strength of your convictions is not dependent on a belief in their absolute status, which would condemn those who disagree with you to blindness to self-evidence or to stubborn ill will. A framework of rational moral argumentation without absolutes is not equivalent to relativism. Not every point of view is equally legitimate simply because it is someone's point of view. A point of view must always be subject to and vulnerable to counterargument and evaluation.

Also, taking part in a discussion within a tradition requires that a person know how to argue within that particular tradition. This means that you have to mas-

10. [This Latin term, used most famously by Baruch Spinoza, can be translated as "from the perspective of eternity."]

ter its language, its literature, and its history in order to participate actively in its cultural debate. Unless you listen carefully to the voices that make up a tradition, you will be unable to think intelligently about its central issues and concerns, let alone present meaningful interpretations that can be organically integrated into its interpretive discussion. The intellectual experience of the Torah scholar is not an isolated, lonely one. There is a community to which you are responsible and with which you are engaged in an ongoing conversation.

A traditional Jew earns the right to speak by listening. Learning is a condition for being taken seriously as a discussant in this tradition. If you don't study or listen with reverence, if you don't feel the burden of the tradition or speak with trepidation about your certainties, you will never gain credibility. The voices of the sages and scholars who participated in the interpretive tradition speak to me. I must be careful and responsible in my interpretations because I have to answer to all those voices that spoke in the past.

By the time German-born Leo Strauss (1899–1983) arrived in the United States in 1937, he had already established a reputation as a leading political philosopher and classicist. This reputation was ensured and enhanced throughout his years in the United States, most particularly during his twenty-five years at the University of Chicago. Among the most resonant aspects of his intellectual legacy are his critique of modern liberalism, his concept of "persecution and the art of writing," and his hermeneutical approach to the reading of texts. His influence on American Jewish thought is enduring.

Leo Strauss, "Jerusalem and Athens: Some Introductory Reflections," *Commentary* 43, no 6 (June 1967): 45–46, 55, 57.

All the hopes that we entertain in the midst of the confusion and dangers of the present are founded, positively or negatively, directly or indirectly, on the experiences of the past. Of these experiences, the broadest and deepest—so far as Western man is concerned—are indicated by the names of two cities: Jerusalem and Athens. Western man became what he is, and is what he is, through the coming together of biblical faith and Greek thought. In order to understand ourselves and to illuminate our trackless way into the future, we must understand Jerusalem and Athens. It goes without saying that this is a task whose proper performance goes much beyond my power; but we cannot define our tasks by our powers, for our powers become known to us through the performance of our tasks, and it is better to fail nobly than to succeed basely.

The objects to which we refer when we speak of Jerusalem and Athens are understood today, by the science devoted to such objects, as cultures; "culture" is meant to be a scientific concept. According to this concept there is an indefinitely large number of cultures: n cultures. The scientist who studies them beholds them as objects; as scientist, he stands outside all of them; he has no preference for any of them; he is not only impartial but objective; he is anxious not to distort any of them; in speaking about them he avoids any "culture-bound" concepts—i.e., concepts bound to any particular culture or kind of culture. In many cases the objects studied by the scientist of culture do or did not know that they are or were cultures. This causes no difficulty for him: electrons also do not know that they are electrons; even dogs do not know that they are dogs. By the mere fact that he speaks of his objects as cultures, the scientific student takes it for granted that he understands the people whom he studies better than they understood or understand themselves.

This whole approach has been questioned for some time, but the questioning does not seem to have had any effect on the scientists. The man who started the questioning was Nietzsche.[11] We have said that according to the prevailing view there were or are n cultures. Let us say there were or are 1,001 cultures, thus reminding ourselves of the 1,001 Arabian Nights; the account of the cultures, if it is well done, will be a series of exciting stories, perhaps of tragedies. Accordingly, Nietzsche speaks of our subject in a speech by his Zarathustra that is entitled "Of 1,000 Goals and One." The Hebrews and the Greeks appear in this speech as two among a number of nations, not superior to the two others that are mentioned or to the 996 that are not. The peculiarity of the Greeks, according to Nietzsche, is the full dedication of the individual to the contest for excellence, distinction, supremacy. The peculiarity of the Hebrews is the utmost honoring of father and mother. Nietzsche's reverence for the sacred tables of the Hebrews, as well as for those of the other nations in question, is deeper than that of any other beholder. Yet since he too is only a beholder of these tables, since what one table commends or commands is incompatible with what others command, he himself is not subject to the commandments of any. This is true also and especially of the tables, or "values," of modern Western culture. But according to him, all scientific concepts, and hence in particular the concept of culture, are culture-bound; the concept of culture is an outgrowth of 19th-century Western culture; its application to the "cultures" of other ages and climates is an act stemming from the spiritual imperialism of that particular culture. There is, then, for Nietzsche, a glaring contradiction between the claimed objectivity of the science of cultures and the subjectivity of that science. To state the case differently, one cannot behold—i.e., truly understand—any culture unless one is firmly rooted in one's own culture or unless one belongs, in one's capacity as a beholder, to some culture. But if the universality of the beholding of all cultures is to be preserved, the culture to which the beholder of all cultures belongs must be the universal culture, the culture of mankind, the world culture; the universality of beholding presupposes, if only by anticipating, the universal culture which is no longer

11. [Friedrich Nietzsche (1844–1900).]

one culture among many. Nietzsche sought therefore for a culture that would no longer be particular and hence in the last analysis arbitrary. The single goal of mankind is conceived by him as in a sense super-human: he speaks of the super-man of the future. The super-man is meant to unite in himself, on the highest level, both Jerusalem and Athens.

However much the science of all cultures may protest its innocence of all preferences or evaluations, it fosters a specific moral posture. Since it requires openness to all cultures, it fosters universal tolerance and the exhilaration which derives from the beholding of diversity; it necessarily affects all cultures that it can still affect by contributing to their transformation in one and the same direction; it willy-nilly brings about a shift of emphasis from the particular to the universal. By asserting, if only implicitly, the rightness of pluralism, it asserts that pluralism is the right way; it asserts the monism of universal tolerance and respect for diversity; for by virtue of being an "-ism," pluralism is a monism.

One remains somewhat closer to the science of culture as it is commonly practiced if one limits oneself to saying that every attempt to understand the phenomena in question remains dependent upon a conceptual framework that is alien to most of these phenomena and therefore necessarily distorts them. "Objectivity" can be expected only if one attempts to understand the various cultures or peoples exactly as they understand or understood themselves. Men of ages and climates other than our own did not understand themselves in terms of cultures because they were not concerned with culture in the present-day meaning of the term. What we now call culture is the accidental result of concerns that were not concerns with culture but with other things—above all with the Truth. . . .

Fifty years ago, in the middle of World War I, Hermann Cohen, the greatest representative of, and spokesman for, German Jewry, the most powerful figure among the German professors of philosophy of his time, stated his view on Jerusalem and Athens in a lecture entitled "The Social Ideal in Plato and the Prophets." He repeated that lecture shortly before his death, and we may regard it as stating his final view on Jerusalem and Athens and therewith on the truth. For, as Cohen says right at the beginning, "Plato and the prophets are the two most important sources of modern culture." Being concerned with "the social ideal," he does not say a single word about Christianity in the whole lecture.

Cohen's view may be restated as follows. The truth is the synthesis of the teachings of Plato and the prophets. What we owe to Plato is the insight that the truth is in the first place the truth of science but that science must be supplemented, overarched, by the idea of the good which to Cohen means, not God, but rational, scientific ethics. The ethical truth must not only be compatible with the scientific truth; the ethical truth needs the scientific truth. The prophets are very much concerned with knowledge: with the knowledge of God. But this knowledge, as the prophets understood it, has no connection whatever with scientific knowledge; it is knowledge only in a metaphorical sense. It is perhaps with a view to this fact that Cohen speaks once of the divine Plato but never of the divine prophets. Why then can he not leave matters at Platonic philosophy? What is the fundamental defect of Platonic philosophy that is remedied by the prophets and only by the prophets? According to Plato, the cessation of evil requires the rule of the philosophers, of the men who possess the highest kind of human knowledge, i.e., of science in the broadest sense of the term. But this kind of knowledge like, to some extent, all scientific knowledge, is, according to Plato, the preserve of a small minority: of the men who possess a certain nature and certain gifts that most men lack. Plato presupposes that there is an unchangeable human nature and, as a consequence, a fundamental structure of the good human society which is unchangeable. This leads him to assert or to assume that there will be wars as long as there will be human beings, that there ought to be a class of warriors and that the class ought to be higher in rank and honor than the class of producers and exchangers. These defects in Plato's system are remedied by the prophets precisely because they lack the idea of science and hence the idea of nature, and therefore they can believe that men's conduct toward one another can undergo a change much more radical than any change ever dreamed of by Plato.

Cohen brought out very well the antagonism between Plato and the prophets. Nevertheless we cannot leave matters at his view of that antagonism. Cohen's thought belongs to the world preceding World War I, and accordingly reflects a greater faith in the power of modern Western culture to mold the fate of mankind than seems to be warranted now. The worst things experienced by Cohen were the Dreyfus scandal and the pogroms instigated by Tsarist Russia: he did not experience Communist Russia and Hitler Germany. More disillusioned than he regarding modern culture, we wonder whether the two separate ingredients of modern culture, of the modern synthesis, are not more solid than the synthesis itself. Catastrophes and horrors of a magnitude hitherto unknown, which we have seen and through which we have lived, were better provided for, or made intelligible, by both Plato and the prophets than by the modern belief in progress. Since we are less certain than Cohen was that the modern synthesis is superior to its pre-modern ingredients, and since the two ingredients are in fundamental opposition to each other, we are ultimately confronted by a problem rather than by a solution....

The fact that both Socrates and the prophets have a divine mission means, or at any rate implies, that both Socrates and the prophets are concerned with justice or righteousness, with the perfectly just society which, as such, would be free of all evils. To this extent Socrates's figuring out of the best social order and the prophets' vision of the messianic age are in agreement. Yet whereas the prophets predict the coming of the messianic age, Socrates merely holds that the perfect society is possible: whether it will ever be actual depends on an unlikely, although not impossible, coincidence, the coincidence of philosophy and political power. For, according to Socrates, the coming-into-being of the best political order is not due to divine intervention; human nature will remain as it always has been; the decisive difference between the best political order and all other societies is that in the former the philosophers will be kings or the natural potentiality of the philosophers will reach its utmost perfection. In the most perfect social order, as Socrates sees it, knowledge of the most important things will remain, as it always was, the preserve of the philosophers, i.e., of a very small part of the population. According to the prophets, however, in the messianic age "the earth shall be full of knowledge of the Lord, as the waters cover the earth" (Isaiah 11:9), and this will be brought about by God Himself. As a consequence, the messianic age will be the age of universal peace: all nations shall come to the mountain of the Lord, to the house of the God of Jacob, "and they shall beat their swords into plowshares, and their spears into pruning hooks: nation shall not lift up sword against nation, neither shall they learn war any more" (Isaiah 2:2–4). The best regime, however, as Socrates envisages it, will animate a single city which, as a matter of course, will become embroiled in wars with other cities. The cessation of evils that Socrates expects from the establishment of the best regime will not include the cessation of war.

Finally, the perfectly just man, the man who is as just as is humanly possible, is, according to Socrates, the philosopher; according to the prophets, he is the faithful servant of the Lord. The philosopher is the man who dedicates his life to the quest for knowledge of the good, of the idea of the good; what we would call moral virtue is only the condition or by-product of that quest. According to the prophets, however, there is no need for the quest for knowledge of the good: God "hath shewed thee, O man, what is good; and what doth the Lord require of thee, but to do justly, and to love mercy, and to walk humbly with thy God" (Micah 6:8).

An outstanding intellectual figure of the twentieth century, Hannah Arendt (1906–75) made her name in her native Germany as a philosopher and political theorist, and her book *The Origins of Totalitarianism* remains a classic work of modern political thought. After eight years of exile in Paris, Arendt came to the United States in 1941. She wrote often on overtly Jewish themes, never shying away from controversial positions. A collection of her works on Jewish topics and affairs has been published.[12]

Hannah Arendt, "The Jew as Pariah: A Hidden Tradition," *Jewish Social Studies* 6, no. 2 (1944): 103–4, 121–22.

It is but natural that the pariah, who receives so little from the world of men that even fame (which the world has been known to bestow even on the most abandoned of her children) is accounted to him a mere sign of *schlemihldom*,[13] should look with an air of innocent amusement, and smile to himself at the spectacle of human beings trying to compete with the divine realities of nature. The bare fact that the sun shines on all alike affords him daily proof that all men are essentially equal. In the presence of such universal things as the sun, music, trees, and children—things which Rachel Varnhagen[14] called "the true realities" just because they are cherished most by those who have no place in the political and social world—the petty dispensations of men which create and maintain inequality must needs appear ridiculous. Confronted with the natural order of things, in which all is equally good, the fabricated order of society, with its manifold classes and ranks, must needs appear a comic, hopeless attempt of creation to throw down the gauntlet to its creator. It is no longer the outcast pariah who

12. Hannah Arendt, *The Jewish Writings*, ed. Jerome Kohn and Ron H. Feldman (New York: Schocken, 2007). See also Richard J. Bernstein, *Hannah Arendt and the Jewish Question* (Cambridge, MA: MIT Press, 1996).

13. [The *schlemihl* (a Yiddish version of a biblical name) is typically understood in Yiddish culture to represent the hapless, awkward, or incompetent person.]

14. [Varnhagen (1771–1833) was a German-Jewish writer about whom Arendt wrote a biography.]

appears the *schlemihl*, but those who live in the ordered ranks of society and who have exchanged the generous gifts of nature for the idols of social privilege and prejudice. Especially is this true of the *parvenu* who was not even born to the system, but chose it of his own free will, and who is called upon to pay the cost meticulously and exactly, whereas others can take things in their stride. But no less are they *schlemihls* who enjoy power and high station. It needs but a poet to compare their vaunted grandeur with the real majesty of the sun, shining on king and beggarman alike, in order to demonstrate that all their pomp and circumstance is but sounding brass and a tinkling cymbal. All of these truths are as old as the hills. We know them from the songs of oppressed and despised peoples who—so long as man does not aspire to halt the course of the sun—will always seek refuge in nature, hoping that beside nature all the devices of men will reveal themselves as ephemeral trifles.

It is from this shifting of the accent, from this vehement protest on the part of the pariah, from this attitude of denying the reality of the social order and of confronting it, instead, with a higher reality, that Heine's spirit of mockery really stems.[15] It is this too which makes his scorn so pointed. Because he gauges things so consistently by the criterion of what is really and manifestly natural, he is able at once to detect the weak spot in his opponent's armor, the vulnerable point in any particular stupidity which he happens to be exposing. And it is this aloofness of the pariah from all the works of man that Heine regards as the essence of freedom. It is this aloofness that accounts for the divine laughter and the absence of bitterness in his verses. He was the first Jew to whom freedom meant more than mere "liberation from the house of bondage" and in whom it was combined, in equal measure, with the traditional Jewish passion for justice. To Heine, freedom had little to do with liberation from a just or unjust yoke. A man is born free, and he can lose his freedom only by selling himself into bondage. In line with his idea, both in his political poems and in his prose writings Heine vents his anger not only on tyrants but equally on those who put up with them. . . .

So long as the Jews of Western Europe were pariahs only in a social sense they could find salvation, to a large extent, by becoming *parvenus*. Insecure as their position may have been, they could nevertheless achieve a *modus vivendi* by combining what Ahad Haam[16] described as "inner slavery" with "outward freedom."

15. [Heinrich Heine (1797–1856) was born to a Jewish family in Germany and converted to Christianity in his twenties. He was highly influential as a poet, essayist, and critic.]

16. [This was the pen name of Asher Ginsberg (1826–1927), a Zionist thinker and essayist most closely associated with the approach known as cultural Zionism.]

Moreover those who deemed the price too high could still remain mere pariahs, calmly enjoying the freedom and untouchability of outcasts. Excluded from the world of political realities, they could still retreat into their quiet corners there to preserve the illusion of liberty and unchallenged humanity. The life of the pariah, though shorn of political significance, was by no means senseless.

But today it is. Today the bottom has dropped out of the old ideology. The pariah Jew and the *parvenu* Jew are in the same boat, rowing desperately in the same angry sea. Both are branded with the same mark; both alike are outlaws. Today the truth has come home: there is no protection in heaven or earth against bare murder, and a man can be driven at any moment from the streets and broad places once open to all. At long last, it has become clear that the "senseless freedom" of the individual merely paves the way for the senseless suffering of his entire people.

Social isolation is no longer possible. You cannot stand aloof from society, whether as a *schlemihl* or as a lord of dreams. The old escape-mechanisms have broken down, and a man can no longer come to terms with a world in which the Jew cannot be a human being either as a *parvenu* using his elbows or as a *pariah* voluntarily spurning its gifts. Both the realism of the one and the idealism of the other are today utopian.

There is, however, a third course—the one that Kafka suggests,[17] in which a man may forego all claims to individual freedom and inviolability and modestly content himself with trying to lead a simple, decent life. But—as Kafka himself points out—this is impossible within the framework of contemporary society. For while the individual might still be allowed to make a career, he is no longer strong enough to fulfil the basic demands of human life. The man of goodwill is driven today into isolation like the Jew-stranger in the castle. He gets lost—or dies from exhaustion. For only within the framework of a people can a man live as a man among men, without exhausting himself. And only when a people lives and functions in consort with other peoples can it contribute to the establishment upon earth of a commonly conditioned and commonly controlled humanity.

17. [Franz Kafka (1883–1924). This leading exponent of European literary modernism was engaged with key questions of Jewish identity and commitment.]

Michael Walzer (born 1935) is Professor Emeritus at the Institute for Advanced Study in Princeton, New Jersey. Through his academic work and his association with *Dissent, The New Republic,* and other journals, as well as his popular works and public appearances, he has become known as a prominent spokesman for a communitarian approach to politics. Walzer is a graduate of Brandeis University who earned his doctorate at Harvard University. His efforts to provide an intellectual basis for the understanding of the Jewish political tradition have been foundational.

Michael Walzer, *Exodus and Revolution* (New York: Basic Books, 1985), 146–49.

Exodus history, as I have said repeatedly, is the source of messianic politics. John Canne, an English Fifth Monarchy man,[18] writing in 1657, makes the crucial claim. "It is a common received opinion: In the Lord's bringing Israel out of Egypt was shadowed out the deliverance of his church and people from all tyranny and oppression in the last days."[19] *Shadowed out* is exactly right, and the shadows are larger than life: not Egypt but the world, not this particular tyranny but all tyranny and oppression, not the future but the Last Days. Without its shadows, however, the Exodus provides the chief alternative to messianism—as Oliver Cromwell's dispute with the Fifth Monarchy suggests. For the Exodus begins with a concrete evil and ends (or doesn't quite end) with a partial success. To be sure, the partial success is a problem. So far is the end of the story from the end of days that there is more than enough room for the backsliding and renewed oppression that repeatedly transform the hope of the Exodus into messianic fantasy. Messianism has its origins in disappointment, in all those Canaans that turn out to be "almost barren." Yet who can doubt that it is better to be in Canaan than in Egypt? And better to work for one more local deliverance than to risk the terrors of the next-to-last days? In every revolutionary movement there are men and women who want to be able to say, with Cromwell: "We are thus

18. [The Fifth Monarchists were an extreme Puritan sect active in England in the 1650s.]
19. John Canne, *The Time of the End* (London, 1641), 9.

far . . ."[20]—and to know, in fact, where they are. For them, Exodus history gives rise to Exodus politics.

Compared with political messianism, Exodus makes for a cautious and moderate politics. Compared with "the old type of social struggle" or with the even more common passivity and acquiescence of the oppressed, it makes for a revolutionary politics. But these terms are misleading. As we have seen, the Exodus story is open to interpretation, and one can imagine social democrats and (some) Bolsheviks at home within it. The biblical text tells a tale of argument and contention, and the commentators read the text in the same spirit; there is always "another interpretation." Political messianism is quite different. One can calculate endlessly the number of days until the Last Days; there is always another calculation; but once a decision has been made to force the End, there is no room for argument. Then politics is absolute, enemies satanic, compromise impossible. Exodus politics slides, sometimes, toward absolutism—as in a sermon preached by the Puritan minister Stephen Marshall to the House of Commons in 1641: "All people are cursed or blessed according as they do or do not join their strength and give their best assistance to the Lord's people against their enemies."[21] The curses and blessing derive, I suppose, from Deuteronomy, but Marshall comes close to the Bolshevik slogan, "You are either for us or against us." It's only when the struggle is an ultimate one that choice can be so radically restricted. For men and women working within the Exodus tradition, however, choice more commonly takes on a different character. There is no ultimate struggle, but a long series of decisions, backslidings, and reforms. The apocalyptic war between "the Lord's people" and "their enemies" can't readily be located within the Exodus.

Absolutism is effectively barred, I think, by the very character of the people, frightened, stubborn, contentious, and at the same time, members of the covenant. The people can't be killed (not all of them anyway) or cast aside or miraculously transformed. They must be led, chastised, defended, argued with, educated—activities that undercut and defeat any simple designation of "enemies." The revolutionary idea of a holy nation does breed enemies, of course, but the struggle is never so melodramatic as Marshall's formula suggests. The presence of the people makes for realism, not only because some among the

20. [This is most likely a reference to a statement attributed to Oliver Cromwell (1599–1658): "A man never goes so far as when he does not know whither he is going."]
21. Marshall, *Meroz Cursed* (London, 1641), 9.

people are tough-minded and skeptical realists, asking hard questions, like the psalmist's "Can God furnish a table in the wilderness?"[22] or the midrashic rabbi's "On what grounds do you slay three thousand men in one day?"[23] The people also make for realism because the pace of the march must be set with their feelings in mind, because their rebellions must be dealt with, leaders chosen from their midst, and the law expounded in their hearing. They can't easily be divided into friends and enemies; their very stiff-neckedness is somehow admirable. Many of them still retained an affection for Egypt, wrote Benjamin Franklin in a "Comparison of the Conduct of the Ancient Jews and of the Anti-Federalists," but "on the whole it appears [from the text] that the Israelites were a people jealous of their newly acquired liberty." They were only inexperienced and, like the Americans, "worked upon by artful men. . . ."[24]

This is a typical piece of Exodus politics, but it doesn't quite suggest the sobering power of the biblical story, for Franklin was hardly disposed to think of the Anti-Federalists as the representatives of Anti-Christ. In the writings of contemporary liberation theologians, the power of the story is more evident. One can feel in their books and essays a constant thrust toward political messianism, but since Exodus is the standard reference for liberation, and the promised land the standard goal, there is also a strong sense of this-worldly complexity. Exodus history and politics work as a constraint on Christian eschatology. Liberation is not a movement from our fallen state to the messianic kingdom but from "the slavery, exploitation and alienation of Egypt" to a land where the people can live "with human dignity." The movement takes place in historical time; it is the hard and continuous work of men and women. The best of the liberation theologians explicitly warns his readers against "absolutizing [the] revolution" and falling into idolatry toward "unavoidably ambiguous achievements."[25] This, again, is Exodus politics.

So pharaonic oppression, deliverance, Sinai, and Canaan are still with us, powerful memories shaping our perception of the political world. The "door of hope" is still open; things are not what they might be—even what they might be isn't totally different from what they are. This is a central theme in Western

22. [Psalms 78:19.]

23. [*Tanna Debe Eliyahu*, Chapter 4, in a discussion of the golden calf episode.]

24. *The Works of Benjamin Franklin*, ed. John Bigelow (New York: Putnam's, 1904), 11, 383, 386.

25. Gustavo Gutiérrez, *A Theology of Liberation: History, Politics, and Salvation*, trans. Sister Caridad Inda and John Eagleson (Maryknoll, NY: Orbis, 1973), 294, 238.

thought, always present though elaborated in many different ways. We still believe, or many of us do, what the Exodus first taught, or what it has commonly been taken to teach, about the meaning and possibility of politics and about its proper form:

first, that wherever you live, it is probably Egypt;

second, that there is a better place, a world more attractive, a promised land;

and third, that "the way to the land is through the wilderness."[26] There is no way to get from here to there except by joining together and marching.

26. W. D. Davies, *The Territorial Dimension of Judaism* (Berkeley: University of California Press, 1982), 60.

Mitchell Cohen (born 1952) earned his doctorate in political science at Columbia University and has served as a professor of political science at Baruch College since 1982. He is a former editor of *Dissent*. Cohen's work straddles the divide between academic insight and personal engagement.

Mitchell Cohen, "In Defense of Shaatnez: A Politics for Jews in a Multicultural America," in *Insider/Outsider: American Jews and Multiculturalism*, ed. David Biale, Michael Galchinsky, and Susannah Heschel (Berkeley: University of California Press, 1998), 36, 50–52.

Let me present it starkly: *Shaatnez*[27] or monism? This is the great intellectual question of Jewish modernity and no less, if you will, of Jewish "postmodernity." Shall Jews and their culture(s) be entwined with, open to, and engaged by the world or shall they turn inward defensively? An ethnocentric vision, as K. Anthony Appiah observes, always implies "an unimaginative attitude to one's own culture."[28] Appiah, an intellectual of mixed African-English parentage who lives in the United States, has written a penetrating book, *In My Father's House*, examining African cultures and identities. He arrives at some important values that are strikingly akin to those articulated four decades earlier by Hayim Greenberg, the Bessarabian-born American Labor Zionist thinker. The source of commonality is clear: both wrestle with contesting demands made of their identities. . . .

An intelligent multiculturalism would envisage an America whose parts are not subsumed by a whole, yet whose parts nonetheless seek to make up a differentiated whole. Its national conversation would be allergic to Jabotinsky's[29]

27. [A biblical Hebrew term denoting forbidden mingling of wool and linen in a garment. Used more widely, the term denotes an approach of "mongrel" interchange between cultures, which Cohen embraces.]

28. K. Anthony Appiah, *In My Father's House: Africa in the Philosophy of Culture* (Oxford and New York: Oxford University Press, 1992), 92.

29. [Ze'ev Jabotinsky (1880–1940), Russian-born poet, writer, activist, and founder of the Revisionist stream within the Zionist movement, whom Cohen discusses earlier in the article, before this excerpted section.]

idiom, to monism, and to any "simple, primal, brutal 'yes or no'" (which is no less the argot of neoconservatives). This America would have no need of Stradivarius's secret;[30] it would need, in its stead, liberality, democracy, tolerance.

Shaatnez would be celebrated and the legitimacy of plural loyalties—of a rooted cosmopolitanism—defended, not just for the enriching possibilities of diversity, as imagined by Bourne[31] or Kallen[32] or Greenberg or Appiah, but also for a contrasting reason: tensions born of overlapping or entwined commitments can educate citizens to tolerance by pressing them to see issues and one another from both cosmopolitan and rooted standpoints, each tempering yet challenging the other. It is true that the value of such tensions may be equal and perhaps be inseparable from the anguish they cause, especially within minorities. W. E. B. DuBois, echoing Goethe's Faust in *The Souls of Black Folk*, spoke of his ever present sense of "twoness—an American, a Negro; two souls, two thoughts, two unreconciled strivings" at war, threatening to tear "one dark body" apart. Harold Rosenberg, in "Jewish Identity in a Free Society," expressed a similar strain when he wrote that being "twice identified" is "embarrassingly ambiguous" because of "a modern impulse"—the oft-made demand—to be "one-hundred-percent-something."[33]

But it is better to live with and through modern ambiguities, to wrestle with unreconciled strivings, than to hanker for the easy, one-sided resolution, just as it is better for a society to accept hyphenated citizens rather than impose homogeneity. Moreover, such one-sidedness and homogeneity cannot be achieved in the end. This doesn't mean that variety, which must come with variance, necessarily stands on its own. If I may borrow from (and modulate) Hegel, diversity in civil society needs a countervailing (though not totalistic) unity in the "political moment." The more pluralism within a society, the more vigorous the sense of political citizenship must be, especially within a democracy.

30. [Earlier in the article (p. 34), Cohen quotes a 1935 letter by Jabotinsky to David Ben-Gurion, in which Jabotinsky describes the delicate process of weaving the disparate threads of Zionism and Socialism into one fabric as something that has been forgotten like the secret of Stradivarius, the famed violin maker. "Stradivarius's secret" is used here as code for the meshing together of unlikely ingredients.]

31. [Randolph Bourne (1886–1918), an American progressive writer and intellectual.]

32. [Horace Kallen (1882–1974), Polish-born American Jewish intellectual. His ideas, such as the term "cultural pluralism" that is often attributed to him, were highly influential.]

33. W. E. B. DuBois, *The Souls of Black Folk* (New York: Signet, 1982), 45; Harold Rosenberg, "Jewish Identity in a Free Society," in Harold Rosenberg, *Discovering the Present: Three Decades in Art, Culture, and Politics* (Chicago and London: University of Chicago Press, 1976), 262.

Furthermore, a robust sense of citizenship needs to extend into the social and economic domains. Just as a part of the left uses multiculturalism as ersatz politics, so many on the right have preoccupied themselves with culture wars so as to avoid addressing widespread social pain in this country. This was revealed starkly in the symposium "The National Prospect," published in *Commentary*, the intellectual flagship of Jewish neoconservatism, on its fiftieth anniversary. Here, while warnings abound of cultural decay and its fragmenting consequences, serious treatment of economic malaise, of the fragmenting, devastating consequences of vast and growing inequality between rich and poor, is absent. Gertrude Himmelfarb and Norman Podhoretz[34] retrieve Disraeli's notion of "Two Nations,"[35] but where this nineteenth-century British conservative meant to warn of what widespread poverty would bring, for today's neoconservative the issue is only cultural. Podhoretz contends that "for all the talk about 'increased economic and social stratification,' prosperity is still more widely shared here than anywhere else."[36] Not two economic nations, but two cultural nations are emerging in America, one with and one without the puritan morals and bourgeois manners championed by neoconservatives.

Yet statistics demonstrate overwhelmingly that the United States has the greatest economic inequality of any Western nation, with 1 percent of the population possessing 40 percent of its wealth and the top 20 percent possessing 80 percent. When it comes to incomes ratio, that of the upper 20 percent to the poorest 20 percent is nine to one.[37] One is tempted to compare the neoconservatives to Jabotinsky: he denounced *shaatnez*, they censure multiculturalism, and in so doing they direct all the focus from other matters, especially economic injustice. There is, however, a significant historical difference. The denunciation of *shaatnez* by Jabotinsky was a rhetorical canard since his Zionism was as "impure" as Ben-Gurion's;[38] but multiculturalism is a genuine issue today because

34. [Gertrude Himmelfarb (born 1922) and Norman Podhoretz (born 1930) are both leading American Jewish neoconservative intellectuals.]

35. [The reference here is to the British statesman Benjamin Disraeli (1804–81), whose 1845 novel *Sybil* warned against the separation of the country into two nations.]

36. Norman Podhoretz, "The National Prospect" (symposium), *Commentary*, November 1995, 99. For Gertrude Himmelfarb, see p. 56 in the same issue.

37. *New York Times*, April 17, 1995, and September 3, 1995; *International Herald Tribune*, July 16, 1996.

38. [David Ben-Gurion (1886–1973), Jabotinsky's ideological adversary and Israel's first Prime Minister.]

of America's pluralism and despite the successes of the melting pot. What is thus needed is some perspective, an ability to recognize when multiculturalism is properly addressed in America, and when it isn't; and also to recognize how urgent it is to address social and economic suffering in this country.

This is to ask, again, of American Jews: In what type of America do you want to live? My answer, as one American Jew, as one rooted cosmopolitan, is that I want to live in an America of democratic citizenship, of social and economic democracy, of liberal tolerance, in a secular state that allows diverse cultures and religions to make of themselves what they will. This America is conceived from a perspective of *shaatnez*; how Judaism fares in it will depend on the cultural life fashioned by American Jews for themselves as a distinct community within the broader society but nonetheless as full participants in it.

Jill Jacobs was born in 1975. She was ordained at the Jewish Theological Seminary and also studied urban affairs at Hunter College. Her rabbinate has been characterized by involvement with social, economic, and political questions at such institutions as the Jewish Council on Urban Affairs, Jewish Funds for Justice, and, for the last several years, T'ruah: The Rabbinic Call for Human Rights, where she has served as Executive Director.

Jill Jacobs, *There Shall Be No Needy: Pursuing Social Justice through Jewish Law and Tradition* (Woodstock, VT: Jewish Lights, 2009), 217–21.

The beauty of America is the opportunity for citizens of varying ethnic, religious, and ideological backgrounds to bring their own beliefs and experiences into the public debate. Ideally, the conversation around public policy issues will become richer as a result of this diversity of opinion, and the resulting public policy will be more successful.

Yet Jews sometimes hesitate to speak as Jews in the public sphere. In contemporary America, public religious space has largely been claimed by the Christian right. Those who speak from a religious standpoint are assumed to care most about banning abortion and limiting the rights of gays and lesbians. In the past decade, the Christian left has grown, as organizations such as Call to Renewal and Evangelicals for Social Action have attempted to redefine Christian politics as a dedication, first and foremost, to poverty relief. Still, many progressives worry that speaking from our own religious tradition will lead to a debate about which religion has the better claim to truth, or will unwittingly legitimize others who claim to know God's political preferences. Others worry that strong Jewish voices in the political sphere will lead to increased anti-Semitism. We are conscious of the large numbers of Jews who play public roles in the U.S. government, and we have seen instances in which this public profile has led to scapegoating and resentment of Jews as a group.

The Jewish community has long been among the strongest voices for the separation of church and state. Jewish communal organizations and individuals have successfully opposed school prayer, the public display of religious symbols, and religious proselytizing in the military. This focus on preventing religious coercion has led many of us to believe that the Constitution calls only for a strict separation between religion and public life. But in addition to limiting the government's ability to provide any favoritism to one religion over another, the First Amendment also guarantees the rights of citizens to express their religious beliefs freely. No single set of religious beliefs should dominate public discourse, but religious beliefs can and should be brought into the public domain, just as any other ideologies, experiences, and insights would. As the theologian Abraham Joshua Heschel commented when explaining his own involvement in justice issues, "We *affirm* the principle of separation of church and state. We *reject* the separation of religion and the human situation."[39] ...

The question for this generation is not how to become an "American in the street,"[40] but how or whether it is possible to be an American Jew in the street, as well as in the home. The answer to this question may determine how Jews can bring Jewish law and tradition into the public square in such a way as to enrich the debate, rather than lead to a head-to-head collision with people of other faiths over the question of how God might vote.

Much of the American conversation about religion in the public square revolves around visible manifestations of religion, such as creches and Christmas trees on public property, or prayer and Bible study in school. The Jewish community expends significant resources on responding to these incidents, either by demanding the strict banishment of religion from public life or by promoting the inclusion of Hanukkah menorahs and other symbols of our own. It is important to protect the boundary between church and state in order for people of all religions to feel comfortable in public space, and in order to ensure that public displays of Christianity do not become coercive. At the same time, such displays of religion are ultimately symbolic, and they are less important than decisions about policies that affect the economic and social welfare of individual citizens and communities.

Many individual Jews play prominent roles in public life, as community organizers, public policy experts, legislators, and government officials. Some of these officials speak proudly of their Jewish commitments and inspirations;

---

39. Abraham Joshua Heschel, "What We Might Do Together," in *Moral Grandeur and Spiritual Audacity*, Susannah Heschel, ed. (New York: Farrar, Straus, and Giroux: 1996), 298.

40. [Jacobs is referring to the phrase coined by poet Judah Leib Gordon and used as a watchword of Jewish enlightenment figures in Europe from the 1860s.]

others keep their Judaism private. Some of these individuals have found a place in a Jewish community; others believe that their own commitments are incompatible with those of most Jewish communities. At the same time, many Jewish organizations are deeply engaged in policy debates at local, state, national, and international levels. In some cases, this involvement focuses on specifically "Jewish issues," such as Israel, separation of church and state, and private school funding. But many Jewish organizations—including local social justice groups, synagogues, and national bodies—devote themselves to issues as varied as reproductive choice, immigration, and international human rights. Many, or even most, of these organizations strive to speak about these issues with a Jewish voice. Most reference the Jewish experience of oppression, quote relevant Biblical verses, and ask prominent rabbis to give sermons and write articles that link Jewish thought to particular issues. Some publish materials aimed at helping individuals, synagogues, and schools to study issues from a Jewish perspective.

What is missing in much of this work is a real public discussion about how Jewish law and tradition might address contemporary policy questions. Those on either side of an issue often quote texts to support their points, but they do so in a way which does not invite debate or discussion. Instead, when Jews engage in the public discourse as Jews, we should bring Jewish law and principles into the conversation in such a way as to enrich, rather than shut down, the discourse. We should also bring into this dialogue Jews and others who are engaged in public life; the conversation among rabbis, public policy experts, grassroots activists, and Jewish communal professionals should generate a nuanced understanding of how the Jewish community might approach individual issues.

This approach precludes quoting a simplified version of Jewish law or text in order to prove a point, or asserting that Jewish law unequivocally demands a certain approach to an issue. Rather, Jewish sources should help us to see various sides of an issue, challenge our assumptions, and enable us to formulate a response that takes multiple factors into account. The commitment to living our Judaism publicly should then push us to take public action in these principles, both as individuals and as a community.

If we succeed in facilitating this rich conversation, we will create a new kind of Jewish politics in America. Rather than trade sound bites, we will continue the talmudic tradition of dialogue, in which various questioners and commentators engage in an often messy conversation that eventually leads to fuller understanding of the situation at hand. Jews who now exercise their commitments to public life outside of the Jewish community will find a place within this community, as they contribute their own wisdom and observations to the conversation. Individual Jews and Jewish institutions will strengthen their commitment to public life, as the question of how to address current issues becomes part of the general Jewish conversation, rather than something separate from it or as an addition to discussion of Shabbat, *Kashrut*, and other aspects of Jewish practice. We will witness the emergence of a Judaism that views ritual observance, study, and engagement in the world as an integrated whole, rather than as separate and distinct practices. The Jewish community's deepened involvement in public life will change the face of religious politics in America, as other communities will recognize the Jewish community as an important and authentic religious voice in the public square of America. Finally, the integration of religion, legal discussion, and participation in public life will instill in the Jewish community the power to have a major impact on the ideologies and policies of the United States.

One of American Judaism's most controversial and divisive figures, Meir Kahane (1932–90) was influenced in his youth by the thinking of Ze'ev Jabotinsky and Hillel Kook. Ordained by the famed Mir Yeshiva, he served as a congregational rabbi before going on to found the Jewish Defense League. He later moved to Israel, where he went on to serve as a member of the Knesset. Kahane headed a political party that was eventually banned on account of its extreme right-wing positions. He was assassinated in New York.

Meir Kahane, "Down with Chanukah!" in Meir Kahane, *Writings 5732–33* (New York: Jewish Identity Center, 1973), 150–52.

If I were a Reform rabbi; if I were a leader of the Establishment whose money and prestige have succeeded in capturing for him the leadership and voice of American Jewry; if I were one of the members of the Israeli Government's ruling group; if I were an enlightened sophisticated, modern Jewish intellectual, I would climb the barricades and join in battle against the most dangerous of all Jewish holidays—Chanukah.

It is a measure of the total ignorance of the world Jewish community that there is no holiday that is more universally celebrated than the "Feast of Lights," and it is an equal measure of the intellectual dishonesty and of Jewish leadership that it plays along with the lie. For if ever there was a holiday that stands for everything that the mass of world Jewry and their leadership has rejected—it is this one. If one would find an event that is truly rooted in everything that Jews of our times and their leaders have rejected and, indeed, attacked—it is this one. If there is any holiday that is more "un-Jewish" in the sense of our modern beliefs and practices—I do not know of it.

The Chanukah that has erupted unto the world Jewish scene in all its childishness, asininity, shallowness, ignorance, and fraud—is not the Chanukah of reality. The Chanukah that came into vogue because of Jewish parents—in their vapidness—needed something to counteract Christmas; that exploded in a show of "we-can-have-lights-just-as-our-goyish-neighbors" and in an effort to reward our spoiled children with eight gifts instead of the poor Christian one;

the Chanukah that the Temple, under its captive rabbi, turned into a school pageant so that the beaming parents might think that the Religious School is really successful instead of the tragic joke and waste that it really is; the Chanukah that speaks of Jewish Patrick Henrys giving-me-liberty-or-death and the pictures of Maccabees as great liberal saviors who fought so that the kibbutzim might continue to be free to preach their Marx and eat their ham, that the split-level dwellers of suburbia might be allowed to violate their Sabbath in perfect freedom and the Reform and Conservative Temples continue the fight for civil rights for Blacks, Puerto Ricans, and Jane Fonda, is not remotely connected with reality.

This is NOT the Chanukah of our ancestors, of the generations of Jews of Eastern Europe and Yemen and Morocco and the crusades and Spain and Babylon. It is surely not the Chanukah for which the Maccabees themselves died. Truly, could those whom we honor so munificently, return and see what Chanukah has become, they might very well begin a second Maccabean revolt. For the life that we Jews lead today was the very cause, the REAL reason for the revolt of the Jews "in those days in our times."

What happened in that era more than 2000 years ago? What led a handful of Jews to rise up in violence against the enemy? And precisely who WAS the enemy? What were they fighting FOR and who were they fighting AGAINST?

For years, the people of Judea had been the vassals of Greece. True independence as a state had been unknown for all those decades and, yet, the Jews did not rise up in revolt. It was only when the Greek policy shifted from mere political control to one that attempted to suppress the Jewish religion that the revolt erupted in all its bloodiness. It was not mere liberty that led to the Maccabean uprising that we so passionately applaud. What we are really cheering is a brave group of Jews who fought and plunged Judea into a bloodbath for the right to observe the Sabbath, to follow the laws of kashruth, to obey the laws of the Torah. IN A WORD EVERYTHING ABOUT CHANUKAH THAT WE COMMEMORATE AND TEACH OUR CHILDREN TO COMMEMORATE ARE THINGS WE CONSIDER TO BE OUTMODED, MEDIEVAL, AND CHILDISH!

At best, then, those who fought and died for Chanukah were naïve and obscurantist. Had we lived in those days we would certainly not have done what they did for everyone knows that the laws of the Torah are not really Divine but only the products of evolution and men (do not the Reform, Reconstructionist, and large parts of the Conservative movements write this daily?). Surely we would not have fought for that which we violate every day of our lives! No, at best Chanukah emerges as a needless holiday if not a foolish one. Poor Hannah and her seven children; poor Mattathias and Judah; poor well-meaning chaps all but hopelessly backward and utterly unnecessary sacrifices.

But there is more. Not only is Chanukah really a foolish and unnecessary holiday, it is also one that is dangerously fanatical and illiberal. The first act of rebellion, the first enemy who fell at the hands of the brave Jewish heroes whom our delightful children portray so cleverly in their Sunday and religious school pageants, was NOT a Greek. He was a Jew.

When the enemy sent its troops into the town of Modin to set up an idol and demand its worship, it was a Jew who decided to exercise his freedom of pagan worship and who approached the altar to worship Zeus (after all, what business was it of anyone what this fellow worshipped?). And it was this Jew, this apostate, this religious traitor who was struck down by the brave, glorious, courageous (are these not the words all our Sunday schools use to describe him?) Mattathias, as he shouted: "Whoever is for G-d, follow me!"

What have we here? What kind of religious intolerance and bigotry? What kind of a man is this for the anti-religious of Hashomer Hatzair,[41] the graceful temples of suburbia, the sophisticated intellectuals, the liberal open-minded Jews, and all the drones who have wearied us unto death with the concept of Judaism as a humanistic, open-minded, undogmatic, liberal, universalistic (if not Marxist) religion, to honor? What kind of nationalism is this for David Ben-Gurion (he who rejects the Galut and speaks of the proud, free Jew of ancient Judea and Israel)?

And to crush us even more (we who know that Judaism is a faith of peace which deplores violence), what kind of Jews were these who reacted to oppression with FORCE? Surely we who so properly have deplored Jewish violence as fascistic, immoral, and (above all!) UN-JEWISH, stand in horror as we contemplate Jews who declined to picket the Syrian Greeks to death and who rejected quiet diplomacy for the sword, spear, and arrow (had there been bombs in those days, who can tell what they might have done?) and "descended to the level of evil," thus rejecting the ethical and moral concepts of Judaism.

Is this the kind of a holiday we wish to propagate? Are these the kinds of men we want our moral and humanistic children to honor? Is this the kind of Judaism that we wish to observe and pass on to our children?

Where shall we find the man of courage, the one voice in the wilderness to cry out against Chanukah and the Judaism that it represents—the Judaism of

41. [A left-wing secularist Zionist movement.]

our grandparents and ancestors? Where shall we find the man of honesty and integrity to attack the Judaism of Medievalism and outdated foolishness; the Judaism of bigotry that strikes down Jews who refuse to observe the law; the Judaism of violence that calls for Jewish force and might against the enemy? When shall we find the courage to proudly eat our Chinese food and violate our Sabbaths and reject all the separateness, nationalism, and religious maximalism that Chanukah so ignobly represents? . . . Down with Chanukah! It is a regressive holiday that merely symbolizes the Judaism that always was; the Judaism that was handed down to us from Sinai; the Judaism that made our ancestors ready to give their lives for the L-rd; the Judaism that young people instinctively know is true and great and real. Such Judaism is dangerous for us and our leaders. We must do all in our power to bury it.

V | The Holocaust and Israel

The twentieth century witnessed two events—the Holocaust and the establishment of the State of Israel—that together had an epoch-making impact on the nature and course of Judaism and the Jewish people.[1] While the Zionist movement unquestionably predated the attempted destruction and genocide of the Jewish people in Europe during the years 1933–45, the scale and fury of the unprecedented hatred and murder that the Nazis and their collaborators and supporters directed at the Jewish people had a radical impact upon American Jewish thought in the years following World War II and into the present. Moreover, the trauma of what Arthur A. Cohen termed "the tremendum"[2] became inextricably linked with the creation of the State of Israel in 1948 in a variety of ways in the minds of countless Jewish thinkers. This linkage is demonstrated in the excerpts included in this part of our book, even as some of the thinkers we have selected challenge its validity.

In the opening selection, Jacob Neusner frames the pieces that follow by arguing that, while classical rabbinic Judaism rested on the myth of a "dual Torah," the Written and the Oral Law, post-Holocaust American Jewish thinking centers on the notions of the Holocaust and the State of Israel, or, to employ his vocabulary, the myth of "destruction" represented by the Holocaust and the reality of "redemption" embodied in the birth of the State of Israel and the restoration of Jewish sovereignty in the land of Israel after two millennia of exile. The symbolic "death" and "rebirth" that these two events represent

1. [The term "epoch-making event" is used by Emil Fackenheim in this context. For a discussion of this usage and its significance, see Zachary Braiterman, "Fideism Redux: Emil Fackenheim and the State of Israel," *Jewish Social Studies* 4, no.1 (Autumn 1997), 105–20.]

2. [This term was the title of an important work by Arthur A. Cohen, *The Tremendum: A Theological Interpretation of the Holocaust* (New York: Crossroad, 1981). See also Steven T. Katz, *Post-Holocaust Dialogues: Critical Studies in Modern Jewish Thought* (New York: New York University Press, 1983); Michael L. Morgan, *Beyond Auschwitz: Post-Holocaust Jewish Thought in America* (Oxford: Oxford University Press, 2001).]

are the foci around which much of modern American Jewish thought orbits, and in the canon of that thought, one event cannot be understood without attention being immediately paid to the other.

The selections that follow Neusner's piece are presented in broad chronological order rather than being grouped in ideological clusters. Not all American Jewish thinkers viewed the grand narrative of destruction and redemption described by Neusner in a positive light. Indeed, the Rebbe of Satmar Joel Teitelbaum, the European Hasidic leader who ultimately came to the United States in 1945, contended that in fact it was Zionism and its heretical character that caused God to punish and destroy six million Jews in Europe. In the selection from his *Vayoel Moshe*, he expresses the view that Zionism and the creation of the State of Israel violated the Talmudic demand that Jews wait patiently for messianic times, when God alone would restore the Jewish people to the land of Israel. Teitelbaum argues that the audacity of Zionist leaders in defying this divine commandment was sinful and that this transgression led to the decimation of the European Jewish community. The linkage that Teitelbaum establishes between the Holocaust and the State of Israel is completely destructive.

Other European refugee rabbi-scholars such as the liberal Emil Fackenheim and the Orthodox Eliezer Berkovits disagreed emphatically with Teitelbaum. In a selection from a famous essay that has achieved iconic status in North American Jewish circles, Fackenheim declares that the "commanding presence" of God at Auschwitz revealed a "614th commandment" to the Jewish people demanding that the people Israel hand Hitler no "posthumous victory" by abandoning their faith, people, or values. We complement this essay by Fackenheim with another in which he explicitly states that the State of Israel has allowed Jews to "recover faith" after the "despair" of the Holocaust. We then include two brief selections in which his thought reinforces the position adopted by Ruth Wisse and others later in Part Five. In them, he argues that powerlessness is no virtue and that Zionism in our day has no right to be "innocent" regarding the threats of destruction that others issue against the State of Israel and the Jewish people. In his *Faith after the Holocaust*, Berkovits adopts a comparable view and declares that the Israeli triumph in the Six Day War bears witness to God acting in history. He sees the State of Israel as the "renewal of biblical times."

David Blumenthal takes exception to Fackenheim's conviction that a ruptured world is in some sense repaired with the Jewish return into history. In a powerful and somewhat shocking use of metaphor and symbolism, he accuses God of "abuse" for the "sin" of permitting European Jewry to perish. Blumenthal states unequivocally that the creation of the State of Israel in no way constitutes adequate "repentance" for the crimes God allowed to be perpetrated against the Jewish people during the Holocaust.

The Orthodox rabbi Irving "Yitz" Greenberg echoes many of the views of Fackenheim and Berkovits in his writings on the meaning of the Holocaust for modern Jewish life. Though he contends that "theological doubts" were inescapable as a result of the Holocaust, Greenberg argues that the events of 1933–45 and the existence of the death camps meant that the exercise of power by the Jewish people was now a "moral necessity" to protect the dignity and existence of Jewish life. Indeed, Greenberg extended this position to argue that all peoples should now possess such power as a guarantor of their own dignity. In "The Ethics of Jewish Power Today," Greenberg expresses this trope unambiguously. Interestingly, he acknowledges that the Palestinians also require such "defense." In so doing, he does not valorize their criticisms of Israel but calls upon Palestinians to see that they have a large share of responsibility for the lack of peace that marks the Israeli-Palestinian conflict. While Greenberg emphasizes the ethical import of Israel for Judaism and the Jewish community after the evil of the Holocaust, a consciousness in his thought that is novel among the "Holocaust theologians" of his generation acknowledges Palestinian suffering. It is a nascent expression of a theme that other Jewish thinkers articulate in a far more condemnatory tone against Israel.

Indeed, Marc Ellis critiques these Holocaust theologians by name for prioritizing the need for Jewish empowerment over the ethical thrust of Jewish tradition. He does not equate Judaism with Zionism and expresses great sympathy for the suffering of the Palestinians. Cultural critic Judith Butler offers an even harsher critique of Zionism, the State of Israel, and their relationship to power than Ellis does. She promotes the centrality of the diaspora as opposed to the land of Israel in Judaism and condemns what she regards as the "aggressive nationalism" inherent in even the most irenic and cooperative forms of Zionism promoted by men like Martin Buber.

Ruth Wisse disagrees completely with Butler and Ellis. Like Fackenheim, Greenberg, and Berkovits, she defends the righteousness of Jewish power after the Holocaust and contends that the Jews and the State of Israel are not going to participate in any type of suicide pact that a surrender of Israeli military power would entail. Daniel Gordis extends this line of thinking, asserting that progressive voices are in fact willing to undermine the case for Israel's very existence, and in this they are to be resisted.

Daniel Boyarin and his brother Jonathan advocate the importance of a particularistic cultural identity while delivering a blistering moral attack upon Israeli political sovereignty. Like Butler, the Boyarins affirm the vibrancy of the diaspora. They see diaspora Judaism as providing an appropriate ethical model for all humanity, one that demonstrates how a people can retain their cultural-religious singularity against the onslaught of universalism, while simultaneously refusing to surrender to the lure of temporal military power. They reject, as do Ellis and Butler, the "redemption" that other thinkers claim the State of Israel provides Jews.

Peter Beinart makes use of another motif that is increasingly expressed in modern American Jewish thought about the Holocaust and Israel. He identifies as a Zionist and states that the Holocaust and the experiences of his refugee grandmother in Europe have convinced him of the necessity of the Jewish state. At the same time, Beinart believes that Israel must be true to the highest ideals of Judaism and condemns the treatment Israel metes out to the Palestinians as a result of the military occupation following the Six Day War.

A selection from the editors of *Commentary* completes Part Five. Writing on February 1, 2015, after the "jihadist siege of a kosher grocery store" in Paris several weeks earlier, the *Commentary* writers charge Beinart and his supporters with being "conditional Zionists" and remark that the tenuous position of Jews in France and Europe makes Zionism and the protection that the State of Israel affords Jews through its military prowess existential necessities. With this argument, this discussion of the relationship between the Holocaust and the State of Israel as seen through the prism Neusner has provided comes to an end.

Jacob Neusner (1932–2016) was educated at Harvard College and Oxford University. He earned his doctorate in religion at Columbia University while studying for rabbinical ordination at the Jewish Theological Seminary. Neusner was probably the most published scholar of Judaic and religious studies in the world during his lifetime, and his contributions to the study of rabbinic literature and history were profound. A professor at Dartmouth College, Brown University, the University of South Florida, and Bard College, among other institutions, Neusner left an indelible impact on American Jewish intellectual life.

Jacob Neusner, *Stranger at Home: "The Holocaust," Zionism, and American Judaism* (Chicago: University of Chicago Press, 1981), 1, 3–4, 6–8, 61–68.

. . . Events, far from America's shores and remote from American Jews' everyday experience, constitute the generative myth by which the generality of American Jews make sense of themselves and decide what to do with that part of themselves set aside for "being Jewish." . . . What is to be called "the myth of Holocaust and redemption" shapes the day-to-day understanding of those who live within the myth. . . . So a sizeable sector of the American people sees the world in and along the lines of a vision of reality beginning in death, "the Holocaust," and completed by resurrection or rebirth, "Israel."

. . . Killing off the bulk of Europe's Jews constitutes a social change of profound and lasting consequence. Setting up a Jewish state in the ancient homeland also presents a social change of equally fundamental character: social change is symbol-change. The shift in the symbolic life of those Jews fortunate enough to find their way to the Jewish state, the use of the destruction of European Jewry in the self-understanding of that state, the formation of a consequent symbolic structure, with its myth and rites of expression of that myth—these expressions of Israel's civil religion are not difficult to describe and to explain. The incapacity of American Jews to make sense of themselves in the aftermath of these same events, except through the appropriation of exactly the same symbolic structure, myth, and rites—this . . . defines the critical problematic of American Judaism.

. . . The myth is that "the Holocaust" is a unique event, which, despite its "uniqueness," teaches compelling lessons about why Jews must be Jewish. . . . The redemptive part of the myth maintains that the State of Israel is the "guarantee" that "the Holocaust" will not happen again, that it is the State and its achievements which give meaning and significance, even fulfillment, to "the Holocaust." The associated ritual is bound up especially in various activities, mostly of a financial character, sometimes of a political one, in support of the State of Israel. The rites of the redemptive myth involve attendance at ritual dinners at which money is given, or, . . . celebrated; endless cycles of work in that same cause; trips to the State of Israel; and, in sum, the definition of the meaning of "being Jewish" around activities in celebration and support of the existence of the State. So if you want to know why be Jewish, you have to remember that (1) the gentiles wiped out the Jews of Europe, so are not to be trusted, let alone joined; (2) if there had been "Israel," meaning the State of Israel, there would have been no "Holocaust"; and so (3) for the sake of your personal safety, you have to "support Israel." Though you do not have to go live there. . . . The issue here is not what happened. It is what people make of what happened. . . .

The other . . . half of the regnant myth of American Judaism . . . is the part about "redemption." That Zionist part speaks of the formation and maintenance of the State of Israel as the compensation and consolation for the death of six million European Jews. . . . The redemptive valence imputed to the State of Israel in American Judaism constitutes a judgment of Zionism. American Judaism must be deemed a wholly Zionist Judaism.

. . . Together this "myth of Holocaust and redemption" makes sense to the American Jew of why he or she is Jewish and explains the world in which "being Jewish" takes place. . . . The issue of the destruction of European Jewry is not theological but psychological and social. . . . Without Zionism, "the Holocaust" is unbearable. . . .

. . . The response to the Holocaust and the creation of the State of Israel differs in form, but not in substance, from earlier [Jewish religious] responses to disaster. The form now is secular. The substance is deeply religious. For the effect of the Holocaust and the creation of the State of Israel is to produce a new myth—by myth I mean a transcendent perspective on events, a story lending meaning and imparting sanctity to ordinary, everyday reactions—and a new religious affirmation.

. . . This . . . myth . . . gives meaning and transcendence to the . . . lives of ordinary people—the myth of the darkness followed by light, of passage through the netherworld and past the gates of hell, then, purified by suffering and by blood, into the new age. The naturalist myth of American Jewry . . . conforms to the supernatural structure of the classic myths of salvific religions from time immemorial. And well it might, for a salvific myth has to tell the story of sin and redemption, disaster and salvation, the old being and the new, the vanquishing of death and mourning, crying and pain, the passing away of former things. The vision of the new Jerusalem, complete in 1967, beckoned not tourists but pilgrims to the new heaven and the new earth. This . . . is the myth that shapes the mind and imagination of American Jewry. . . .

. . . They do not need to believe in or affirm the myth, for they know it to be true. . . . They are confident of the exact correspondence between reality and the story that explains reality, they are the saved. . . . We know this is how things really were and what they really meant. We know it because the myth of suffering and redemption corresponds to our perceptions of reality, evokes immediate recognition and assent. It not only bears meaning, it imparts meaning precisely because it explains experience and derives from what we know to be true.

But one must ask whether experience is so stable, the world so unchanging, that we may continue to explain today's reality in terms of what happened yesterday. The answer is that, much as we might want to, we cannot. The world has moved on. . . . We cannot, because our children will not allow it. They experience a different world—perhaps not better, perhaps not so simple, but certainly different. . . .

Joel Teitelbaum (1887–1979), the Satmar Rebbe, was the founder and Grand Rabbi of the Satmar Hasidic dynasty. An ultraorthodox rabbi born in what was then Austria-Hungary (today Romania), Teitelbaum was a religious conservative who strongly opposed the Enlightenment and Zionism. He arrived in the United States in 1946. Teitelbaum established his community first in Brooklyn and years later in Kiryas Joel in Monroe, New York. A fierce anti-Zionist, he expressed his opposition to Zionism and his condemnation of it as a heretical movement in his halakhic work *Vayoel Moshe*.

Joel Teitelbaum [The Satmar Rebbe], *Vayoel Moshe: Maamar Shalosh Shavuot* (Brooklyn: New Edition, 5776 [2006]), Section 110, 123, accessed April 5, 2019, https://www.etzion.org.il/en/lecture-04c-satmar-rebbes-understanding-reason -holocaust. This translation is based on the translation by Kaeren Fish of a lecture by Rabbi Tamir Granot in which Teitelbaum's teaching is cited.

No one takes note of the fact that six million Jews were killed because of these [Zionist] groups, who drew the hearts of the nation [to their cause] and violated the oath of hastening the end[3] by claiming sovereignty and freedom before the time. For aside from this being the bitter punishment set forth in the Gemara for [violating the oaths]—"I shall abandon your flesh. . . ."[4]—and by oath they and the whole world are punished, and no punishment comes to the world except on account of the wicked, nor does it begin except with the righteous. But they also performed terrible actions to bring this about; for aside from the fact that even

3. [This refers to an oath found in Babylonian Talmud Ketubot 110b–111a, where God forces the Jewish people to swear that they will not establish Jewish political sovereignty in the land of Israel until the messiah comes. To do so would be an act of absolute heresy and is taken by many in the Jewish tradition, including Rabbi Teitelbaum, to indicate that the Zionist movement, with its political goal of establishing such sovereignty, is at its root a severe violation of Jewish tradition and God's command. On this oath and the implications it held for Jewish political quiescence, see Aviezer Ravitzky, *Messianism, Zionism, and Jewish Religious Radicalism* (Chicago: University of Chicago Press, 1996).]

4. [Babylonian Talmud Ketubot 111a.]

at the very beginning of their establishment for many years they "informed" terribly on the Jews to the nations, and spoke of them badly to the authorities, as though [the Jews] were highly dangerous to the nations and they had to be expelled from their countries, [which the Zionists did] thinking that it would thereby be easier for them to carry out their scheme to come to the land of Israel and to organize a government there. We saw already then, in their letters, that great rabbis were greatly, deathly fearful that [the Zionists'] informing would bring about that which, for our many sins, did come to be afterwards.

Aside from this, there are verified reports of several cruel actions that they performed that indirectly brought about the entire terrible catastrophe. Concerning Hungary some of these activities came to light in the court case that was held in Eretz Yisrael in this regard [i.e., the Kastner trial],[5] and thus there were several clear actions throughout that period, because they thought that they would thereby achieve more of their aim of obtaining government.

But I do not wish to elaborate on this here, for my intention in this booklet is only to clarify Halakha, and I write this only in order to show that it is clear that the impure idea of establishing a State prior to the proper time has caused us all of the tribulations and troubles that have come upon us, aside from the tens of thousands of Jews who have been killed needlessly in [the Zionists'] wars.

Furthermore, among those who have moved to Eretz Yisrael in these times, most of the immigrants from Arab countries were living peacefully and tranquilly in their countries, lacking nothing, until the establishment of the heretical kingdom in Israel. Through the establishment of that State they began to suffer hatred and persecution in their countries, and the Zionists themselves aided this through their wiles, so as to increase the persecution until they would be forced to emigrate to Eretz Yisrael, destitute and with nothing, and they glorified their saviors, but the truth was the opposite—that [the Zionists] had brought about all of the destruction in the first place.

5. [The Kastner trial was a libel case held in Jerusalem in 1954–55. Rudolf Kastner, a Hungarian Jew and Zionist who later became a civil servant in Israel, was accused of collaboration with the Nazis and Adolf Eichmann during the Holocaust. Those who condemned Kastner contended that he knew Jews were not being deported from Hungary to be "resettled," as the Nazis had said, but were being taken to death camps. Rabbi Teitelbaum took this as a sign of Zionist perfidy against the whole of the Jewish people.]

Emil L. Fackenheim (1916–2003) was one of the most prominent Jewish philosophers of the twentieth century. Born in Germany, he was ordained as a Liberal rabbi at the Hochschule in Berlin. After Kristallnacht on November 9, 1938, he was interned by the Nazis in the Sachsenhausen prison camp during 1938 and 1939. In 1940, Fackenheim came to Canada and received his doctorate in philosophy from the University of Toronto. There he had a distinguished academic career and became a prominent public Jewish intellectual whose writings on the Holocaust and insistence that Jews not hand Hitler "a posthumous victory" by abandoning either Jewish life or the State of Israel gained him wide public acclaim. The first excerpt that follows includes what is perhaps his most famous statement of this position.

a. "The 614th Commandment," in Emil L. Fackenheim, *The Jewish Return into History* (New York: Schocken, 1978), 22–24.

b. "The Holocaust and the State of Israel: Their Relation," in Emil L. Fackenheim, *The Jewish Return into History*, 273, 284–86.

c. "A Reply to My Critics: A Testament of Thought," in *Fackenheim: German Philosophy and Jewish Thought*, ed. Louis Greenspan and Graeme Nicholson (Toronto: University of Toronto Press, 1992), 284–85.

d. Emil L. Fackenheim, *A Political Philosophy for the State of Israel: Fragments* (Jerusalem: Jerusalem Center for Public Affairs, 1988), 8–9.

A.

. . . In the present situation, [the] question becomes: can we confront the Holocaust, and yet not despair? Not accidentally has it taken twenty years for us to face this question, and it is not certain that we can face it yet. . . . *For we are forbidden to turn present and future life into death, as the price of remembering death in Auschwitz. And we are equally forbidden to affirm present and future life, as the price of forgetting Auschwitz.*

We have lived in this contradiction for twenty years without being able to face it. Unless I am mistaken, we are now beginning to face it, however fragmentarily and inconclusively. And from this beginning confrontation, there emerges what

I will boldly term a 614th commandment: *the authentic Jew of today is forbidden to hand Hitler yet another, posthumous victory.* . . .

And I think he hears it whether, as agnostic, he hears no more, or whether, as believer, he hears the voice of the *metzaveh* (the commander) in the *mitzvah* (the commandment). Moreover, it may well be the case that the authentic Jewish agnostic and the authentic Jewish believer are closer today than at any previous time. . . .

If the 614th commandment is binding upon the authentic Jew, then we are, first, commanded to survive as Jews, lest the Jewish people perish. We are commanded, second, to remember in our very guts and bones the martyrs of the Holocaust, lest their memory perish. We are forbidden, thirdly, to deny or despair of God, however much we may have to contend with him, or belief in him, lest Judaism perish. We are forbidden, finally, to despair of the world as the place which is to become the kingdom of God, lest we help make it a meaningless place in which God is dead or irrelevant and everything is permitted. To abandon any of these imperatives, in response to Hitler's victories at Auschwitz, would be to hand him yet other, posthumous victories. . . .

At least twice before—at the time of the destruction of the First and of the Second Temples—Jewish endurance in the midst of catastrophe helped transform the world. We cannot know the future. . . . But this ignorance on our part can have no effect on our present action. The uncertainty of what will be may not shake our certainty of what we must do.

B.

"Our Father in Heaven, the Rock of Israel and her Redeemer, bless Thou the State of Israel, the beginning of the dawn of our redemption. . . ."

This prayer by the Israeli Chief Rabbinate does not hesitate to describe the state of Israel as "the beginning of the dawn of redemption" of the Jewish people . . . what is positively astonishing . . . is its wide acceptance by Jews everywhere. Religious Jews inside and outside Israel recite it in the synagogue, and secularist Israelis . . . recite *this* prayer, as it were, not with their lips but with their lives. . . .

. . . Mordecai Anielewicz was to perish in the flames of the [Warsaw] Ghetto [battling against the Nazis]. . . . In his last letter he wrote, "My life's aspiration is fulfilled. The Jewish self-defense has arisen. Blissful and chosen is my fate to be among the first Jewish fighters in the Ghetto." . . .

Mordecai Anielewicz died in May 1943. Named after him, kibbutz Yad

Mordekhai was founded in the same year. Five years after Mordecai's death . . . a small band of members of the kibbutz bearing his name held off a well-equipped Egyptian army for five long days—days in which the defense of Tel Aviv could be prepared, days crucial for the survival of the Jewish state. . . .

Their hope, however, had not been a rational one, much less a calculated prediction. It had been a blessed self-fulfilling prophecy. . . . The battle for Yad Mordekhai began in the streets of Warsaw. To this day the justly larger-than-life statue of Mordecai Anielewicz dominates the kibbutz named after him, remind-ing the forgetful and teaching the thoughtless . . . that what links the Ghetto fighters with Yad Mordekhai is neither a causal necessity nor a divine miracle, if these are thought of as divorced from human believing and acting. . . . It is an acting which through despair has recovered faith.

Behind the statue stands the shattered water tower of the kibbutz, a mute re-minder that even after its climax the combination of hatred of Jews and Jewish powerlessness has not come to an end. However, the shattered tower is dwarfed by the statue, and is at its back. The statue faces what Mordecai longed for and never despaired of—green fields, crops, trees, birds, flowers, Israel.

"Our Father in Heaven, the Rock of Israel and her Redeemer, bless Thou the state of Israel, the beginning of the dawn of our Redemption. Shield her with the wings of Thy love, and spread over her the Tabernacle of Thy peace. . . ."

C.

Zionism in our time . . . has no right to be "innocent." . . .

Moral high-mindedness towards Arabs once caused Buber and his friends to argue for a binational state in which Jews would exceed Arabs in number only with the latter's consent. . . . Was this view, high-minded towards Arabs, moral towards Jews? That Arab consent to Jewish immigrants in excess of the quota would not come was predictable. What then of the morality of the envisaged binational state that would close its doors to homeless Jews, much more firmly than, say, postwar America, Canada, or Australia?

One such as Achad ha-Am could think of Zionist growth as proceeding little-by-little, and of Jewish statehood, rarely if at all. After the Holocaust, the Jewish people did not enjoy this particular luxury: for them, it was no Zionism with-out a state—and either then or not at all. Had it not been for that inescapable choice of emergency—who knows?—the Arab-Jewish conflict, if not avoided, might by now be resolved. The Holocaust, then, far from a boon to the Zionist enterprise, was—continues to be!—a burden, one that is often all but unbearable.

D.

One Jewish way of living with powerlessness has been to make it into a virtue. At the time [Hermann] Cohen and [Martin] Buber were arguing about Zionism,[6] it was a widely accepted view that the destruction of the ancient Jewish state had been a blessing in disguise, that Jewish powerlessness made for greater moral purity.

. . . Whereas in some circumstances powerlessness may indeed be made a moral virtue, in others it is indulgence in a moral luxury. That, despite forty years of Jewish statehood, this ambivalence about Jewish power has not vanished, even within the confines of the Jewish state itself, was expressed in a moving Jewish *cri de coeur* in the midst of the unrest that at the time of writing has not yet ended. "We used to suffer the anguish of powerlessness," a Jewish woman wrote in the Jerusalem Post. "Now we suffer the anguish of power." This statement is completely false. That there is deep Jewish anguish as Jewish soldiers club stone-throwing Arab youths is evident on every side. (It speaks well for the moral fiber of the State that it should be so, even after forty years of siege. . . .) The anguish is caused, however, not by Jewish power but by an insufficiency of it.

6. [For a description of this 1915–16 debate, see Jeffrey Andrew Barash, "Politics and Theology: The Debate on Zionism between Hermann Cohen and Martin Buber," in *Dialogue as a Trans-Disciplinary Concept: Martin Buber's Philosophy of Dialogue and Its Contemporary Reception*, ed. Paul Mendes-Flohr (Berlin: de Gruyter, 2015), 49–60.]

For a biographical sketch, see Part One, p. 18.

Eliezer Berkovits, *Faith after the Holocaust* (New York: Ktav Publishing House, 1973), 1, 144–45, 153–54.

The main thesis of this volume was worked out during the critical weeks that led up to the Six Day War between Israel and the Arab nations, and this was completed during those drama-filled six days; the last word of its heart was written practically when the last shot was fired in that war. It was written under almost unbearable tension, and against dark fears and anxieties. The threat of another holocaust was hanging over the Jewish people. This destruction would have been the final for all Israel the world over, and not only for the Jewish people in the State of Israel. Our generation could not have survived another holocaust and, certainly, not this one. The State of Israel was a Jew's only comfort—although not really quite a healing one—after the extermination of six million of his people.

In spite of the fears and notwithstanding the tension, carried along by one's faith in the immortality of Judaism and the Jewish people, it was possible to write. Not once did I have to ask myself whether this faith in the eternity of Jewish survival was, perhaps, only a latter-day version of the "lying words," so radically rejected by the prophet Jeremiah: "The temple of the Lord, the temple of the Lord, the temple of the Lord."[7] No, the State of Israel is not the temple of the Lord. But God can do without his temple; he cannot do without Israel, the people, nor can he, in this post-holocaust phase of world history, do without Israel the State. It was this faith that I was affirming with every word I wrote in those critical weeks before the war and during the six days of the war. To wait and see what was going to happen and then to write, would have been a betrayal and a desecration. . . .

When in the early spring of 1967, we decided to set down our thoughts on the

7. [Jeremiah 7:4, which states, "You should not trust in lying words and say, 'This is the temple of the Lord, the temple of the Lord, the temple of the Lord!'"]

problem of faith raised by the European holocaust, we could not anticipate that by the time the task was brought to a conclusion, a threat, in its consequences even more fateful than Auschwitz itself, would becloud the skies of Jewish existence. The Arab nations resolved to wipe the small State of Israel off the map of the earth. . . . The fact that the frightening drama of perhaps ultimate extinction would find its redemptive denouement in the awe-inspiring return of the Jewish people to Zion and Jerusalem could not have been visualized by the wildest imagination as being within the realm of historical possibilities. We started our discussion with the theological and religious problems arising from the darkest hour in the history of Israel's exile. Soon after our task was finished, we stepped into the brightest hour that God, in His unexpected mercy, bestowed upon Israel since the inception of its dispersion. But, that, of course, is the question. Was it indeed "from God"? Was it in truth—to use the phrase from Isaiah—the "hiding" God of Israel who acted as the savior?[8] . . . Did we really experience one of those rarer occasions, when God—almost as in biblical times—made his presence manifest as the Redeemer of Israel?

. . . Military victory alone does not prove divine involvement in Jewish history, just as the crematoria are not proof of divine indifference. Defeat and suffering need not mean being abandoned by God and worldly success in the affairs of man is not proof of divine support. Nevertheless, the Jew the world over, and especially in the State of Israel, experienced the speedily developing crisis, followed by the lightning transformation of the Six Day War as history on a metaphysical level. This was not a conscious reaction to what had happened; not an interpretation of the events, nor a considered judgment. As a conscious reaction, the sensing of metaphysical meaning might be questioned. But the realization that through the events of those few days all Israel was addressed from beyond the boundaries of time was not in the realm of conscious reaction. It was a spontaneous experience, borne in upon the Jew with the power of inescapable revelational quality. Can this revelational character of the experience be proved? Revelation is never provable. One can only testify to its occurrence: Ye are my witnesses! says God.[9] Once again the words of Isaiah have found their realization in world history. . . .

The overwhelming majority of [contemporary Jews] experienced the recent confrontation between the State of Israel and the Arab nations as a moment of

8. [See Isaiah 45:15.]
9. [Isaiah 43:10.]

messianic history. It was an event not on the purely man-made level of history, but one that took place in conformity with the divine plan. Especially in the land of Israel the widest section of the population were convinced that "this is God's doing; it is marvelous in our eyes." . . . There was a Presence about in the land. What is there in these events of unique Jewish destiny that we are able to discern from afar?

For the first time since the destruction of the ancient Jewish commonwealth the City of David is once again the capital of a Jewish state. Undoubtedly, this is a moment in Jewish history that takes its place beside the classical occasions as recorded in the Bible. For the Jew this is the renewal of biblical times.

David R. Blumenthal, *Facing the Abusing God*

David Blumenthal (born 1938) has been the Jay Leslie Cohen Professor of Judaic Studies at Emory University for the bulk of his academic career. A graduate of the University of Pennsylvania, he was ordained as a rabbi at the Jewish Theological Seminary of America and received his PhD in religion from Columbia University. A scholar of medieval Judaism, Blumenthal has also written on Jewish mysticism and Jewish thought.

David R. Blumenthal, *Facing the Abusing God: A Theology of Protest* (Louisville: Westminster John Knox Press, 1993), 263–64, 248.

In the inner reaches of Jewish religious reflection, the question is asked whether God can make a mistake, whether God can sin. The biblical evidence is that God *can* make a mistake: God changes God's mind in the case of Noah and in the desert regarding the rebellious people. In the Rosh Ha-Shana liturgy, God prays that God's mercy overcome God's anger, implying, if not stating, . . . that God can be overwhelmed by factors in Godself. And in the Zoharic strain of Jewish mystical thinking, God's inner stability can be destroyed, provoking great destruction. In a personalist theology, then, God can sin.

But how does God repent? How does God do *teshuva*? If the echoes of the book of Lamentations and the book of Job are heard seriously, God repents by talking to us, by taking notice of us, by acknowledging us in some concrete way. For some Jews, the creation and continued existence of the State of Israel are such an acknowledgement. For others, this is insufficient on three grounds: First, the trauma has simply been too great, the loss too severe. Second, the very historicism that allows us to rationalize away certain texts also forces us to see history for what it really was; we can no longer paradigmatize history and count this suffering in with all the others. The Holocaust is abuse, and there is no excuse for it. Finally, we know from a study of repentance in Jewish tradition and from an examination of the therapy on healing from abuse that acknowledgement of the abused by the abuser is simply not enough. Both Jewish teaching and proper therapy require much more: they require knowledge by the abuser of the grounds and causes of the abusing behaviors; and a commitment, acceptable to the abused, never to abuse again. They require self-empowerment of the abused and reestablished inter-subjectivity and interrelatedness between the abused and the abuser. With God this has not happened, and while reconciliation may not be possible in cases of abuse, it is nonetheless the goal and the ideal in . . . religious healing.

. . . When God acts abusively, we are the victims, we are innocent. When God acts abusively, we are the hurt party and we are not responsible for God's abuse. Our sins—and we are always sinful—are in no proportion whatsoever to the punishment meted out to us. . . . Abuse is unjustified, in God as well as in human beings.

But God is not always abusive. God is often loving and fair, even kind and merciful. . . . Our gratitude for God's fairness, love, kindness, and mercy, however, does not stop us from acknowledging God's abusiveness.

To have faith in a post-Holocaust, abuse-sensitive world is, first, to know—to recognize and to admit—that God is an abusing God, but not always.

Irving "Yitz" Greenberg (born 1933) was ordained a rabbi by Yeshiva Beis Yosef and earned his doctorate in history at Harvard University. He was head of the Jewish Studies Program at the City College of New York and taught at Yeshiva University. Greenberg has been an outstanding figure on the Jewish scene as a scholar, a theologian, and an activist. He has promoted cross-denominational Jewish dialogue and tolerance, and interfaith Jewish-Christian dialogue as well. His writings have been highly influential, and his 1976 essay, "Cloud of Smoke, Pillar of Fire: Judaism, Christianity, and Modernity after the Holocaust," is a major statement of post-Holocaust Jewish thought.

Irving Greenberg, "The Ethics of Jewish Power Today," (speech to the United Jewish Communities General Assembly, Chicago, IL, November 11, 2000), published in a pamphlet by CLAL, 2001, 5–8.

For the last 60 years, the Jewish people has sought to establish its own right, its own ability to live and create and build on the side of life. . . . After a long period of living in a state of powerlessness and marginality to society, the Jewish people ran into the greatest disaster in its history; a disaster that essentially was made possible by its own powerlessness. . . . We discovered that all our teaching about the dignity and value of life could not sustain itself in the real world. . . . When, in fact, others chose death for us, we didn't have enough power to stop it. When others chose to degrade the value of Jewish life, we didn't have enough power and influence to assert its value, to get people to commit money to buy Jewish captives who could have been saved, to get enough energy to bomb rail lines that would have stopped the construction, etc. etc. So, in a certain sense the whole Jewish people came to a simple conclusion that if we believe in our cause, and if we still believe in the future of life itself, and if we believe in the future of our dream, the only way we are going to change that dream fully is with national dignity. . . . If you want your full personal dignity, you have to be part of . . . a national unit which creates a society within which you can live properly and appropriately. And where your dignity might be established. . . . That whatever my function, whatever my capacity for . . . full dignity, I will need some society of like-minded people who share my values and are prepared to work with me to create living conditions under which I can achieve my full dignity. . . . For the Jewish people, obviously Zionism had claimed this. . . . For 60 years now we have struggled with the fact that our recognition of this need . . . took place in a world where there was no choice but to take power and to have a national structure. As you well know, it turned out that we are located, at least in Israel, in a neighborhood in which the Arab world around us did not agree necessarily on our right to national existence and [that our] dignity was compatible with theirs. . . .

[Yet], not only will we create a democracy for ourselves, but . . . we can make a society in which others can live in security and dignity. . . . Our experience, we think, can serve as a model for others of how to wrestle with these questions.

When this struggle started 60 years ago, . . . there was no serious Palestinian national identity. . . . In other words, the Jews . . . discovered that their dignity and their ability to create a better world depends on creating a national framework where their dignity is assured. . . . And . . . the Palestinians . . . at first really did not think in these terms, [but] became increasingly convinced: no maybe I should think in these terms. That their chance for culture and personal dignity depends on creating a nation in which they can express their own values, their own priorities, and their own equality and dignity. So again, I say, ironically enough we should be complimented or feel complimented.

But, . . . this is the tragedy of the whole situation: from the beginning the Arab conclusion [was] that their dignity and their equality [meant that] . . . we have no right to exist in that world. . . . In essence the Palestinian national identity [developed] in the context in which they believe that their dignity is compromised and not fully realizable if the Jewish state and Jewish power exists.

Now, I want to be . . . fair here. A Palestinian standing here would say that that is too self-serving a version; that in fact the Palestinians went through a catastrophe, namely that Israeli independence led to . . . flight and refugee status for hundreds of thousands of Palestinian Arabs. . . . I know we could answer right back. You invited it upon yourself; you didn't let us live in peace; you tried to invade and destroy us; you invited people to flee. All that is true. But for the moment I am trying to hear what they would say if they were standing here. A) You[r coming into being was] a great setback to us. B) During this period of refugee status, we have suffered continuously because of inequalities and all kinds of persecution and suffering. Again, our answer was: you chose to stay in those camps; we offered to set you up; we offered to help you resettle. A lot of [that] suffering came [from] self-inflicted [acts]. I am not trying to load the picture either way. I am trying to give a framework for our judgments.

This is the exchange that has come to a head now in the last two decades in which Palestinian self-definition matured, became ever more insistent. But it became ... ever more insistent under circumstances in which it was them against us. Basically there was no trust, no confidence, that they are prepared to find room for our right to exist, and our dignity....

... I put this text ["The Ethics of Jewish Power," which was written in 1984] before you.... There are three sentences I wanted to read to you ... [which I wrote then], "The ethical idea would be a balance of power in the Middle East in which Israel cannot dominate the Arab nations and the Arab nations cannot dream of destroying Israel by force. Ideally the Palestinian Arabs should have their own state and should treat the Jews living on the West Bank with dignity. They should respect Jews' rights and cultures just as the internal Arab minority in the Jewish [State] has a vital inner life and real political power to protect itself."

The second paragraph made the point there is a serious flaw in the statement of the ideal—namely that major elements were unreconciled to Jewish sovereignty and would destroy us if they could. I said then, "a balance of power under these circumstances is not morally acceptable." The third point [I made] ... was that "in the interim, Israel should seek maximum Arab autonomy in Judea and Samaria by encouraging the emergence of indigenous leadership. Let the word go out unequivocally that Palestinian Arabs can earn autonomy and even a state by seeking peace and taking risks. In theory, the PLO could also earn the status of a negotiating partner with Israel. The PLO would have to disavow its call for the destruction of Israel." The point, of course I am making is that there was a period, . . . only one to five years ago, when the notion of a peace based on a Palestinian state and a PLO renunciation of destruction of Israel appeared to be ... a kind of fond hope.... I think we have to keep that perspective ... and realize that time does play a role, and one should not assume that the present moment will go on forever and ever.

Marc H. Ellis, *Toward a Jewish Theology of Liberation*

Marc Ellis (born 1952) received his doctorate at Marquette University. Previously, he earned his BA and MA degrees at Florida State University, where he studied with Richard Rubenstein. Ellis taught for a number of years at the Maryknoll School of Theology, and in 1999 came to Baylor University, where he headed the Center for Jewish Studies. Ellis is a well-known peace activist and critic of the political policies of the State of Israel.

Marc H. Ellis, *Toward a Jewish Theology of Liberation* (Maryknoll, NY: Orbis, 1987), 110–11; 118–21.

Jewish theology arises out of and is accountable to the experience of the people. . . . Richard Rubenstein, . . . Emil Fackenheim, [and] Irving Greenberg quite rightly place the Holocaust alongside the Exodus event and . . . rabbinic interpretations [as a central event in Jewish history]. . . . [These] Jewish theologians [also] presented the story of Israel as intrinsic to the renewal of Jewish life [after the Holocaust]. As theologians . . . [they] spoke publicly about the need for empowerment as a religious response to destruction. . . .

The Holocaust theologians portray a Jew today as one who remembers the Holocaust and participates in the survival and empowerment of the Jewish people. A secondary although important theme is the pursuit of the ethical. As we have seen, a Jewish theology of liberation raises the ethical again to a primary status. . . . Holocaust theologians thus have redefined the notion of practicing Jew from one who engages in ritual and observance of the Law to one who cherishes memory, survival, and empowerment. . . .

We must also assert quite clearly that identification with the State of Israel is not, in and of itself, a religious act. The contrary is also true: the refusal to see the State of Israel as central to Jewish spirituality is not, in and of itself, an offense warranting excommunication. A practicing Jew within the liberationist perspective sees the State of Israel as neither central or peripheral, but rather as a necessary and flawed attempt to create an autonomous presence within the Middle East. . . . A Jewish liberationist perspective denies that Jewish history revolves around a return to the Land and that Israel is *the* important Jewish community. . . .

The equation of Zionism with Judaism is clearly inappropriate. . . . Solidarity with one's own people is hardly exhausted by one's position on the issue of Zionism and Israel, though the framers of the discussion would have us believe this to be the case. So much energy and emotion have been spent on equating Zionism and Israel that an understandable fear exists when even an adjustment is suggested. But what if Israel as a state ceased to exist, either involuntarily through military force, or voluntarily through confederation with the Palestinian community? . . . The Jewish people existed long before the State of Israel and will exist long after the nation-state ceases to exist.

A true Jewish liberationist believes that Palestine and the support of a Palestinian state formed by the Palestine Liberation Organization need to be part of any discussion of Israel. . . . Our fear for survival seems to cover over a deeper fear: the discovery that we are less and less in touch with our own witness. Instead of the affluent and relatively empowered lecturing powerless peoples on the importance of uncritical support for Israel, perhaps it is time for us to be silent and listen to the painful, moving, and sometimes contradictory stories that emerge from the underside. By listening instead of lecturing we might find that we are increasingly complicit in their suffering. . . .

Judith Butler (born 1956) attended Bennington College and received both her undergraduate and doctoral degrees from Yale University. A major American philosopher and gender theorist whose work has had tremendous influence on philosophy and ethics as well as the fields of literary and queer theory, Butler is the Maxine Elliot Professor in the Department of Comparative Literature and the Program in Critical Theory at the University of California at Berkeley and holds the Hannah Arendt Chair at the European Graduate School. She is a noted critic of Zionism.

Judith Butler, *Parting Ways: Jewishness and the Critique of Zionism* (New York: Columbia University Press, 2012), 4, 15, 34–37.

My proposal is that the vast and violent hegemonic structure of political Zionism must cede its hold on those lands (West Bank and Gaza) and populations, and that what must take place is a new polity that would presuppose the end to settler colonialism and that would imply complex and antagonistic modes of living together, an amelioration of the wretched forms of binationalism that already exist.

. . . One needs to contest the hegemonic control Zionism exercises over Jewishness. . . . One needs equally to contest the colonial subjugation Zionism has implied for the Palestinian people. In fact, one would not be concerned with the first hegemonic move (Jewish = Zionist) if one were not primarily concerned with ending the history of subjugation.

. . . The "exilic"—or more emphatically, *the diasporic*—is built into the idea of the Jewish: in this sense, to "be" a Jew is to be departing from oneself, cast into a world of the non-Jew, bound to make one's way ethically and politically there within a world of irreversible heterogeneity. . . . The diasporic . . . depends upon cohabitation with the non-Jew and eschews the Zionist linkage of nation to land. . . . Jewish populations, when not explicitly destroyed, were certainly dispossessed from home and land under the Nazi regime, but not from Palestine. The idea that a forcible dispossession of others might rightfully compensate for having been forcibly dispossessed follows no legitimate ethical or legal line of reasoning.

. . . Disputing the legitimacy of Israel's founding and its continued claims to certain lands . . . implies that the injustices of expulsion, killing, disenfranchisement not only characterize the founding of the state, but have continued, and continue still, as the basic modes of reproducing the state and its legitimacy. . . .

. . . [Hannah] Arendt was perhaps the most avid secular Jewish critic of Zionism in the twentieth century. . . . Although she was a Jew, she insisted that Israel ought *not* to be a Jewish state and thought its efforts to legitimate its claims to the land through state violence were racist forms of colonization that could only lead to permanent conflict. . . .

Her criticisms of the State of Israel followed from her critique of the nation-state and colonialism. Martin Buber, on the other hand, was a cultural Zionist, no secularist, and though he was an advocate of cooperative ventures [between Jew and Arab], he failed to criticize Israel as a form of settler colonialism. His version of Zionism has become so anathematic in light of contemporary framings of Zionism that it now reads as "post-Zionist" or simply anti-Zionist. His political position [in opposition to the creation of a Jewish political state] was rather resolutely defeated by the establishment of Israel as a Jewish state. . . .

. . . The most consequential blindness in [Martin Buber's] position . . . was that he could not see the impossibility of trying to cultivate certain ideals of cooperation on conditions established by settler colonialism. Buber did not seem to understand that the project of settler colonialism, with its seizure of lands and subjugation of Palestinian laborers, undermined the possibility of realizing his cooperative ideals. . . . He sought, paradoxically, humane forms of colonization, arguing for what he called concentrative colonialism rather than "expansionist" colonialism. . . . It becomes all the more worrisome when we see the "success" of concentrative colonialism in the West Bank and, most emphatically, in Gaza, where living conditions are cramped and impoverished in accord with the concentrative model. . . . What Buber failed to see is that no "common projects" could set aside the land seizures that had already taken place and that the basis on which he claimed Jewish right to the land installed an aggressive nationalism at the heart of the notion of cooperation.

Ruth R. Wisse was born in 1936 in Ukraine and grew up in Montreal, Canada. She received her doctorate in English literature at McGill University but soon turned her attention to Yiddish and Jewish texts. Wisse is the Martin Peretz Professor of Yiddish Literature and Professor of Comparative Literature Emerita at Harvard University, a post to which she was appointed in 1993. In addition to her many academic publications, she has spoken out often on political matters.

Ruth R. Wisse, *Jews and Power* (New York: Schocken, 2007), 137–76.

Arab leaders *created* the crisis for which they blamed the Jews. In denying the partition of Palestine, Arab governments also refused to allow the resettlement of the Palestinians so that they could create perpetual evidence of Jewish iniquity: "The refugees are the cornerstone in the Arab struggle against Israel. The refugees are the armaments of the Arabs and Arab nationalism." Arab rulers refused to absorb or to resettle the refugees "because it meant the final disposal of a moral asset." Israel could be charged for the suffering of the Palestinians only as long as their suffering could be sustained.

The universal refugee crisis is one of the most disturbing and pervasive phenomena of the modern period. . . . Palestinian Arabs are to be pitied along with the tens of millions of refugees of the twentieth century. But Palestinians are doubly unfortunate because theirs is the only such displacement that is prolonged for political advantage. Originally, the Palestinians who fled from their homes in 1948 were a relatively small and easily assimilable group, moving often no more than several miles among people who spoke their language and shared their religion and culture. Leaving aside the refugees of the two world wars, as well as Jews driven from Arab lands in numbers equal to the Arabs who fled from Israel, the two massive conflicts that framed Israel's War of Independence—India's war over the creation of Pakistan in 1947 and the Korean War of 1950-1953—produced more than 10 million refugees between them, yet most of these refugees were reabsorbed within a generation. Only in the Arab case did a coalition of rulers, with millions of square miles and great wealth at their disposal, foster and cultivate the state of emergency as a means of sustaining a casus belli. . . .

Jews were required to assess as never before the strategic options available to them on the home front, in their region, and in the family of nations. Whom could they hope to enlist as allies in their asymmetrical struggle? What defensive boundaries would provide the greatest security for their citizens? How could they expose Arab exploitation of the Palestinian refugee crisis and coerce the Palestinians into building rather than destroying? With what symbols and signs of strength, confidence, determination, and power could they convince the Arab and Muslim world that the disposition of Israel was not negotiable? . . .

Two opposite movements arose in Israel in response to this political impasse —Gush Emunim, the Bloc of the Faithful, and Shalom Achsav, Peace Now. Neither of them articulated the unique political dilemma facing their country or developed a strategic plan of national defense. The Gush prepared to annex once and for all the disputed territories of Israel up to the natural boundary of the Jordan River; Peace Now, to return . . . most of the disputed territories on the grounds that their sizable Arab population would otherwise prolong the conflict. Gush Emunim cast its project as a religious obligation, claiming that the disputed lands were part of the Jews' biblical inheritance. Shalom Achsav insisted that unilateral concessions of the territories would result in regional "peace." The first group professed to satisfy the will of God, the second, the will of the Arabs. The first assertion was not subject to proof, and the second was demonstrably bogus. The West Bank had been in Jordan's hands before the combined Arab attacks on Israel. One could legitimately argue for strategic withdrawal from the captured territories on defensive grounds, but there could be no expectation of peace in a return to status quo ante. Since the disputed territories were Israel's as a *result* of Arab aggression, they could not retroactively have become its *cause*. . . .

In the aftermath of [the 1977] election [that brought Menachem Begin and the Likud Party to power], . . . it became fashionable in the liberal media to claim that peace would break out were it not for the Israeli "occupation" [of the West Bank]. The Pan-Arab war against the Jews was obscured and displaced by focus on Israeli wrongdoing. The political Left revived the slogans of the 1930s charging Israel with imperialist expansion. State departments and businessmen with an eye on Arab oil and Muslim markets found it convenient to blame Israel for Arab aggression against it. Following two suicide bombings by Hamas in 1995 (one of whose victims was Aliza Flatow of New Jersey), Israel's most prominent writer, Amos Oz, appeared in the *New York Times* to accuse Likud for engendering an atmosphere of "religious, chauvinistic egoism" that benefited from Arab violence and replicated its extremism.

The usual protest against such analogies between Hamas and Likud, or between Arab aggressors and Israel defenders, is that they create a false *moral* equivalence between the instigators of hostility and those required to guard against it. Some monitors of "honest reporting" point out that "though not all Arabs are haters and not every Israeli is a paragon of tolerance, there is simply no comparison between what goes on in terms of learning about peace and hate between Israel and its neighbors." Well intentioned as such distinctions may be, it is the phony *political* rather than moral equivalence between a culture of blame and a politics of accommodation that stands in the way of grasping what is at stake in the Middle East. Moral standards are subject to interpretation, political contrasts are manifest in deeds. . . . Palestinian Arabs are hardly blind to the ways they have been exploited in the war against Israel. One rueful Arab refugee of 1948 compared the hospitable welcome Palestinians used to offer other Arab immigrants with the cold shoulder *they* were given when they left Israel. He deplored the absence of any public movement in the Arab world to promote welfare services to the refugees. Yet, when it came to ascribing blame for their condition, most Palestinians followed their leaders in reproaching Israel and the Jews rather than the Arab governments that kept them homeless. Assigned the role of contesting Israel, and indulged by their fellow Arabs only to the extent that they fulfilled their function, Palestinians, once said to be the most highly accomplished in the Arab world, forged their identity to an unprecedented degree in obsessive opposition to another people. . . .

Predictably, the Law of Return looms on the Palestinian calendar for July 15 (1950) as an act of discrimination against Arabs. Because no Arab country shares Israel's sense of responsibility for its co-religionists, because Arabs passed no Law of Return but instead prevented their resettlement, Palestinians must interpret [Jewish] solidarity as a crime or else admit the crime Arabs committed against them. . . .

If historians once mistook the absence of [Jewish] sovereignty to mean that Jews stood outside politics, modern students of the problem too often assumed that the resumption of sovereignty guaranteed political parity between Israel and the nations. Jews were said to have reversed their political fortunes once they began governing themselves and an Arab minority in a country of their own. Equating "statehood" with "power," the new experts confused Zionism's potential with its achievement, as if the acquired option of Jewish self-defense has erased Arab advantages of numbers, resources, and land.

This misdiagnosis deepened in 1982 when Israel entered Lebanon to destroy the terrorist bases of the Palestine Liberation Organization. This incursion was seized upon as proof of Israel's offensive as well as defensive capability, as well as its potential corruption as an aggressor state. Observers expressed their concern about the "rapidity with which Jews have moved from powerlessness to power," citing Israel's military capability as a major threat to traditional Jewish values. In an effort to chasten modern Israel, the historian David Biale[10] . . . offered a beguilingly contrarian recital of history, locating "power" in situations of prolonged political dependency and "powerlessness" in situations where Jews ruled themselves. Thus, he considers periods of Jewish sovereignty merely preludes to political defeat: "Ultimately, the history of the Hasmoneans led to the destruction of the Temple itself." Defeat, on the other hand, leads to advantageous political dependency: "The failure of the revolt against the Romans ultimately led to a greater stability and greater Jewish power." By "stability," Biale means the internal Jewish governance of the rabbis under foreign control; the function of "ultimately" in these judgments is to make Diaspora the preferred condition of Jewish political life because it lacks the anxieties of political self-rule.

Critics like Biale were right to hold Israel accountable for its political actions, some of which have been regrettable, though not necessarily in the ways that they imply. His book is useful as an articulation of something larger, hearkening back to the politics of complementarity as though accommodation were part of the moral essence of Judaism itself. In the wake of the First World War, the writer and ethnographer S. An-sky theorized that Jewish folklore differed fundamentally from its Gentile counterparts in its aversion to any kind of physical heroism or strength. . . . But An-sky's insight, like Biale's, ignored that premodern Jews ascribed to the Almighty, Lord of the Universe, all the physical prowess that they lacked. No daily reader of the Psalms could underestimate the might of God, whose indignation blazed like fire, who avenged the spilled blood of His servants the Jews and would pay back their enemies sevenfold. The glorification of powerlessness was as antithetical to Judaism as belief in the son of God. Jews did not think themselves powerless in the most meaningful sense: Had they not reckoned on ultimate vindication, they could not have claimed

---

10. [David Biale, *Power and Powerlessness in Jewish History* (New York: Schocken, 1986).]

to believe in justice—one of the cardinal tenets of civilization. The power of God, emphatically including his eventual action in history, was the guarantee that justice would ultimately triumph. Lacking such faith in God's intervention, modern Jews could not claim to be moral unless they themselves intended to supply the missing dimension of power. Otherwise, they were signing up Jews for a suicide pact with every new set of enemies.

Daniel Gordis (born 1959), Senior Vice President and Koret Distinguished Fellow at Shalem College in Jerusalem, immigrated to Israel from Los Angeles in 1999. He received his BA from Columbia University, rabbinical ordination at the Jewish Theological Seminary, and a PhD in religion from the University of Southern California. A prolific author of books, essays, and op-eds, Gordis remains a prominent commentator and popular lecturer in North America on issues relating to Israel.

Daniel Gordis, *We Stand Divided: The Rift between American Jews and Israel*
(New York: HarperCollins Publishers, 2019), 129–33.

The question that matters most may not be whether force is good or evil; the real question is whether the Jews deserve to have a state. One of J Street's founders . . . said no; if maintaining a Jewish state requires endless conflict, then the state is a bad idea. Only a Jewish state at peace is a Jewish state worth having.[11] Moderate Zionists, however, do not go there. Yes, they admit. The fight is horrific, the costs often unbearable to all, but if not fighting means the end of the state, then the alternative is worse.

The classic statement of this worldview is a eulogy that Moshe Dayan delivered in memory of a young man named Roi Rotberg. On April 29, 1956, twenty-one-year-old Rotberg was patrolling the fields of Nachal Oz, the Gaza-adjacent community in which he lived, on horseback. Accustomed to seeing Gazans picking the kibbutz's fields, Rotberg, seeing a group of Arabs in the fields, rode toward them to get them to leave. But it was an ambush, and as Rotberg approached the "farmers," they shot and killed him, then dragged his body into Gaza, where it was horrifically mutilated.

Coincidentally, Dayan had met Rotberg a few days earlier. He attended the funeral and delivered a brief eulogy (merely 238 words in total) that became one of Israel's classic speeches, still oft-quoted. Dayan reminded his listeners that there was nothing surprising about Arab resentment and violence. "Let us not cast

---

11. [J Street is a political advocacy group promoting a liberal approach to the Israeli-Palestinian conflict.]

the blame on the murderers today," he said. "Why should we deplore their burning hatred for us? For eight years they have been sitting in the refugee camps in Gaza, and before their eyes we have been transforming the lands and the villages, where they and their fathers dwelt, into our estate."

Yet if mere Israeli survival was going to evoke Arab anger, Dayan warned both his listeners and his entire newborn nation, Israelis had better be prepared to live by the sword. In language filled with biblical imagery, as if to remind his listeners that the battle to stay in the land was not new but was a story that had begun thousands of years earlier, Dayan continued: "Let us not fear to look squarely at the hatred that consumes and fills the lives of hundreds of Arabs who live around us. Let us not drop our gaze, lest our arms weaken. That is the fate of our generation. That is our choice—to be ready and armed, tough and hard—or else the sword shall fall from our hands and our lives will be cut short."

Some forty-five years later, from 2000 to 2004, Israel was embroiled in the Second Intifada. . . . At that point, one of the intellectual darlings of Israel's left was Ben-Gurion University professor Benny Morris, whose research on the War of Independence and Israel's early years had exploded the myth that the Arabs had simply "fled" Palestine. No, Morris showed, they had left for many reasons. Some fled, some were intimidated into fleeing, and others, though many Israelis did not want to hear it, had been forcibly exiled as part of Ben-Gurion's explicit desire to address security issues during the war and diminish the number of Israel's Arabs so that the state he was creating would have a Jewish majority.

In a 2004 interview in *Ha'aretz*, Morris was clear about what Ben-Gurion did. "Ben-Gurion was a transferist. He understood that there could be no Jewish state with a large and hostile Arab minority in its midst. There would be no such state. It would not be able to exist."

What was astonishing about the interview was the fact that Morris, then the doyen of Israel's New Historians (a group of scholars—embraced by the left and reviled by the right—who had upended much of the mythology on which generations of Israelis had been raised and sought to "strip Israel's history of its grandeur," as historian Martin Kramer puts it), seemed unwilling to critique Ben-Gurion. "Ben-Gurion was right," Morris insisted. "If he had not done what he did, a state would not have come into being. That has to be clear. It is impossible to evade it. Without the uprooting of the Palestinians, a Jewish state would not have arisen here."

Morris further insisted that what happened was not a war crime. "In certain conditions, expulsion is not a war crime. I don't think that the expulsions of 1948 were war crimes." He continued: "A society that aims to kill you forces you to destroy it. When the choice is between destroying or being destroyed, it's better to destroy."

Here was Benny Morris, the intellectual hero of Israel's left, echoing sentiments usually associated with Jabotinsky and Klausner. And herein lies one of the core differences between Israelis and many American Jews. American Jews, and particularly progressives and millennials, are so deeply troubled by Israel's use of force that they would give up the state in order to end the violence. . . . Simply put, for American progressives, the conflict is a human rights issue. For Israelis, even Israelis on the political left, it is first and foremost about security and survival.

In language that would infuriate many American Jews, even those committed to Israel, Morris minced no words. If Ben-Gurion wanted to found a Jewish state, some of the Arabs simply had to go, he said. "You can't make an omelet without breaking eggs. You have to dirty your hands." To a large extent, the divide between American Jews and Israelis is over who is willing to say that, and who is not.

Daniel Boyarin (born 1946) and Jonathan Boyarin (born 1956) are brothers. Daniel was educated at Goddard College and received rabbinical ordination and his doctorate in Talmud at the Jewish Theological Seminary of America. He has taught at Bar-Ilan, Ben-Gurion, Harvard, Yale, and Yeshiva Universities, among other institutions, and has been Professor of Talmudic Culture at the University of California, Berkeley, in the Departments of Near Eastern Culture and Rhetoric. His scholarship has enjoyed prodigious influence in the academy worldwide. Jonathan Boyarin received his undergraduate degree from Reed College and his PhD in anthropology from the New School for Social Research. He is also a graduate of Yale Law School. Currently, he is the Thomas and Diann Mann Professor of Modern Jewish Studies in the Departments of Anthropology and Near Eastern Studies at Cornell University. Like his brother, he is a highly influential scholar who also writes often on public matters.

Daniel Boyarin and Jonathan Boyarin, "Diaspora: Generation and the Ground of Jewish Identity," *Critical Inquiry* 19 (Summer 1993): 695, 708, 710–23.

In early patristic writings . . . Paul's project has been understood as one of universalizing the Torah, breaking through the "particularism" of the Jewish religion. Galatians 3:26–29 is taken as the moral center of Paul's work: "For as many of you as were baptized into Christ have put on Christ [saying]: 'There is neither Jew nor Greek; there is neither slave nor free man; there is no male or female. For you are all one in Christ Jesus.' If . . . you belong to Christ, then you are Abraham's offspring, heir according to the promise." . . .

The Rabbis' insistence on the centrality of peoplehood can thus be read as a critique of Paul, for if the Pauline move had within it the possibility of breaking out of the tribal allegiances and commitments to one's own family, . . . it also contains the seeds of an imperialist and colonizing missionary practice. The very emphasis on a universalism expressed as a concern for all the families of the world turns very rapidly . . . into a doctrine that they must all become part of our family of the spirit with all of the horrifying practices against Jews and others that Christian Europe produced. . . .

Critics of Zionism, both Arab and others, along with both Jewish and non-Jewish anti-semites, have often sought to portray Jewish culture as essentially racist. This foundational racism is traced to the Hebrew Bible. . . . Critics who are otherwise fully committed to constructionist and historicist accounts of meaning and practice abandon this commitment when it comes to the Hebrew Bible. . . . Frederick Turner writes, "But the distinctions raised in the covenant between religion and idolatry are like some visitation of the khamsin to wilderness peoples as yet unsuspected, dark clouds over Africa, America, the Far East, until finally the remotest islands and jungle enclaves are struck by fire and sword and the subtler weapon of conversion-by-ridicule (Deuteronomy 2:34, 7:2, 20:16–18; Joshua 6:17–21)."[12] The historically and materially defined local practices of a culture far away and long ago are here made "naturally" responsible . . . for the colonial practices entirely other to it simply because later cultures used these practices as their authorization. One effect of this sudden dehistoricization of hermeneutics has been an exoneration of European Christian society that has been . . . the religious hegemonic system for virtually all of the imperialist, racist, and even genocidal societies of the West, but not, of course, Judaism. . . . It should be clearly recognized . . . that the attempt of the integrationist Zionist Gush Emunim to refigure the Palestinians as Amalek and to reactivate the genocidal commandment is an act of religious revisionism and not in any way a continuation of historical rabbinic Judaism.

Does this mean that rabbinic Judaism qua ideology is innocent of either ethnocentric or supremacist tenets? Certainly not. What it argues is rather that Jewish racism, like the racism of other peoples, is a . . . dispensable aspect of the cultural system. . . . Perhaps the primary function for a critical construction of cultural (or racial or gender or sexual) identity is to construct it in ways that purge it of its elements of domination and oppression. . . .

. . . To our understanding, it would be an appropriate goal to articulate a theory and practice of identity that would simultaneously respect the irreducibility and positive value of cultural differences, address the harmfulness, not of abolishing frontiers but of dissolution of uniqueness, and encourage the mutual fructification of different life-styles and traditions. . . . The solution of Zionism —that is, Jewish state hegemony, except insofar as it represented an emergency and temporary rescue operation—seems to us the subversion of Jewish culture

12. [The reference here is to Frederick W. Turner and his 1980 book *Beyond Geography*. A *khamsin* is a desert wind.]

and not its culmination. It represents the substitution of a European, Western cultural-political formation for a traditional Jewish one that has been based on a sharing, at best, of political power with others and that takes on entirely other meanings when combined with political hegemony. . . .

For those of us who are equally committed to social justice and collective Jewish existence, some other formation must be constituted. . . . Reversing A. B. Yehoshua's famous pronouncement that only in a condition of political hegemony is moral responsibility mobilized, we would argue that the only moral path would be the renunciation of Jewish hegemony. . . . This would involve first of all complete separation of religion from state, but even more than that the revocation of the Law of Return and such cultural, discursive practices that code the state as a Jewish state and not a multinational and multicultural one. The dream of a place that is ours founders on the rock of realization that there are Others. . . . Any notion of redemption through Land must either be infinitely deferred (as the Neturei Karta[13] understands so well) or become a moral monster. . . . Race and space together form a deadly discourse.

Genealogy and *territorialism* have been the problematic and necessary . . . terms around which Jewish identity has revolved. In Jewish history . . . these terms are more obviously at odds with each other than in synergy. This allows a formulation of Jewish identity not as a proud resting place . . . but as a perpetual, creative, diasporic tension. . . .

. . . It is crucial to recognize that the Jewish conception of the Land of Israel is similar to the discourse of the Land of many . . . "indigenous" peoples of the world. Somehow the Jews have managed to retain a sense of being rooted somewhere in the world through twenty centuries of exile from that someplace. . . .

It is profoundly disturbing to hear Jewish attachment to the Land decried as regressive in the same discursive situations in which the attachment of native Americans or Australians to their particular rocks, trees, and deserts is celebrated as an organic connection to the Earth that "we" have lost. The uncritical valorization of indigenousness (and particularly the confusion between political indigenousness and mystified autochthony) must come under critique, without wishing to deny the rights of native Americans, Australians, and Palestinians to their Lands precisely on the basis of real, unmysterious political claims. If, on the one hand, Jews are to give up hegemony over the Land, this does not mean

13. [An Ultra-Orthodox group virulently opposed to the State of Israel.]

that the profundity of our attachment to the Land can be denied. This must also have a political expression in the present, in the provision of the possibility for Jews to live a Jewish life in a Palestine not dominated by one ethnic group or another.

On the other hand, the biblical story is not one of autochthony,[14] but one of always coming from somewhere else. . . . At the same time that one vitally important strain . . . within biblical religion promotes a sense of organic, "natural" connectedness between the People and this Land—a settlement in the Land— in another sense . . . Israelite and Jewish religion is perpetually an unsettlement of the very notion of autochthony. Traditional Jewish attachment to the Land . . . thus provides a self-critique as well as a critique of identities based on notions of autochthony. . . .

One modern story of Israel, the Israeli Declaration of Independence, begins with an imaginary autochthony—"In the Land of Israel this people came into existence"—and ends with the triumphant return of the People to their natural Land, making them "re-autochthonized," "like all the nations." . . . An alternative story of Israel, closer . . . to the readings of the Judaism lived for two thousand years, begins with a people forever unconnected with a particular land, a people that calls into question the idea that a people must have a land in order to be a people. . . .

The Rabbis produced their cultural formation within the conditions of Diaspora. . . . The point is not that the Land was devalued by the Rabbis but that they renounced it until the final redemption. . . . [The scholar W. D.] Davies [of Duke University] phrases the positions just rightly when he says, "It was its ability to detach its loyalty from 'place,' while nonetheless retaining 'place' in its memory, that enabled Pharisaism to transcend the loss of its Land."[15] Our only addition would be to argue that this displacement of loyalty from place to memory of place was necessary not only to transcend the loss of the Land but to enable the loss of the Land. Political possession of the Land most threatened the possibility of continued Jewish cultural practice and difference. Given the choice between an ethnocentricity that would not seek domination over others and a seeking of political domination . . . , the Rabbis chose ethnocentricity. Zionism is thus a subversion of rabbinic Judaism, and it is no wonder that

14. [The term is used here to denote connection with a place by virtue of birth or origin.]

15. [W. D. Davies, *The Territorial Dimension of Judaism* (Minneapolis: Fortress Press, 1991), 69.]

until World War II Zionism was a secular movement to which very few religious Jews adhered, seeing it as a human arrogation of a work that only God should or could perform....

The dialectic between Paul and the Rabbis can be recuperated for cultural critique. When Christianity is the hegemonic power in Europe and the United States, the resistance of Jews to being universalized can be a critical force and model for the resistance of all peoples to being Europeanized out of particular bodily existence. When, however, an ethnocentric Judaism becomes a temporal, hegemonic political force, it becomes absolutely, vitally necessary to accept Paul's critical challenge—although not his universalizing, disembodying solution—and to develop an equally passionate concern for all human beings.... Within the conditions of the Diaspora, . . . [a]bsolute devotion to the maintenance of Jewish culture and the historical memory was not inconsistent with devotion to radical causes of human liberation.... The "chosenness" of the Jews becomes, when seen in this light, not a warrant for racism but precisely an antidote to racism. This is a Judaism that mobilizes the critical forces within the Bible and the Jewish tradition rather than mobilizing the repressive and racist forces that also subsist there....

... Diasporic identity is a disaggregated identity.... Jewishness disrupts the very categories of identity because it is not national, not genealogical, not religious, but all of these in dialectical tension with one another....

... [The] Diaspora is not the forced product of war and destruction—taking place after the downfall of Judea—but that already in the centuries before this downfall, the majority of Jews lived voluntarily outside of the Land. Moreover, given a choice between domination by a "foreign" power who would allow them to keep Torah undisturbed and domination by a "Jewish" authority who would interfere with religious life, the Pharisees and their successors the Rabbis generally chose the former....

... The rabbinic answer to Paul's challenge was to renounce any possibility of domination over Others by being perpetually out of power....

... The Neturei Karta, to this day, refuse to visit the Western Wall, the holiest place in Judaism, without PLO "visas" because it was taken by violence.

This response has much to teach us. We want to propose a privileging of the Diaspora, a disassociation of ethnicities and political hegemonies as the only social structure that even begins to make possible a maintenance of cultural identity in a world grown thoroughly and inextricably interdependent.... We would suggest that Diaspora, and not monotheism, may be the most important contribution that Judaism has to make to the world. . . . The renunciation of sovereignty (justified by discourses of autochthony, indigenousness, and territorial self-determination), combined with a fierce tenacity in holding onto cultural identity, might well have something to offer a world in which these two forces, together, kill thousands daily.

Peter Beinart (born 1971) is a journalist, professor, and liberal political commentator who was educated at Yale College. He was a Rhodes Scholar at Oxford, where he earned an MPhil in international relations. Beinart was formerly an editor at the *New Republic* and currently teaches journalism and political science at the City University of New York. He is a major figure on the contemporary Jewish and American political and cultural scenes.

Peter Beinart, *The Crisis of Zionism* (New York: Henry Holt and Company, 2012), 1–4, 10.

I wrote this book because of my grandmother, who made me a Zionist. And because of Khaled Jaber, who could have been my son.

I remember walking back with my grandmother one night from synagogue, past the loquat trees of Pretoria, South Africa, the most beautiful Jewish ghetto in the world. I was a kid, and was boasting about the United States, the country to which her daughter—my mother—had immigrated. She grew annoyed. "Don't get too attached," she announced. "The Jews are like rats. We leave the sinking ship. One day, please God, we'll all join Isaac in Israel."

Isaac was her brother. They had parted ways four decades earlier, as the ancient Jewish community of Alexandria, Egypt, broke under the strain of economic depression, Arab nationalism, and world war. . . .

When the war ended, my grandmother moved . . . to South Africa. . . . Fifteen years later, the Congo erupted in civil war, and the Jews there fled. Now, in her old age, racial violence was bloodying South Africa, too, and all around her, Jews were again packing their things. Only later did I realize that my grandmother had spent her life burying Jewish communities. So did her parents. She suspected I would do the same.

Yet she was at peace, because of Israel. . . . Israel's existence calmed her, comforted her, rooted her. It made her feel that Jewish history was more than an endless cycle of estrangement and dislocation; it actually led somewhere. It made her feel that not all Jewish homes need be temporary. . . .

My life has been very different than my grandmother's. But I have seen enough to understand how she feels. When I was thirteen, I watched footage of thousands of emaciated Ethiopian Jews, isolated from the rest of their people since the days when the first Temple stood, trekking through the Sahara to reach the planes that the Jewish state had sent to take them home. When I was fourteen, I saw a squat, bald Russian named Anatoly Sharansky—fresh from eight years in a Soviet jail—raise his hands in triumph as he descended the steps at Ben-Gurion Airport. In those soul-stirring scenes, I saw my grandmother's Zionism —the Zionism of refuge—play out before my eyes. It became my Zionism, too. Like her, I sleep better knowing that the world contains a Jewish state.

But not any Jewish state. Roughly eighteen months ago, an Israeli friend sent me a video. It was of a Palestinian man named Fadel Jaber, who was being arrested for stealing water. His family had repeatedly asked Israeli authorities for access to the pipes that service a nearby Jewish settlement. But the Jabers have little influence over the Israeli authorities: like all Palestinians in the West Bank, they are subjects, not citizens. Partly as a result, West Bank Palestinians use roughly one-fifth as much water per person as do Jewish settlers, which means that while settlements often boast swimming pools and intensive irrigation systems, Palestinians fall far below the World Health Organization's recommended daily water consumption rate.

In the video, Israeli police drag Fadel toward some kind of paddy wagon. And then the camera pans down, to a five-year-old boy with a striped shirt and short brown hair, Khaled, who is frantically trying to navigate the thicket of adults in order to reach his father. As his father pulls away, he keeps screaming, "Baba, Baba."

As soon as I began watching the video, I wished I had never turned it on. For most of my life, my reaction to accounts of Palestinian suffering has been rationalization, a search for reasons why the accounts are exaggerated or the suffering self-inflicted. In that respect, I suspect, I'm like many American Jews. But in recent years . . . I had been lowering my defenses and Khaled's cries left me staring in mute horror at my computer screen.

Perhaps it is because my son is Khaled's age. He attends a Jewish school, has an Israeli flag on his wall, and can recount Bible stories testifying to our ancient ties to the land. When he was younger, we thought he would call me *Abba*, the Hebrew word for father. But he couldn't say Abba, so he calls me Baba, the same name Khaled calls his father.

One day when they're old enough to understand, I'll tell his sister and him how my grandmother made me a Zionist. And one day, if they see a video like this, I'll tell them that unless American Jews help end the occupation that desecrates Israel's founding ideals, this is what Zionism will become, a movement that fails the test of Jewish power. . . .

Israel's survival is bound up with its ethical survival. Whether or not Israel's nuclear weapons and antimissile shields can protect it from Iran, Hezbollah, and Hamas, they will be of no use on the day that hundreds of thousands of Palestinians march, nonviolently, to demand the very "equality of social and political rights" that Israel promises in its declaration of independence. And if American Jewish leaders continue to defend the Israeli government at the expense of Israeli democracy, they may find their own children and grandchildren cheering these protesters on.

I will try to give my son and daughter a sense of the immensity of what they have been given, of the agony that prior generations endured so that Jews could have a state. And I will tell them their duty is to help ensure that . . . Jewish sovereignty does not fail. I will tell them, if they see the video of Khaled Jaber calling for his father, that I learned of his story because brave young Israelis chronicled it, Israelis who believe in the promise of Israel's independence declaration, which envisions a nation that pursues "freedom, justice, and peace as envisaged by the Hebrew prophets." I will tell them that that pledge, made when the stench of Jewish death still hung over Europe, and amid a war for Israel's very existence, is their patrimony. If Israel betrays that promise, it will be a stain upon their lives. . . .

The Editors of *Commentary*, "The Existential Necessity of Zionism after Paris"

Commentary is a monthly American magazine on religion, Judaism, and politics, as well as social and cultural issues. It is now neoconservative in orientation and its present-day editor is John Podhoretz.

Editors of *Commentary*, "The Existential Necessity of Zionism after Paris," *Commentary* 139, no. 2 (February 2015): 14–16.

For all the opinions among the Zionist leaders who followed Herzl as to what form Jewish self-rule should take—and there were many—there was one thing on which they all agreed. Any debate over *what kind of state* Israel should be was irrelevant unless *there was a state*. This was a practical nationalism. . . . What Israel needed was not to *become* but to *be*. . . .

Today, within the Jewish community, anti-Zionist Jews do not pose much of a challenge. Now the real challenge comes from within Zionism itself—with the way practical Zionism has disappointed some Jews. These are people who have replaced practical Zionism with what might be called "conditional Zionism." For the conditional Zionists, Israel was once the port of call for Jews adrift. Now, they say, the storm is over and the threat to Jewry comes more from what they see as the calamity that the storm has wreaked on the port. . . .

In his 2012 book *The Crisis of Zionism*, Peter Beinart insists he sleeps better at night "knowing that the world contains a Jewish state." His very next words, however, might count as a succinct motto of the conditional Zionists: "But not any Jewish state." If Israel does not behave as the conditional Zionists wish it to behave, if it does not enact policies the conditional Zionists wish it to enact, if it does not confront its own external challenges in a manner that salves the consciences of the conditional Zionists, then it is not deserving of their support. . . .

The conditional Zionists have a way of mistaking a lull in the waves [of anti-Semitism] for a permanent low tide. Consider this sentence Beinart wrote only three years ago: "For the most part, young American Jews don't experience their campuses as hostile or anti-Semitic." . . .

So what happens to the conditional Zionists' arguments when anti-Semitism reasserts itself with a vengeance? The answer comes from the academic Alan Wolfe. His latest book, *At Home in Exile*,[16] purports to explain "why Diaspora is good for the Jews." Wolfe accepts, to some degree, the premise of practical Zionism. But then he caricatures it, asserting that the credibility of the Zionist project, at least as its most dedicated adherents see it, depends on the complete collapse of Diaspora life:

> Intentionally or not, a focus on diasporic success undermines that unity, for if Jews can flourish outside the Jewish state, the fundamental rationale for that state's existence is inevitably brought into question. Zionists did not build a home for some Jews so that others could treat it as a place to go on vacation.

According to Wolfe, then, the Zionists' response is threat inflation in the service of particularism at the expense of universalism. Wolfe says Jews don't appreciate, or don't permit themselves to appreciate, their good fortune. "Far from representing an appeal for the rights of powerless minorities to live in dignity," Wolfe writes, "repeated accusations of anti-Semitism under such conditions all too often lose their innocence."

It is, we fear, Wolfe and the conditional Zionists who must now lose their innocence, if innocence it ever was. The conditions in France reveal the dangerous complacency of conditional Zionism. Israel was not established as a messianic project or a secular haven. It is not a socialist workers' paradise. It is not a capitalist-imperialist outpost. It is, instead, a country, now 66 years of age, freer than most, fairer to minorities than most, in which 6.2 million Jews now live.

"Home is the place where, when you have to go there, / They have to take you in," wrote Robert Frost. For every French Jew at risk, for every Jew everywhere at risk, and for every Jew who chooses, Israel is home. Its existence before the Holocaust would have saved millions. Its existence after the Holocaust saved and created millions. Seventy years after the Holocaust, Jews in Europe are in need of it again.

Alas, the promise Herzl offered at the conclusion of *The Jewish State* was dreadfully naive: "The Jews, once settled in their own State, would probably have

16. [Alan Wolfe, *At Home in Exile: Why Diaspora Is Good for the Jews* (Boston: Beacon Press, 2014).]

no more enemies," he wrote. In two months, Jews will gather for the Passover seder and sing: "In every generation they rise up against us to destroy us." Anti-Semitism is a disease for which there is likely no cure.

The existential necessity of Zionism after Paris is not only a fact. It is a charge for the future.

VI | Feminism, Gender, and Sexuality

When she published *The Feminine Mystique* in 1963, Betty Friedan ushered in a revolution in American life in which the voices of women in the public sphere would no longer be silenced. Her influence was felt in the larger world through organizations like NOW (the National Organization for Women) and publications like *Ms.*, and feminism emerged as a full-blown movement in the United States during the 1960s and 1970s.[1]

As a result of the effervescence of this cultural and political moment, the impact of feminism was felt in the Jewish community as well. The year 1970 saw Trude Weiss-Rosmarin write an essay titled "The Unfreedom of the Jewish Woman" in *The Jewish Spectator*, where she was the editor,[2] and the then-Orthodox Rachel Adler shortly thereafter wrote an article in the countercultural periodical *Davka* that issued a major indictment against the status of Jewish women in Jewish law.[3] Sally Priesand was ordained as a rabbi by Hebrew Union College–Jewish Institute of Religion in 1972, and at the same time women activists from a group named *Ezrat Nashim* began to make their presence felt in the larger Jewish community through protests against the silence and discrimination women had to endure in public Jewish life. By 1976, Elizabeth Koltun had edited an influential volume, *The Jewish Woman: New Perspectives*,[4] and *Lilith*, the enduring feminist journal coedited by Susan Weidman Schneider and Aviva Cantor, appeared that same year for the first time. *The Jewish Woman in America*, coauthored by Paula Hyman, Charlotte Baum, and

1. [See Joyce Antler, *Jewish Radical Feminism: Voices from the Women's Liberation Movement* (New York: New York University Press, 2018).]

2. [Trude Weiss-Rosmarin, "The Unfreedom of the Jewish Woman," *Jewish Spectator* 35, no. 7 (October 1970): 2–6.]

3. [Rachel Adler, "The Jew Who Wasn't There: Halakhah and the Jewish Woman," *Davka* 1, no. 4 (Summer 1971): 6–11. This article has been reprinted on a number of occasions.]

4. [Elizabeth Koltun, ed., *The Jewish Woman: New Perspectives* (New York: Schocken, 1976).]

Sonya Michel, also was published in 1976.[5] The prominence of women in the life of the Jewish community, their demands for inclusion and ritual innovation, and the intellectual ferment supporting such changes grew increasingly common and prominent in the years that followed.

These calls for expansion of the community needed thoughtful articulation and, in the decades following the 1970s, the writings and influences of Jewish feminism on the thought of American Jews and Judaism have been many and pronounced. Increasingly, sophisticated statements of Jewish faith and culture have appeared, and the work of Jewish feminists has arguably represented the most exciting and vital dimension of contemporary American Jewish thought. The creativity and urgent demands for justice these women and their allies have contributed to the public life of the Jewish people have captured the attention of many.

These thinkers also established a trajectory of expansion in the realms of American Jewish thought. Supported by more recent developments leading to rights for LGBTQ persons in the larger world, the formerly closeted voices and concerns of gays, lesbians, bisexuals, trans-gender people and queer persons have promoted an awareness of issues of gender and sexuality in the lives of American Jews. Many have noted the connections between feminist thought and gender awareness,[6] and this section of our book brings them together to bear witness to this relatively new chapter in American Jewish thought.

Part Six begins with the work of Susannah Heschel, who provides a brilliant introduction to the nature and demands of Jewish feminism from her perspective as both a historian and religious thinker. She places the demands of the feminist movement in American Judaism within the larger context of Judaism's struggle with the challenges of modernization during the past two hundred years, and her selection ends with a call for justice and assertiveness. The writer Cynthia Ozick then asks what is the "right question" that Jewish feminists should be asking of the tradition and the community. While she has no doubt that an injustice has been done to Jewish women by their consignment to the domestic sphere in Jewish life, she offers several perspectives on

5. [Charlotte Baum, Paula Hyman, and Sonya Michel, *The Jewish Woman in America* (New York: Dial Press, 1976).]

6. [The challenges and complexities of this connection are discussed in Judith Butler, "Against Proper Objects: Introduction," *Differences: A Journal of Feminist Cultural Studies* 6, no. 2–3 (1994): 1–26.]

whether the solution to this injustice demands a sociological or theological remedy. In contrast, Judith Plaskow in her response to Ozick has no doubt that the question is fundamentally a theological one, and she calls upon the Jewish community to correct religious usage that enshrines patriarchy, in addition to male metaphors, language, and imagery for naming and conceptualizing God. Such theological change is requisite for repair of the Jewish community and tradition. The Ozick-Plaskow dialogue can be seen as a foundational document of Jewish feminist discourse.

The passage from the Orthodox Blu Greenberg echoes many of the concerns that Heschel, Ozick, and Plaskow have expressed, but in tones that seem somewhat more moderate. Her insistence upon and her case for equality for women in Judaism are surely apparent in the selection she has written. In it, she uses a phrase that has famously come to be associated with her in Jewish feminist circles ever since when, in speaking of the arbiters of Jewish law throughout history, she asserts, "where there is a halakhic will, there is a halakhic way." At the same time, she contends that her call for gender inclusion and justice for women reflects a vector that has long been present in Jewish jurisprudence. The fifth selection, authored by Rachel Adler, who at the time of writing was Orthodox, questions this last claim and argues that a patriarchal "methodolatry" that has previously marked Jewish life must be uprooted if a vision of a just Jewish community is to be realized.

Two essays by Julia Watts Belser follow. In the first, Belser indicates how a contemporary feminist envisions God. In the second selection from her work, Belser draws upon her knowledge as a Talmudist and rabbi to argue on behalf of a "feminist environmental ethics." Both these selections by a contemporary feminist reveal the directions the community has taken over the past fifty years, as feminist Jewish thought has developed. Her writings reflect the hopes that earlier feminists such as Plaskow and Adler had for the role that feminist sensibilities could play in American Jewish thought, and Belser surely epitomizes the confidence in their own voices that present-day feminists possess.

From Belser we turn to the Orthodox rabbi Steve Greenberg and begin to hear the words and thoughts of those in the LGBTQ sectors of the Jewish world. In the selection drawn from his *Wrestling with God and Man*, Greenberg argues that while patriarchy emerged as dominant from the biblical accounts found in Genesis, God's original vision of the world was not one marked by a male-female binary. Rather, with the creation of a single *Adam*, the divine ideal for the world was a nonhierarchical androgyny. Furthermore, he lays the groundwork for opposition to the notion that God unequivocally prohibited male-male anal intercourse in accord with the usual interpretations of Leviticus 18 and 20. In so doing, Greenberg attempts to provide for a broader reading of Jewish tradition on matters of sexuality and the treatment of gays and others in the Jewish community. Jay Michaelson walks in much the same path as Greenberg and echoes the Orthodox rabbi when he argues that his own homosexuality is determined by God and nature and must therefore not be condemned. Rabbi Benay Lappe then provides an approach to Jewish law and interpretation based on the Talmudic concept of *svara* to indicate how LGBTQ interpretations of the Torah are authentically Jewish.

Rabbi Jane Litman moves in a slightly different direction. She critiques figures such as Greenberg and Michaelson and questions the wisdom and legitimacy of a "determinist" ethics in creating a Jewish sexual ethic. The influence of "transgender" thinking on her own position causes her to reject absolutely any notion of a male-female binary, which she sees as too narrow to capture the reality of human sexuality. Furthermore, she does not agree that sexual attraction is always "determined." Rather, drawing on texts found in Jewish tradition, Litman feels that sexuality is often chosen. Finally, Part Six concludes with a selection from Joy Ladin, who contends that "our humanity does not depend on gender." Indeed, "male or female limits our understanding of who we are and what we can be." Ladin concludes, "the biblical account of the genesis of gender lays the ground for accepting the dazzling variety not just of transgender people, but of humanity." With confidence that other voices will be heard on these topics in the years to come, we can predict that these revolutionary changes will continue to have an indelible impact on American Jewish thought. In the words of Marcia Cohn Spiegel, "[t]he silence has been broken.... We are speaking out in clear voices, not concealing the truth from one another.... We are changing Jewish life forever."[7]

7. [Marcia Cohn Spiegel, "Foreword" in *Celebrating the Lives of Jewish Women: Patterns in a Feminist Sampler*, ed. Rachel Josefowitz Siegel and Ellen Cole (New York: Routledge, 2013).]

Susannah Heschel (born 1956) is the Eli Black Professor of Jewish Studies at Dartmouth College. Heschel received her undergraduate education at Trinity College in Hartford, Connecticut, and her doctorate at the University of Pennsylvania. She is famed as a scholar of modern Jewish intellectual history and of Jewish-Christian relations in Germany during the nineteenth and twentieth centuries. Heschel also enjoys a reputation as a highly prominent Jewish public intellectual, and she has written often on matters of feminism.

Susannah Heschel, "Introduction" in *On Being a Jewish Feminist*, ed. Susannah Heschel (New York: Schocken, 1983), xxi–xxv, xxxi–xxxiii.[8]

Opponents who protest feminism's social and psychological ramifications, as well as many feminists proposing change through halakhic procedures, are not confronting core arguments and insights of the feminist critique. Feminism is not calling for a renunciation of womanhood . . . nor for simple equality between men and women. . . . Rather, feminism's central insight contends that not only do women not shape and control their own lives, but that our most basic understandings of human nature are drawn primarily from men's experiences. A patriarchal outlook begins by making men's experiences normative, equating the human with the male. Not only are women excluded from the process of shaping the outlook, but women's experiences are projected as something external, "other" to that norm. As Virginia Woolf long ago pointed out, the vast literature that attempts to define "woman's nature" clearly reveals the assumption that women lie outside the general definitions of humanity and constitute a separate category in need of explication. No comparable literature exists to define "men's nature," since that is equated with all intellectual endeavors generally. Simone de Beauvoir writes, "This humanity is male and man defines woman not in herself

8. [While we have chosen to present excerpts from the original introduction, since it provides a pathbreaking articulation of the issues Jewish feminism would confront in the following years, Heschel's revised introduction to a later edition of this work (New York: Schocken, 1995) is also of great interest.]

but as relative to him; she is not regarded as an autonomous being. . . . He is the Subject, he is the Absolute—she is the Other."[9]

. . . The Jewish feminist writers represented in this volume have moved beyond criticizing specific traditions and institutions to recognize the marginality of Jewish women extending beyond the synagogue, tradition, and *halakhah*. The problem, as today's writers see it, runs throughout the course of Jewish history, penetrating the basic theological suppositions of Judaism: its imagery of women and men, its liturgy, its conceptions of the Jewish people and community, its understanding of God as Father and King. Woman as Other is expressed, for instance, by Judaism's "purity" laws, in which women convey impurity not to themselves or to other women, but only to men with whom they come into contact. Similarly, women enter into discussions in Judaism's law codes only as they affect men's lives; there exists no Talmudic tractate discussing the experience of women's lives, how they are to be guided halakhically and interpreted religiously. In another example, women are placed behind a curtain in some synagogues, or denied *aliyot* and positions of leadership, not for any reasons concerning them, but because their visible presence might affect the concentration of men at prayer.

These issues, all concerning the authority and relevance of key aspects of Judaism, lie at the root of the feminist challenge. Here the question arises: if feminists do indeed bring about all the changes their critique implies, what will remain as recognizably Judaism? What criteria, what grounds of authority, will be used to retain some aspects of Judaism while rejecting or radically modifying others?

The implications of the feminist inquiry clearly involve more than the repair of particular laws or traditions. . . . The very bases of Judaism are being challenged—from *halakhah* to the prayer book to the very ways we conceive of God. The challenge today demands a Copernican revolution: a new theology of Judaism, requiring new understandings of God, revelation, *halakhah*, and the Jewish people in order to support and encourage change.

To an extent, the conflict emerging between feminism and Judaism today parallels the conflict between Jews and Western culture that began to take shape with the Emancipation of Jews in Europe two hundred years ago. Just as none of the great ideological movements of the modern period—from liberalism to Marxism to nationalism—seemed able, ultimately, to incorporate and accept Jews and Judaism, so, too, none of the religious movements of modern Juda-

9. Simone de Beauvoir, *The Second Sex* (New York: Knopf, 1953), 16.

ism seems capable of coming to terms with women and feminism. And just as Jews became the crucible of modern political thought, so, too, feminism is the crucible for modern Judaism. Today's confrontation with feminism exposes the failure of modern religious movements to cope with modernity's challenges to theology and respond effectively to them. . . .

The issue is not that feminism poses insoluble problems to Jewish law, but that Judaism has long ago died in the way it had existed for two thousand years. The crisis has not been brought on by feminism, but feminism clearly discloses the morbid condition of Judaism that has continued, untreated, throughout the modern period.

Thus, from Judaism's perspective, the conflict emerges not so much from the particular agenda of feminism, but from the weakness of Jewish theological responses to modernity, which are thrown into relief by the challenges of feminism. In reality, a large part of the opposition to feminism arises from a displaced concern over the impact of secularism. Attacks on feminist demands for changes in *halakhah* simply reveal the absence of a coherent position regarding the authority of Jewish law in an age of relativism. Claims that feminism violates Jewish principles and values reveal general confusion over what constitutes Judaism in today's context of pluralism and free choice.

. . . Feminists may be misdirecting their efforts by attempting to remain within the frameworks of the denominations, whose confrontations with feminism raise the question whether these branches of Judaism have succeeded in their ostensible goal of meeting modernity's challenges. Modernity strikes not so much at the specifics of traditional theology, but at the general concept of theological absolutism. Yet these Jewish denominations have responded to modernity by substituting new dogmas for the old traditional ones. For Orthodoxy, the absolute core is *halakhah*, while Reform lays claim to a spirit or an idea, and Conservatism and Reconstructionism adhere to an historical consciousness or civilization of the Jewish people.

Yet none of these approaches provides clear, normative criteria for implementing the changes called for by feminism. In fact, the changes made by these denominations in response to particular feminist demands were not made by applying the central principles of each movement. Whatever progress made during the past decades by feminists was not because of, but in spite of, the core ideas of the movements.

. . . Clearly, there is a need for theological reinterpretations to transform women in Judaism from object to subject. For only theology can offer the solution to the present problem, determining the role of rabbinic tradition in contemporary Judaism and its application to the lives we lead. Theology must apply feminism's concern for women's dignity and humanity in examining the meanings of religious symbols, traditions, and beliefs, and strive to give answers to humankind's ultimate questions.

. . . In helping to create a new theology, women will become receivers and transmitters of Judaism, not onlookers. That shift can be illustrated in a parable by Franz Kafka, "Before the Law." In Kafka's parable, a man from the country arrives at a door, seeking entry into the law, but the doorkeeper tells him it is impossible; a guard sits before each of many doors, and each guard is larger and fiercer than the one before. The man from the country sits down before the open door and remains there for years, until his death, begging and bribing the doorkeeper for permission to enter. Finally, as the man faces death, he asks why no one else has ever sought admission during the many years. The doorkeeper informs him that this door was intended solely for him—and then shuts it.

Although the doorkeeper forbids entry into the law to the man from the country, in reality he cannot prevent it. The man from the country fails to gain entry when he passively assumes that authorities are obstacles to the law, instead of taking the initiative and walking through the door himself. His error becomes twofold: first, he believes he can achieve his aim only through the guard and only if he begs and bribes him correctly, and second, he blames his failure to gain entry on the doorkeeper, whose refusal to give help is seen as unfeeling and evil.

Many women in recent years have come seeking entry into Judaism. Some give up and eventually leave. Others plead and argue for admission, and are offered counterarguments, warnings, barriers, and a few ameliorating changes.

By assuming a posture like that of the man from the country, women continue their relation to Judaism as outsider or Other—even if they walk past the guards and through the doors. A profound error underlies this approach. Kafka's parable applies well to the situation of modern Judaism, which has built the doors of denominations, guarded by rabbis, institutions, and ideologies. But Judaism is not an edifice lying behind doors and guards and we should not have to go through a denomination to reach it. Rather, our relations should be with the diversity and totality of Judaism, unmediated by one of its modern forms. There are no doors, there are no guards. Through theological exploration Judaism can belong to all who desire it.

Cynthia Ozick, "Notes Toward Finding
the Right Question"

Cynthia Ozick (born 1928) is one of the most significant Jewish literary figures
of the past century. She is a prolific writer of short stories and novels as well as an
outstanding essayist. Her fame is worldwide. Ozick has also become one of the
foremost commentators on Jewish affairs in her lifetime.

Cynthia Ozick, "Notes toward Finding the Right Question," in *On Being
a Jewish Feminist*, 143–51. First published in *Lilith* 6 (1979): 19–29.

BUT SUPPOSE THE QUESTION IS SACRAL?
THE MISSING COMMANDMENT; THE TWO
WALLS OF SCANDAL

Up to this point, in these *Notes toward Finding the Right Question*, I have taken the
position that the status of Jewish women flows from societal, not sacral, sources.
But suppose this position is dead wrong? And suppose the opponents of this position, who believe that the status of women is in fact, a sacral question, are right?

Clearly, it would be narrow-minded, as well as metaphysically risky not to
pay close attention to those who insist that one cannot look at the question of
women without the imperative of looking simultaneously into the profoundest
intent, deeper than social practice merely, of Torah itself.

And clearly one cannot reflect on the meaning of Torah without also reflecting on justice and injustice.

What is injustice? We need not define it. Justice must be defined and redefined,
but not injustice. How to right a wrong demands ripe deliberation, often ingenu-
ity. But a wrong needs only to be seen, to be seen to be wrong. Injustice is instantly
intuited, felt, recognized, reacted to. That there is injustice with regard to women
is well understood; otherwise there would be, to take only three illustrations
centuries apart, no *halitzah*,[10] no *ketubah*,[11] and no current agitation over *agunah*.[12]

10. [When a woman's husband dies without male offspring, Jewish law prescribes levirate marriage and requires the woman to marry her husband's brother in the hope that
this union will produce a surrogate son and heir to the deceased brother so that his name

The fact that injustice can be instantly identified raises a strange question. Each of the great offenses is recognized and dealt with in the broadest way in the Decalogue by means of a single all-encompassing "Thou shalt not." But the Decalogue is silent about the status of women except insofar as women are perceived as part of the web of ownership. We are not told not to covet our neighbor's husband; a husband is not property. And the injunction against adultery, while applying to both women and men, is to protect husbands from theft. But just as "Thou shalt not covet thy neighbor's wife" is a refinement of "Thou shalt not commit adultery," so are both of these refinements of "Thou shalt not steal."

So the question arises: if, in the most fundamental text and texture of Torah, the lesser status of women is not worthy of a great "Thou shalt not," then perhaps there is nothing inherently offensive in it, then perhaps there is no essential injustice, then perhaps the common status of women is not only sanctioned, but, in fact, divinely ordained?

Yet, if this were so, why are there any attempts at all in rabbinic history to repair the status of women? It is as if the Oral Law is saying to the Written Law: *there is something missing*. In fact, whoever believes that the Oral Law is implicit in the Torah is already saying that something is missing: obviously, if the missing element were explicit, the Oral Law would not have to derive it.

What we receive through Torah is the eternality and immutability of certain moral principles, beyond social custom and even despite nature.

When we accept this standard—that Torah gives precepts for the elevation of humanity—as endemic in Torah, and when we posit the giving of such precepts

---

"may not be blotted out in Israel" (Deuteronomy 25:6). Should the living brother reject his dead brother's widow and opt not to fulfill his levirate duty, he may perform the ritual of *halitzah*, "unshoeing," whereby he releases the levirate widow from her automatic levirate tie to him. His sister-in-law is then free to remarry or not at will.]

11. [A *ketubah* is a Jewish marriage contract signed prior to the wedding ceremony that delineates the financial obligations of the groom to his bride. It is signed in traditional circles by two male witnesses in the presence of the groom and offers the wife financial protections.]

12. [An *agunah* is literally "a chained or anchored woman." It refers to a woman whose recalcitrant husband refuses to issue her a Jewish writ of divorce (*get*) or whose marriage has been terminated de facto (for instance, her husband is missing in war), but not de jure. As husbands alone possess the right to initiate divorce in Jewish law, the *agunah* is "chained" to her husband and prohibited from remarrying. Debate over the status of the *agunah* is the subject of great moral anguish in contemporary Judaism.]

as a kind of general definition of Torah, as in effect the essence of Torah, then we run into a wall of scandal.

. . . The *point* of the Commandments is that the world isn't like them, that the commandments are contrary to the way the world really is. That is why we value them; that is how they come to elevate us above merciless nature and unjust social usage. It is because Torah makes us and our usages different and separate from the way things appear to be given, that we have found meaning in being human.

How, then, does this relate to a wall of scandal? It would seem that, in every instance, Torah can be trusted to say its timeless and holy "Thou shalt not" to the lenient, cruel, and careless indifference of both society and nature—to the way human beings unmediated by conscience behave, and even to the continuum of conscienceless nature as it passes through undifferentiated days.

With one tragic exception. In one remarkable instance only there is lacking the cleansing force of "Thou shalt not," and the abuses of society are permitted to have their way almost unchecked by Torah.

With regard to the condition of women, we speak of "abuses of society"—but these abuses are so wideflung on our planet that they seem, by their undeviating pervasiveness, very nearly to have the sanction of nature. If we look only into Torah, we see that the ubiquitousness of women's condition applies here as well, with as much force as elsewhere. Women's quality of lesser-ness, of other-ness, is laid down at the very beginning, as a paradigm and as a rule: at the start of the Creation of the World woman is given an inferior place. In Scripture, it is true, whenever we hear her speak in her own voice, she is uttering a protest against being put upon: Sarah arguing with Abraham, for instance, over Hagar, or Zelophehad's daughters arguing with Moses over their inheritance. In each case, God is moved by injustice and enjoins both Abraham and Moses to redress the abuse. In both accounts the injustice-contradicting texture of Torah prevails over the offenses of the ruling social order.

But mostly the social order as given—woman dehumanized, woman as inferior, woman as chattel—remains untouched by the healing force of any grand principle of justice. . . .

On the whole, it turns out the status of women under Torah is not remarkably or radically different from the status of women in the world at large. And when we consider the world at large, what we see is steady and incontrovertible. A society of Amazons and primeval matriarchs is a fantasy, a myth, one of those wishful dreams that result in sphinxes and gryphons and that inner universe of poetical fancy against which Torah turns its face. As far as we can tell, history, archaeology, and anthropology combine to persuade us in every place, in every time, in every tribe, women have been set aside as lesser, and in that assumption of inferiority have suffered dehumanization, because inferiority is dehumanization. . . .

Why did "Thou shalt not steal" come into being? It came into being because in every place, in every time, in every tribe, then or now, whatever the social or economic or political order, there have been thieves. It came into being because it was necessary to set a precept against the-way-the-world-ordinarily-is.

And that is the salient meaning of Torah, to give precepts against the-way-the-world-ordinarily-is.

With, as I have said, a single tragic exception. We look at the-way-the-world-is with regard to women, and we see that women are perceived as lesser, and are thereby dehumanized. We look into Torah with regard to women, and we see that women are perceived as lesser, and are thereby dehumanized. Torah, in this one instance, and in this instance alone, offers no precept against the-way-the-world-ordinarily-is. There is no "Thou shalt not lessen the humanity of women!" to echo downward from age to age. There is no immutable moral principle to countermand what humankind will do if left to the willfulness and negligence and indifference and callousness of its unrestraint.

This is the terrifying scandal built within the tower of Torah itself. In creating the Sabbath, Torah came face to face with a nature that says, "I make no difference among the days." And Torah made a difference among the days. In giving the Commandment against idolatry, Torah came face to face with a society in competition with the Creator. In making the Commandment against the dishonor of parents, Torah came face to face with merciless usage of the old. And Torah ordained devotion to parents. In every instance, Torah strives to teach *No* to unrestraint. *No* to victimization. *No* to dehumanization. The Covenant is a bond with the Creator, not with the practices of the world as they are found in reality.

With one tragic exception. With regard to women Torah does not say *No* to the practices of the world as they are found in actuality; here alone Torah confirms the world, denying the meaning of its own Covenant.

This wall of scandal is so mammoth in its centrality and its durability that, contemplating it, I can no longer believe in the triviality of the question that asks about the status of Jewish women. It is a question, which reflected on without frivolity, understood without arrogance, makes shock itself seem feeble, makes fright itself grow faint. The relation of Torah to women calls Torah itself into question. Where is the missing Commandment that sits in judgment on the world? Where is the commandment that will say, from the beginning of history until now, *Thou shalt not lessen the humanity of women?* . . .

So what we must do is find, for this absent precept, a Yavneh that will create the conditions for the precept. . . .

To do this is necessary—but it is not necessary for the sake of a more harmonious social order; it is least of all necessary for the sake of "modern times"; it is not necessary for the sake of women; it is not even necessary for the sake of the Jewish people. It is necessary for the sake of Torah: to preserve and strengthen Torah itself.

Judith Plaskow (born 1947) received her undergraduate education at Clark University and her doctorate at Yale Divinity School, writing on the thought of Reinhold Niebuhr and Paul Tillich. A cofounder of the Jewish feminist group B'not Esh in 1981 and the *Journal of Feminist Studies in Religion*, Plaskow was the first Jewish feminist to identify herself as a theologian. A longtime professor at Manhattan College in New York, Plaskow has been a prolific author. Her influence on Jewish and Christian feminist theological discourse has been immense for more than forty years. An excerpt from her pivotal *Standing Again at Sinai* can be found in Part Seven.

Judith Plaskow, "The Right Question Is Theological," in *On Being a Jewish Feminist*, 223–27, 230–32.

The fact that Ozick . . . is reluctant to explore the theological underpinnings of women's status, places her in the mainstream of Jewish feminism. The Jewish women's movement of the past decade has been and remains a civil-rights movement rather than a movement for "women's liberation."[13] . . . It has focused on getting women a piece of the Jewish pie: it has not wanted to bake a new one!

. . . Of the issues that present themselves for our attention, *halakhah* has been at the center of feminist agitation for religious change, and it is to *halakhah* that Ozick turns in the hope of altering women's situation. But while this issue has been considered and debated frequently in the last ten years, it is specific *halakhot* that have been questioned and not the fundamental presuppositions of the legal system. . . . Underlying specific *halakhot*, and *outlasting their amelioration or rejection* is an assumption of women's Otherness far more basic than the laws in which it finds expression. If women are not part of the congregation, if we stand passively under the *huppah*, if, even in the Reform movement, we have become rabbis only in the last ten years, that is because men—and not women with

13. Judith Hole and Ellen Levine, *Rebirth of Feminism* (New York: Quadrangle Books, 1971), ix–x.

them—define Jewish humanity. Men are the actors in religious and communal life because they are normative Jews. Women are "other than" the norm: we are less than fully human.

This Otherness of women is a presupposition of Jewish law in its most central formulations. In the last section of her article on Jewish women, finally turning to the sacral nature of women's status, Ozick points out that the biblical passion for justice does not extend to women. Women's position in biblical law as "part of the web of ownership" is taken as simply the way things are: it is not perceived as or named "injustice." One great "Thou shalt not"—"Thou shalt not lessen the humanity of women"—is absent from the Torah. . . .

. . . Our legal disabilities are a *symptom* of a pattern . . . that lies deep in Jewish thinking. They express and reflect a fundamental stance toward women that must be confronted, addressed and rooted out at its core. While it is Jewish to hope that changes in *halakhah* might bring about changes in underlying attitudes, it is folly to think that justice for women can be achieved simply through halakhic mechanisms when women's plight is not primarily a product of *halakhah*.

But this is just one issue. The Otherness of women is also given dramatic expression in our language about God. Here, we confront a great scandal: the God who supposedly transcends sexuality, who is presumably one and whole, is known to us through language that is highly selective and partial. The images we use to describe God, the qualities we attribute to God, draw on male pronouns and male experience and convey a sense of power and authority that is male in character. . . . The hand that takes us out of Egypt is a male hand—both in the Bible and in our contemporary imaginations.

Perceiving the predominance of male language is not the same as understanding its importance, however. Ozick, for instance, begins her article with the question of God and dismisses it quickly. She does not deny the dominance of male imagery, but argues that reflection on the absence of female imagery "can only take us to quibbles about the incompetence of pronouns." If the Jewish-woman question is unrelated to theology, theological questions can only lead to dead ends. But as with Ozick's treatment of *halakhah*, this position seriously underestimates the depth of the issue. . . . The maleness of God is not arbitrary—nor is it simply a matter of pronouns. It leads us to the central question . . . of the Otherness of women, just as the Otherness of women leads to the maleness of God. . . .

Women are not educated as creators of tradition because we are Other, but of course we remain Other when we are seen through the filter of male experience without ever speaking for ourselves. The maleness of God calls for the silence of women as shapers of the Holy, but our silence in turn enforces our "Otherness" and a communal sense of the "rightness" of the male image of God. There is a "fit" in other words, a tragic coherence between the role of women in the community, and its symbolism, law, and teaching. The Otherness of women is part of the fabric of Jewish life.

Once again, and now most clearly, we are brought up against the impotence of halakhic change. For *halakhah* is part of the system that women have not had a hand in creating, neither in its foundations, nor as it was developed and refined. Not only is this absence reflected in the content of *halakhah*, it may be also reflected in its very form. How can we presume that if women add their voices to the tradition, *halakhah* will be our medium of expression and repair? How can we determine in advance the channels through which the tradition will become wholly Jewish, i.e., a product of the whole Jewish people, when women are only beginning consciously to explore the particularities of our own Jewishness? To settle on *halakhah* as the source of justice for women is to foreclose the question of women's experience when it has scarcely begun to be raised.

Clearly, the implications of Jewish feminism, while they include halakhic restructuring, reach beyond *halakhah* to transform the bases of Jewish life. Feminism demands a new understanding of Torah, God, and Israel: an understanding of Torah that begins with acknowledgement of the profound injustice of Torah itself. The assumption of the lesser humanity of women has poisoned the content and structure of the law, undergirding women's legal disabilities and our subordination in the broader tradition. This assumption is not amenable to piecemeal change. It must be utterly eradicated by the withdrawal of projection from women—the discovery that the negative traits attributed to women are also in the men who attribute them, while the positive qualities reserved for men are also in women. Feminism demands a new understanding of God that reflects and supports the redefinition of Jewish humanity. The long-suppressed femaleness of God, acknowledged in the mystical tradition, but even here shaped and articulated by men, must be recovered and reexplored and reintegrated into the Godhead. Last, feminism assumes that these changes will be possible only when we come to a new understanding of the community of Israel which includes the whole of Israel and therefore allows women to speak and name our experiences for ourselves. The outcome of these new understandings is difficult to see in advance of our turning. It is clear, however, that the courage, concern, and creativity necessary for a feminist transformation of Judaism will not be mustered by evading the magnitude of the required change.

Blu Greenberg, *On Women and Judaism*

Blu Greenberg (born 1936) has long been the most prominent voice for gender equality and feminism in the Orthodox Jewish community. Founder of JOFA (Jewish Orthodox Feminists of America), Greenberg has written widely on a host of modern Jewish issues related to women and other topics.

Blu Greenberg, *On Women and Judaism: A View from Tradition* (Philadelphia: Jewish Publication Society, 1981), 39–42, 43–44, 46.

We who are committed to traditional Judaism are standing today at the crossroads on the question of women. Feminism disturbs our previous equilibrium, for it makes a fundamental claim about women contrary to the model generated by Halakhah.

The feminist ideology can be summed up as follows:

1. Women have the same innate potential, capability, and needs as men, whether in the realm of the spirit, the word, or the deed.

2. Women have a similar capacity for interpretation and concomitant decision making.

3. Women can function fully as "outside" persons, in broader areas of society beyond the home.

4. Women can and should have some control over their own destinies, to the extent that such mastery is possible for anyone.

Let us reduce these broad statements from the level of generalization to a theology of woman as Jew:

1. A woman of faith has the same innate vision and existential longing for a redemptive-covenantal reality as a man of faith.[14] She has the same ability and need to be in the presence of God alone and within the context of the community. Such a woman is sufficiently mature to accept the responsibilities for this relationship and the rights that flow from these responsibilities. . . .

14. [Greenberg here adopts the language found in Joseph B. Soloveitchik, "The Lonely Man of Faith," *Tradition* 7:2 (Summer, 1965), pp. 5–67.]

2. Jewish women, as much as men, have the mental and emotional capacities to deal directly with the most sacred Jewish texts and primary sources. Jewish women are capable of interpreting tradition based on the sources. They can be involved in the decision-making process that grows out of the blending of inherited tradition and contemporary needs.

3. Some women, as some men, are capable of functioning in the positions of authority related to the religious and physical survival of the Jewish people.

4. Woman as a class should not find themselves in discriminatory positions in personal situations. In such matters as marriage and divorce, a woman should have no less control or personal freedom than a man, nor should she be subject to abuse resulting from the constriction of freedom.

. . . What I am saying is that Halakhah, contrary to the feminist values I have described above, continues to delimit women. In some very real ways, halakhic parameters inhibit women's growth, both as Jews and as human beings.

I do not speak here of all of Halakhah. One must be careful not to generalize from certain critical comments and apply them to the system as a whole. In fact, my critique could only grow out of a profound appreciation for the system in its entirety—its ability to preserve the essence of an ancient revelation as a fresh experience each day; its power to generate an abiding sense of kinship, past and present; its intimate relatedness to concerns both intimate and other-worldly; its psychological soundness; its ethical and moral integrity. On the whole, I believe a Jew has a better chance of living a worthwhile life if he or she lives a life according to Halakhah. Therefore, I do not feel threatened when addressing the question of the new needs of women in Judaism or admitting the limitations of Halakhah in this area. Indeed, it is my very faith in halakhic Judaism that makes me believe we can search within it for a new level of perfection, as Jews have been doing for three thousand years. . . .

There are certain external and internal factors that explain the insufficiency of the tradition with regard to women. The stratification of men and women in Judaism simply reflects the male-female hierarchical status in all previous societies in human history. Moreover, in light of the primary model of Jewish women as domestic creature—as wife, mother, dependent, auxiliary—all other roles and responsibilities that seemed to conflict with the primary model simply were eliminated.

I do not wish to imply that Jewish women were oppressed. This is far from the truth. Given the historically universal stratification of the sexes, plus the model of the Jewish woman as enabler and the exclusive male (rabbinic) option of interpreting the law, there could have been widespread abuse of the powerless. But this did not happen. In fact, the reverse is true; throughout rabbinic history one observes a remarkably benign and caring attitude toward women.

Nevertheless, there is a need today to redefine the status of women in certain areas of Jewish law. First, a benign and caring stance is not discernible in every last instance of rabbinic legislation. Second, paternalism is not what women are seeking nowadays, not even the women of the traditional Jewish community. Increasingly, such women are beginning to ask questions about equality, about a more mature sharing of responsibility, about divesting the power of halakhic interpretation and legislation of its singular maleness.

The techniques of reinterpretation are built right in the system. It was the proper use of these techniques that enabled rabbinic Judaism to be continuous with the past, even as it redefined and redirected the present and future. The techniques also allowed for diversity, for allowances based on local usage, for a certain kind of pluralism....

... [W]here there was a rabbinic will, there was a halakhic way. This is not to say that Talmudic and post-talmudic literature is not "the law of Moses at Sinai." It is that, but it is also the substance of rabbinic will finding a halakhic way. What shall we call it? Continuing revelation? Wise, interpretive judgment based on inherited tradition? An understanding, divinely given or intuited, of the appropriate moment for greater restraint, or relaxation of the rules, or heightened responsibility?...

It would seem, then, that the full equalization of women in Judaism should be consistent with the wider principles of Torah. In fact, we ought to go one step further. If the hierarchy of the sexes serves no religious function, if Halakhah has the capacity for reinterpretation, if equality is a basic positive value in Judaism, then it behooves the community and its leaders to take the initiative; together they must search for new ways to upgrade religious expression and new means by which to generate equality for women in tradition. No longer shall we hear the argument that women are demanding this or that of the Halakhah. Rather, the issue should be set forth in the following terms: Halakhah, the Jewish way, cries out for reinterpretation in the light of the new awareness of feminine equality, feminine potential.

For a biographical sketch, see Part Two, p. 78.

Rachel Adler, "I've Had Nothing Yet So I Can't Take More," *Moment* 8, no. 8
(September 1983): 22, 24, 26.

"Take some more Tea," the March Hare said to Alice very earnestly.

"I've had nothing yet," Alice replied in an offended tone: "so I can't take more."

"You mean you can't take less," said the Hatter: "it's very easy to take more
than nothing."

    LEWIS CARROLL, *Alice's Adventures in Wonderland*

The Mad Hatter, I have always felt, was guilty of a fallacy in the passage above.
At a tea party where the rules are constant and have been assented to by all the
guests, people can help themselves freely. At the Mad Hatter's sort of tea party,
however, it is not so easy to take more than nothing.

Being a Jewish woman is very much like being Alice at the Hatter's tea party.
We did not participate in making the rules, nor were we there at the beginning
of the party. . . . When our external reality is absurdity and madness, it is difficult
for us to retain internal coherence. We begin to ask, "Who are we, really?" We
are being invited by Jewish men to re-covenant, to forge a covenant which will
address the inequalities of women's position in Judaism, but we ask ourselves,
"Have we ever had a covenant in the first place? Are women Jews?"

. . . I never ask myself, "Am I, Rachel Adler, a Jew?" just as I never ask myself,
"Is there really a God?" These are both facts I know from my internal experience.
They form the core of my selfhood. My pain and the pain of other committed
Jewish women lies in the discrepancy between our internal and external realities.

. . . We are confronting what Mary Daly called methodolatry.[15] In a method-

---

    15. [Mary Daly (1928–2010), who described herself as "a radical lesbian feminist," was
a prominent feminist philosopher who taught at Boston College. In her book *Beyond God
the Father: Toward a Philosophy of Women's Liberation* (Boston: Beacon Press, 1973), she coined
the term "methodolatry."]

olatrous system, the choice of problems to be addressed is determined by the method being shaped to address questions. Questions that do not fit the categories of the method are simply classified as non-data. Patriarchal methods, says Daly, have obliterated women's own questions about the sanctification of their experience....

... When the tradition is brought to bear on the problems of Jewish women, it prefers to address the problems on which it has the most information: namely, the status problems of marriage, desertion, divorce, and *chalitzah*[16] which the tradition itself created and from whose consequences it now seeks to "protect" women since by its own rules they can never protect themselves.

The problem of "methodolatry" cannot be dismissed as an "Orthodox problem." It is a meta-halakhic problem, touching all Jews who believe the tradition possesses some relevance to modern Jewish life. Any wedding, for example, at which the groom says, "Behold, you are sanctified to me with this ring according to the laws of Moses and Israel," and any divorce issued unilaterally by the husband . . . is utilizing the categories of acquisition and manumission in which men are actors and women are their objects. A model of Jewish marriage and divorce in which men and women are equals could be constructed only by uprooting those entire categories of the tradition.[17]

... The problems I have outlined here are huge and painful, and I do not know how they are to be solved. Although it is hard for me to remember, I remind myself that I do not have to know how to solve them alone. I did not cause these problems by being a feminist. As Heschel demonstrates, what feminism exposes is Judaism's unfinished adjustment to the relativism and pluralism of the post-Enlightenment world.[18] The questions, then, are the following:

1. If the process of Judaism depends upon the continuous transformation of a body of received knowledge . . . to render it contextually relevant, and if this

16. [See footnote 10 on pp. 221–22.]

17. [Adler ultimately addressed this issue directly, and in her 1999 book *Engendering Judaism* she offered a novel, egalitarian form of the Jewish marriage contract, a *brit ahuvim* (lovers' covenant), for use by heterosexual and gay couples in lieu of the classical Jewish wedding contract, the *ketubah*. In this work, Adler explicitly rejected *kinyan* (acquisition) on the part of the husband toward his bride in the Jewish wedding ceremony as inherently patriarchal and unjust.]

18. [The reference here is to Susannah Heschel, "No Doors, No Guards: From Jewish Feminism to a New Judaism," *Menorah* 4 (March 1983): 1–2. See also the selection on pp. 217–19 of the present book, where Heschel also makes this point.]

knowledge excludes the experiences, perceptions, and concerns of women, then from where are Jewish women to derive their religious understandings and behavior, and how will these be authentically Jewish?

2. What shall be our stance toward the method and categories of the tradition, seeing that they have precluded the equality of women and men?

3. If the content of the tradition is in question, how will we retain our sense of commandedness, and how will we determine what we have been commanded?

4. How can we fashion a method that will systematically frame and name the Jewish experience of both men and women?

5. How can women be included as full and equal participants in the covenant, and through what sort of ritual observance will they be brought into the covenantal community?

6. Recognizing that it is idolatrous and blasphemous to behave as if God were inherently masculine, how will we expand our God-language both for theology and for prayer so that both masculine and feminine words and metaphors will be used to *name toward* God?

Until we answer these questions and formulate a just and consistent Judaism for our time, we must, to borrow a phrase from Adrienne Rich, "dive into the wreck." I dive into this shattered rotting hulk of the tradition which I have loved and hated, and I salvage pieces to keep: Sarah's laughter, Miriam's dancing, Deborah's song, *Mitzrayim* and *Y'tziat Mitzrayim*,[19] matzah, the journey-bread of a travelling woman; Shabbat, my grandmother's dented candlesticks; the story of the *Shechinah*, because her experience is mine. I, too, know what it is to be in exile, a stranger, an Other, in a land not my own. I, too, feel my incompleteness and seek to be whole. I, too, bear within me a ruined Temple and am always hoping to rebuild it.

May the *Shechinah* soon be restored to her place, and I to mine.

19. [Egypt and the Exodus from Egypt. The Hebrew word *Mitzrayim* is often linked to the notions of narrowness and entrapment.]

Julia Watts Belser, "Making Room for the
Divine She" / "Privilege and Disaster"

Julia Watts Belser (born 1977) was ordained a rabbi by the Academy for Jewish
Religion in California and received her doctorate in Talmud and religious studies
at the University of California, Berkeley. A professor at Georgetown University,
Belser is also on the board of Nehirim, a community of LGBTQ Jews and their allies.
A prominent activist for the rights of disabled and LGBTQ persons, Belser is also an
accomplished academic in the field of rabbinics.

a. Julia Watts Belser, "Making Room for the Divine She," accessed June 20,
2019, http://www.zeek.net/708she/.
b. Julia Watts Belser, "Privilege and Disaster: Toward a Jewish Feminist Ethics
of Climate Silence and Environmental Unknowing," *Journal of the Society of
Christian Ethics* 43, no. 1 (Spring/Summer 2014): 87–89.

A.

Goddess and Judaism are not irreconcilable. Jews can and do experience the
Divine as a feminine presence. Jews can and do serve Her as an expression of
their Jewish practice. The reality that most Jews through most of Jewish history
have related to and experienced God as He does not obligate all of us to do so.
In fact, Jewish ways of gendering the Holy have shifted considerably over the
course of our history. Yet regardless of how an individual soul experiences the
Holy Presence, claiming the freedom to know God as She can throw open a window on God that has long been closed. Understanding the Jewishness of *God who
is She* calls us to cut through constructs of language and culture, artifacts of old
metaphors and misperceptions—a process that can help us come closer to the
living Presence that reveals Itself in so many ways.

Goddess *is*. Goddess is a being, not a belief. Goddess is the name I give to the
Presence who births, sustains, and cradles this world and everything in it. She is
the One who binds us together, the fabric of the universe that surrounds us, and
the Being who forges us. She is the Holy that I know, the face of the Divine who
illuminates my life and guides my way. She is a Presence, not a theology. She is
the living core on which my life is built.

... Gender matters. But gender does not make a split in the fabric of the ultimate. Rather than splitting off Goddess from God and declaring them distinct and separate spheres, Jewish affirmations of divine unity and wholeness suggest that God is Goddess—a Goddess who is God who is Goddess. Gender matters. But gender is not a discontinuity that separates me and my Holy from the tapestry of my people. The discomfort the pronoun She provokes in certain quarters —and the rejoicing that it brings in others—testifies to the power gender has in our world. The panic the pronoun causes exposes a silence that often goes ignored. It calls into question the false neutrality of the masculine and opens wide a window of possibility and profound responsibility.

The presence of Goddess as an authentic and integral part of Jewish life emerges in community, as Jews who know and love Goddess craft our religious insights into the larger Jewish narrative. Religious experiences are not "born Jewish." They *become* Jewish as individuals and communities learn to express them Jewishly, to find a Jewish context for understanding and sharing them, to seam them into the larger tapestry of Judaism's sacred stories. When communities engage intentionally in this process, when we wrestle with the new and strive to integrate it into our understanding and practice of Judaism, we create Jewish authenticity.

Ultimately, I suspect, in a realm that is far removed from our own, gender *is* actually insignificant. *Ehiyeh Asher Ehiyeh*—the ultimate divine force that will be whatever it will be—has neither a womb nor a phallus to tangle our thoughts. But we live in a world in which gender matters. We live in a world scarred by the denial of the feminine sacred. Wounded by our loss of Goddess.

But She is present, no matter how the vagaries of history and tradition may have hidden Her. She is not erased, no matter how sacred scriptures may have silenced Her story. She is the stones and the sea, each leaf of every tree and the lines that lace up every human hand. She is the letters of Torah, if not always the words we read. She dwells within the soul of everyone who's ever searched for Her. She cradles this world and all the realms beyond it, just as she holds the hearts of all who love Her.

Those who love me, I love; and those who seek me will find me. (Proverbs 8:17)

B.

As a Jewish feminist ethicist, I ground my work in the call to commitment that Adrienne Rich lays out in the final lines of her long poem, "Natural Resources":

My heart is moved by all I cannot save:
so much has been destroyed
I have to cast my lot with those
who age after age, perversely,
with no extraordinary power,
reconstitute the world.[20]

From Rich's words, I draw vision for a Jewish feminist ethics that is a "recon-stituative ethics," an ethics that aims first and foremost toward the fashioning of a life-giving word and world. Central to this task is a commitment to the critical analysis of social power and structural violence, a commitment to disrupting oppression and alienation, a commitment to the practice of cultivating beauty, integrity, and awe. The task of engaging Jewish texts and traditions for the ser-vice of reconstituative ethics is not simply a call to comment upon or critique existing texts and traditions but a call to bring creative agency to bear in shap-ing a contemporary encounter with inherited tradition. It approaches religious inheritance with a commitment to create anew. Traditional texts serve as a goad, a provocation to consider unexpected dimensions of the question—not as a straightforward source of normative instruction about Jewish obligation. . . .

. . . Rabbinic and medieval texts had no way to envision the realities of the an-thropocene; they did not anticipate the scope and scale of present human capac-ity to alter the ecosystem. In light of the unprecedented nature of contemporary environmental devastation, traditional sources that urge ecological responsibil-ity do not always provide sufficient moral guidance for forging a twenty-first century environmental ethic.

Rather than seeking texts that address the subject of environmental distress, I look for narratives that capture continuities of social power and emotional re-sponse that can speak to the contemporary situation. To examine more closely the social politics of environmental ignorance, I turn to an unlikely source: a series of disaster stories in the Babylonian Talmud, commonly known as the Bavli. . . . A lengthy narrative sugya (section of text) from Bavli Gittin 55b–58a recounts the aftermath of the destruction of the Second Temple and the Bar Kokhba revolt in the first and second centuries CE, which resulted in profound Roman military and political domination in Judea. . . . These narratives of de-struction reveal the imprint of both rabbinic power and powerlessness. These

20. Adrienne Rich, "Natural Resources," in *The Dream of a Common Language: Poems, 1974–1977* (Repr., New York: W. W. Norton, 1993), 67.

Talmudic tales show the rabbis simultaneously constructing and exercising their own authority while also resisting the domination of Rome. Rabbinic tales of the destruction of Jerusalem represent a potent resource for grappling with religious response to unprecedented contemporary environmental disasters. Bavli Gittin's sugya[21] sheds light on critical ecojustice concerns: the estrangement from sacred land and the experience of exile; the coercive power of colonialism and the violence of empire; the difficulty of assessing the scope and stakes of crisis; the need to radically reconfigure religious meaning and practice; and the experience of cataclysmic loss—coupled with the possibility of resilience.

While Talmudic stories are often read as didactic literature designed to convey a straightforward moral message, I follow a trend in contemporary rabbinic scholarship that aims to parse the cultural tensions expressed through rabbinic narratives. Rather than drawing proscriptive ethical conclusions from rabbinic literature, I highlight the power of rabbinic story to convey moral complexity and to facilitate a deeper, more compelling engagement with ethical questions. Yet my work also takes a critical stance toward traditional literature, aiming to illuminate (and resist) hegemonic elements within rabbinic culture. While a feminist reconstituative ethics reaches back to tradition for insight, it does not privilege the values of the text as an unquestioned source of ethical authority. It remains always attuned to the way the tradition has been used to silence and wound....

As a feminist ethicist, rabbinic narratives make for uneasy conversation partners. These stories were crafted in the thoroughly masculinist environment of the rabbinic study house, within a Jewish subculture forged in large part through the Otherness of women. Yet these stories are also crafted in the shadow of Roman domination, by the empire's uneasy subjects. Rabbinic stories reflect both the experience of subjugation and domination. They reveal rabbinic resistance to the imprint of Roman power while they also betray the rabbis' own participation in hegemonic enterprises. Not uncommonly, rabbinic storytellers attempted to fashion their own sense of self as empowered and vigorous (colonized) men, often by constraining the place of their wives and effacing the voices of their daughters. Because they are neither unalloyed heroes nor victims; because they are resisting and refashioning power, dominance, and authority; because they are committed to their own reconstituative project, their stories are a compelling resource for reflecting on the contemporary moment.

21. [A passage in the Talmud discussing a specific issue in the Mishnah.]

Steven Greenberg (born 1956) was ordained an Orthodox rabbi by the Rabbi Isaac Elchanan Theological Seminary (RIETS) of Yeshiva University. The first openly gay Orthodox rabbi, he serves as Senior Teaching Fellow and Director, the Diversity Project at CLAL, the National Jewish Center for Learning and Leadership.

Steven Greenberg, *Wrestling with God and Men: Homosexuality in the Jewish Tradition* (Madison: University of Wisconsin Press, 2004), 49, 53–54, 135–38.

However one works it out, at least according to our two sages,[22] heterosexuality as we know it was not the original plan for humanity.

With this reading of Genesis the sages have not provided a positive mythic foundation for homosexual love, but what their reading offers is immensely important for us. First, this reading affirms that heterosexuality is not original. If anything was original, it was the androgynous *adam*, the first effort of creation. This first androgynous *adam* was perhaps too whole, too much like God. Having no distance to overcome, the creature perhaps began to long for longing, for a wholeness not to possess but to realize. The prohibition to eat of the tree of knowledge of good and evil introduced Adam to the very possibility of lack. The threat of death gave birth to the desire for union, for a love that cannot be conquered by death.

Second, there is no romance in two. Romantic love can comfort, but it cannot redeem. The pain of loneliness is not fixed with the healing of heterosexual union. For Adam and Eve, the experience of being one flesh does not defend them against mutual recriminations. . . . With a great deal of effort, the earth can be made to bear fruit, children can be born, a life of partnership can be negotiated, and love can be sustained, but nothing is whole or certain.

Last, this reading offers a trajectory for those of us eager to see the world

22. [The reference here is to rabbinic interpretations in *Genesis Rabbah* 8:1 of the apparent anomaly in the Genesis creation accounts, according to which it seems that the Adam, the first earthling, was both male and female. Greenberg concludes that the original plan for creation was a singular androgynous being. The more familiar version of Adam and Eve is developed in the second chapter of Genesis.]

healed when it comes to gender. The subjugation of females to males, punishment for the sin in the garden, is seen by the sages as a fracture in the plan, a
distortion of God's original intent. It must not be denied that in the larger corpus of the rabbinic tradition the rabbis most often enforced the power hierarchy
between the genders. In various ways, women were silenced and controlled,
infantilized and disempowered, as they were cared for, idealized, and protected.
However, the cracks in the fortress are visible, and the same sages point them
out to us, reminding us that the world is not as it ought to be. Since the gender
hierarchy is a broken condition, try as they may, they cannot fully contain the
desire to fix it. For all the limitations of their efforts, the sages often increased
the power of women beyond what was normative in the cultures around them.
Later generations of rabbis found ways to provide even greater independence for
women than did their predecessors. While the rabbinic record hardly conforms
to contemporary egalitarian standards, one finds the desire to see the hierarchy
healed and the moon restored.

> "Thinking again?" the Duchess asked.... "I have a right to think," said Alice....
> "Just about as much right," said the Duchess, "as pigs have to fly."
> LEWIS CARROLL, Alice in Wonderland

In many social worlds asking questions would be considered traitorous, bait
for the enemy. Such questions no one is permitted to ask....

In our moment to ask why two people of the same sex ought not be permitted to build a life together has become the epitome of such a question in the
Orthodox community. This was not always so. The law against homosexual
relations for nearly two thousand years was a rule like any other. Over the last
two generations liberal governments, psychologists, and even clergy of some
denominations have legitimated what was once deemed to be criminal, patho-
logical, or at the very least immoral behavior. The increased public presence of
gays and lesbians in day-to-day life, the rising political demands for equality and
legitimacy and the support that gay liberation has garnered among liberal Jews
has turned the question into a threat and raised the stakes enough to demand a
response from a great American Orthodox scholar, not merely on homosexuality, but on the very legitimacy of asking why.

In the 1970s, a Swiss publisher found a previously unknown manuscript of
a Torah commentary attributed to the revered Rabbi Yehudah HeHasid of Re-
gensberg, a German pietist of the twelfth century. Publication had begun when

Rabbi Daniel Levy, concerned about certain "heresies" that he found in it, sent a copy to a number of religious authorities. Rabbi Feinstein and others tried to halt the publication of the book,[23] claiming that it was a forgery. . . .

Among the alleged heresies found in the Torah commentary of Rabbi Yehudah is his comment on the prohibition in Leviticus of homosexual intercourse in which he addresses its rationale. Here Rav Moshe makes his opinion known concerning the legitimacy of asking why.

> When the manuscript was sent to me by Rabbi Daniel, I saw in it another matter. The wicked had intended to weaken the prohibition of male sexual intercourse, first by the question of why the Torah had prohibited it. In itself this is a great evil that weakens the prohibition for the wicked ones who have this ugly craving, which is so detestable that even the nations of the world know that there are no abominations like it. It needs no reason since it is an abomination, despised by all the world. All understand that transgressors of this sin are corrupt and not members of civilization at all. And when the reason is sought for this prohibition, the asking of such a question removes [from the prohibition] all the obscenity, shame, and disgrace, and completely disparages it. Moreover, his rationale [for the prohibition] is to ensure that men marry women and fulfill the commandment to reproduce. . . . It is prohibited to publish this, just as if it were heresy, since it reads a Torah text in a fashion contrary to the Halakha. . . .[24]

The diatribe of this responsum is caustic and painful. However, putting that factor aside for the moment, one must admit that politically speaking, Rav Moshe is right. Reasons undermine taboos. As I read this responsum for the first time, I had a very unsettling feeling. I realized that I was doing exactly what Rav Moshe feared would be done. Among my central tasks in this book is to ask why homosexual intercourse is forbidden in the first place and then to theorize about the prohibition in ways that shed new light on it, its meaning, and application. According to his description, my work would seem to be an elaborate justification of vice, an attempt to halakhically rationalize sexual license.

So how does one respond in a meaningful way to a taboo? One way, of course, is to insist that the whole frightful mess is superstitious hogwash. There is no

---

23. [Rabbi Moshe Feinstein (1895–1986) was a leading halakhic authority in the United States, where he arrived in 1937, and his reputation and influence were international.]

24. *Iggerot Moshe, Yoreh De'ah* 3:115.

curse, no ruination, no cosmic blight attendant to homosexual sex. A demysti-fication of sexuality in general and of gay sex in particular seems imperative in order to proceed thoughtfully toward understanding.

However, as a religious person, I am caught at this juncture, unable to chase away the old sacred narratives which map a holy and mysterious world and replace them with objective data. Demystification or disenchantment, as Peter Berger would call it, is one of the calling cards of the modern era. When mys-tery and transcendence are washed away and only the scientifically observable and the bureaucratically definable are left, we are perhaps easily freed from our demons; however, we are also deprived of a spiritual life. Where there is no won-der, no mystery, no meandering, no sense of a Presence hiding in the wings, then life is deprived of its deepest meanings.

And, of course, it is no surprise that sex is one of the things that we have the most trouble demystifying. Even though contraceptives have spliced sex from inevitable life-making, we still feel that the sexual experience is much more than can be accounted for by the physiology of orgasmic release. Sex is always a mat-ter of the soul. The Jewish mystics believed that sexual desire did not originate in the person, but was sent down from above.

It remains for us then to explore the tools of demystification, in this case the un-tabooing of a prohibition, in the service of knowledge, in a way that will not exile us from a holy world. The rabbis of the first and second centuries aimed their efforts at just such a paradoxical goal. They invented a way of thinking and talking about scripture that unhinged certainties, opened up multiple meanings and, by doing so, demystified the biblical law—and then they turned around and remystified it by finding, inside their conversational Torah study, the very workings of the Divine.

Jay Michaelson, "Toward a Queer
Jewish Theology"

> Born in 1971, Jay Michaelson is a graduate of Columbia College and Yale Uni-
> versity Law School. He is currently the legal affairs columnist at the *Daily Beast*.
> He was the founder and from 2004 to 2013 the Executive Director of Nehirim,
> an LGBTQ Jewish organization. His PhD thesis in Jewish thought from the Hebrew
> University of Jerusalem relates to the thought of the eighteenth-century anti-
> nomian heretic Jacob Frank.

> Jay Michaelson, "Toward a Queer Jewish Theology," *Sh'ma* December 1, 2005,
> accessed August 21, 2019, http://shma.com/2005/12/toward-a-queer-jewish
> -theology/.[25]

Notwithstanding the rhetoric of denial prevalent in some religious circles,
sexual orientation is known, by those with firsthand experience of homosexuality as well as by scientists who study it, to be either genetically determined or
so deeply developmentally ingrained as to be fundamentally unchangeable. For
Jews, this reality of gay and lesbian identity presents a theological question: why
does God make some people gay?

For many people today, the question is only the first half of a larger dilemma
—namely how, if God makes some people gay, we ought to read the prohibitions of Leviticus 18 and 20. Quite a lot of ink has already been spilled on this
subject. Most who maintain that the prohibitions extend beyond anal intercourse between men—the extent of the p'shat of the Levitical text—still insist
that sexuality is not fundamentally determined (which is what I mean by "God
makes people gay"), but is, in some way, chosen. This despite the lived experience of gay and lesbian people, the overwhelming evidence of neurological science, and, not least, shocking rates of suicide among gay and lesbian youth (it's
odd to kill yourself for a choice, is it not?). Others, recognizing that sexuality is

---

25. Dr. Michaelson presented a significantly expanded version of the reflections in
this essay in the 2017 Gilberto Castañeda lecture at Chicago Theological Seminary. That
lecture is available online at https://youtube/VOo5vrt67Wo.

not chosen, feel compelled to take a more restrictive reading of Leviticus 18 in order to maintain our fundamental beliefs about God and the mitzvot: e.g., that God loves human beings and does not want them mutilated or distorted, or that the commandments are meant to govern responsible behavior, or that they are meant to be kept at all. Still others, of course, simply avoid the theological problem by denying the Divine origins of the biblical text and bringing our ancient holiness codes in line with contemporary thinking.

But homosexuality itself presents a theological question apart from how we read two verses of the Torah. Is being gay like having brown eyes—a biological quirk of no religious significance? Or, given the central status in Judaism of procreation, family, patrimony, and gender binarism, is there something more theologically significant about people who, because of their souls' physiognomies, defy the traditional constructions of each?

Other religious traditions provide a wealth of possible answers to the theological riddle of homosexuality. For example, several Native American traditions believed that people whom we might call gay or lesbian possessed both male and female souls and assigned to them roles as priests, shamans, and healers. This is the phenomenon Europeans called the berdache, described at length in the work of anthropologists Walter L. Williams, Will Roscoe, and others. Mirroring similar phenomena in Japan, India, Africa, the classical Mediterranean, and, in a perverse way, the campaigns against witches (i.e. lesbians) and fairies (gay men) in Europe, the berdache was seen as special, or kadosh—literally, set aside, in Hebrew. Not only was s/he set apart from ordinary life but s/he lived in a state of liminality, and that in-between-ness was itself regarded as a hallmark of the sacred. In such societies, gays and lesbians existed to be sacred priests of the liminal.

Within Judaism, we are warned against speculating why God creates or manifests in a particular way; to do so can lead to a dehumanizing reductivism and a dangerous claim to know the will of the Divine. But we can approach the question of homosexuality by observing some distinctive, theologically-relevant experiences of gay and lesbian people. The yield is abundant. On a spiritual level, how we experience love of humans shapes how we experience love of God. On an intellectual level, it colors how we conceive God. On a physical level, it changes how we manifest and seek the Divine in the world. And on an emotional level, it gives form and meaning to the yearnings of the heart. When I chant Yedid Nefesh,[26] the moving, homophilic, medieval love song for God, I

26. [This liturgical poem is attributed to Elazar Azikri (1533–1600).]

think of my relationship to the yedid, the (male) beloved that is distinctively flavored by my love of men. When I read of the receptivity of Isaac, the effeminate beauty of Joseph, or the love between David and Jonathan, I find a resonance between my own experience and these nontraditionally-gendered Jewish heroes. As described in Daniel Boyarin's work on the "effeminate" Jewish man, this ideal resounds through the generations.[27]

Theology—thinking rigorously about God—is necessarily impacted by such "queer" self-images, images of the Divine, conceptions of how Divine relates to the world, readings of text, and experiences of how love, religion, and spirituality manifest in the world. The point is not, trivially, that David and Jonathan were lovers; the point is that when a kabbalist imagines his soul to be a female entity uniting with the male godhead, ordinary assumptions about gender are disrupted, with theologically interesting consequences—kal v'chomer[28] when that God is both male and female and is constantly shifting gender roles and attitudes. Both in our tradition and in the lived experience of gay, lesbian, bisexual, and transgender people, God/dess is not only male, not only transcendent; S/he is not only female, not only immanent; there is a unity of sames as well as opposites, and we are all God in drag. In other words, the conversation is about soul, not genitals.

Even the non-normativity of LGBTQ identity can be a productive contributor to theological discourse. Most Jewish theology, philosophical and mystical, tells us that the more we upset familiar assumptions and ways we think about God, the closer we are to God. Labels that come from our own experience—God is male, God is just, God is the source of wonder—are projections. They can reduce the ineffability of the transcendent and flatten our experience of the immanent into categories shaped by desire and aversion. In this light, to "queer" (invoking that term as it is used in the academic discipline of queer theory: i.e., as rejecting the notion that binary gender and normative sexuality are natural categories) theology helps to undermine normative tendencies in theological thinking. Removing assumptions of Divine gender, reading Kabbalah as positing a Divine hermaphrodite hiding in the closet of the world, denying that categories of gender even exist ultimately at all—all move us closer to the Infinity and Divine Oneness. The farther we get from our preconceived notions of what

27. [Here the reference is to Daniel Boyarin, *Unheroic Conduct: The Rise of Heterosexuality and the Invention of the Jewish Man* (Berkeley: University of California Press, 1997).]

28. ["All the more so."]

"identity" is supposed to be and the more open we are to categories beyond our imagination or experience, the closer we are to realization.

Or, moving from negative theology to positive experience, there is what Franz Rosenzweig called the "first primary word"—love. All Western mystics express their relationship to God in erotic terms, and it is no mere metaphor; in the Oneness of the One, the mystics report a great knowing love. To be holy, the Kabbalists write, is to be on fire with love for God. Thus, on a superficial level, if a gay man experiences love of "like" rather than love of "unlike," this changes how he conceives, embraces, and loves God. On a deeper level, if he experiences unity not as union-with-an-opposite, but of an internal embrace of his own masculine and feminine natures—which is what the Zohar calls the essence of mystical practice—that, too, reconfigures (in a provocative, nondualistic way) what unio mystica is really about.

Another aspect of love: to be a self-accepting gay or lesbian person, one generally must go through a certain process of negation and affirmation. In homophobic societies, gays or lesbians are told that how they love is wrong. Yet at some point, to live a full life, they must learn for themselves that these statements are wrong and that love is right. This inversion forms a moral conscience and teaches what it is to love God b'chol levavcha, b'chol nafeshecha, u'v'chol me-odecha, with the whole heart, body, mind, and spirit. The result is a distinctively complex, self-aware mode of religious erotic consciousness, which resonates in the queer mysticism of Rumi, Hafiz, and Judah Halevy; the poems of Whitman, Wilde, Sappho, and Shakespeare; the art of Michelangelo and Da Vinci.

The process of relating to sacred text, liturgy, and teshuvah is indelibly colored by the same process of "coming out" morally, intellectually, and spiritually. At first, the religious lesbian or gay man loves religion and thus hates him/herself. Then, s/he may either affirm the self and hate religion, continue to repress the self and "love" religion, or, somehow, reconcile religion with the reality of love and sexual expression. Even if the third option is chosen, though, gay religious consciousness is necessarily distrustful, because it has seen—and more importantly, felt—how rules, codes, and even the operation of conscience itself can actually be tools of oppression and self-repression. Of course, straight people may come to this realization also. But religious gay people must.

Images of the ineffable are always projections, and relationships to the transcendent always carry the character of myth. Yet to the extent that we conceptualize the One at all, we have no choice but to do so from our conceptions of love, self, and world; tradition, text, and tribe. Questions of boundary, models of the soul, ideals of human behavior, experiences of love, and relationships with sacred text—these are but a few of the areas in which sexuality matters to theology, and I have stated them here only by way of a prolegomenon. Really, if theology is thinking about God, the only way sexuality couldn't matter would be if we really believed that how we love has nothing to do with how we think, imagine, dream, and create. What an impoverished life that would be.

Benay Lappe (born 1960) is a Talmudist who graduated from the University of Illinois and earned her MA in rabbinic literature from the University of Judaism (now the American Jewish University). Lappe was ordained a rabbi at the Jewish Theological Seminary of America and is CEO and Rosh (Head of) Yeshiva at Svara in Chicago.

Benay Lappe, "The New Rabbis: A Postscript," in *Torah Queeries: Weekly Commentaries on the Hebrew Bible*, ed. Gregg Drinkwater, Joshua Lesser, and David Shneer (New York: New York University Press, 2009), 311–13.

The visionaries who picked up the pieces of a shattered Judaism two thousand years ago, after the destruction of the Second Temple and the crashing of Biblical Judaism, were courageous, creative, out-of-the-box thinking, fringy radicals. Queer, if you will. Not in the sense of sexuality or gender, perhaps, but in what *being* those very kinds of people usually makes you: courageous, creative, out-of-the-box thinking, fringy, and radical. And deeply attuned to that still, small voice inside and confident of the truth it is telling you even when the whole world is telling you something else. These guys called themselves Rabbis. Teachers. They were the architects of a Judaism that would have been virtually unrecognizable to those practicing Judaism of the Temple era.

Their Judaism, like ours, was crashing. Theirs, in many ways, was no longer physically possible. Ours, in many ways, is no longer morally plausible. They had a new take on what it meant to be a human being and took a shot at playing it out. Their radically transformed Judaism survived and we are its descendants. In a way, it was easier for them than it is for us. The Judaism they knew was over. They had nothing to lose. No one could pretend that sitting in (the) Temple was "working for them" any more—there was no more Temple. It's harder for us. We've got a lot to lose. But much of what we are afraid to lose is illusion, the illusion that Judaism today is working for us all even when it's not working for most of us. And it cannot work for most of us until it understands all of us.

Queer people (along with women, the deaf, the disabled, and people of color, among many others) have important—*essential*—things to say about what life is really like and the Tradition needs to hear. And although the Rabbis may have delegitimated the God-spoke-to-me kind of prophecy as a source of new Jewish law two millennia ago, they elevated our informed ethical impulse to the status of Torah itself and called it *svara*.

These queer rabbis took their outsider insights—their sensitivity to those marginalized and oppressed by the Torah itself, their courage to stand up for them and mess with the Tradition to incorporate them—and declared their informed internal ethical impulse an authentic source of God's will. They deemed it a source of Jewish legal change as authoritative as a verse in the Torah itself —so much so that a law that they created out of *svara* has the same status as one that appears verbatim in Torah itself—*d'oraita*. And they even went further than that. They declared that one's *svara* could even trump a verse in the Torah when the two conflicted.

Svara is a term and a concept that has been kept virtually secret—certainly in its far-reaching implications—for over fifteen hundred years. It is not taught even to rabbis or rabbinical students today. In my six years of rabbinical school at the Conservative Movement's flagship, The Jewish Theological Seminary, the word was never uttered. Not once. We were never assigned a text that contained it—though hundreds do. Instead, we were taught, as if it were Jewish dogma, the lie that our leaders have succeeded in conveying to most Jews: that when it comes to certain verses in the Torah, "There's nothing we can do," "Our hands are tied," "If we could change it, we would." Understanding the talmudic concept of *svara* exposes these excuses as the untruths that they are.

That is why queer Jewish learning must begin with an understanding of the game-changing concept of *svara*. Yet it is understandable that *svara* would not be taught in seminaries. Seminaries (particularly movement-affiliated ones) are typically in business to perpetuate the status quo of an era long gone—not to teach mechanisms of potentially radical change. *Svara* allows *any* change—even to the point of uprooting the entire Tradition itself—to create a system that better achieves the Tradition's ultimate goals. It is a mechanism of change that arguably should be entrusted only to those who are committed stakeholders in the Jewish enterprise. My reading of Talmud also tells me that the Rabbis who came up with this potentially dangerous and potentially chaos-creating source of change required its practitioners to be learned in the Tradition. This cannot be overstated. They did not believe that *svara* was merely one's uneducated "gut feeling" but that it was one's moral impulse that was deeply influenced by having been steeped in the intricacies of the values, principles, and concerns of the entire Jewish Tradition as well as by a broad exposure to the world and its people....

You cannot be a Jewish ignoramus and claim that "what I think is right" is *svara*. It is not. And neither can you have never met a queer person and presume to legislate on matters of, well, just about anything in Jewish law. The Rabbis of the Talmud were explicit, though, that exercising one's *svara* to upgrade the Tradition—to play the game, as it were—did not require rabbinic ordination. It didn't for them, nor should it for us. But it did require learning.

Like that small band of queer Tradition-changers and inventors two thousand years ago, most of the new Tradition-changers and inventors of this next era of Judaism may not be ordained. They will, though, like their predecessors, have to possess learning and *svara*. The queer Jews who take up the challenge will be Judaism's new Rabbis.

The fact that each queer person is still alive is a testament to a willingness to heed the truth of one's inner voices when the world would have queer people silence them, and to do so at great personal cost. Queers have been willing to face inconvenient truths to live fuller, more human lives. The prophetic insight of queer Jews is ultimately less about sexuality and gender than it is about the imperative to live by one's *svara*. And that, it turns out, is a very old Jewish idea.

My dream is that when every queer Jewish kid comes out, he or she or ze will know—having already learned about the concept of *svara* in Hebrew school—that the voice they are choosing to listen to does not only place them *outside* of Jewish tradition or in conflict with God's will but is the most authoritative manifestation of both....

... Go and learn, refine and develop your *svara*, and use it to make Judaism ... places where we are all freer to live more *fully human* lives.

Jane Rachel Litman (born 1955) was ordained a rabbi in 1989 by the Reconstructionist Rabbinical College. Openly bisexual, Litman has taught in many academic settings and has written widely on LGBTQ rights.

Jane Rachel Litman, "Born to Be Wild: A Critique of Determinism," in *Balancing on the Mechitza: Transgender in Jewish Community*, ed. Noach Dzmura (Berkeley, CA: North Atlantic Books, 2010), 229–34.

One common political strategy of contemporary gay and trans rights advocates is to maintain that people who are variant from the norm in their sexual or gender identities are "born that way," and have no volition in the matter. This strategy is a response to years of oppressive theory that pathologizes LGBT identity as an illness, or—worse still—vilifies it as a sin. . . .

However, though the determinist argument may afford short-term political gains, I believe that a mindful examination of this claim is important. In my view the secular political doctrine that gender/sexual identity is invariably determined (the mechanism remains unspecified) at birth has unintended and detrimental consequences for both LGBT people and the movement for gender/sexual identity freedom.

There are also several Jewish versions of the deterministic discourse. One Jewish approach rests on the rabbinic doctrine that if one is physically unable to perform a certain mitzvah, one is not obligated to do so. The classic example is a person without hands. Such a person is not halakhically obligated to perform the mitzvah of laying tefillin. . . . Proponents of this idea argue that male homosexuality . . . is a physical bodily disability that renders a man unable to engage in a fulfilling sexual relationship with a woman. He is therefore not required to engage in one, just as the person with no hands is not required to lay tefillin.

Rabbi Steven Greenberg, in his book *Wrestling with God and Men*, presents a similar though not identical approach. Greenberg suggests that homosexuality falls into the halakhic (Jewish legal) category of *oness*, a compulsion or power beyond control. In certain cases, for example a Sabbath medical emergency an *oness* allows [for] a transgression of normal halakhic boundaries. It is not my aim to engage either of these arguments halakhically, but rather to note their determinist foundations and to examine the moral implications of any determinist approach for LGBT and in particular transgender people.

According to secular and halakhic "born that way" arguments, both gender and sexual identity are binary categories. There are only two genders—male and female—and two and only two sexual identities, heterosexual and homosexual. Anyone who does not fit the sexual binary . . . undermines the binary determinist discourse. Self-identified trannies and genderqueers need not apply.

What's wrong with a determinist "born that way" approach? Most importantly, it doesn't reflect reality. It displaces real human experience with a political theory. I'm reminded of the midrash about the sin of Sodom (Sanhedrin 109b). According to Jewish tradition, the people of Sodom had a community guesthouse with a single bed. If a guest to the city was too short for the bed, the citizens of Sodom put the person to the rack. If the person was too tall, they cut off the guest's feet and legs to fit. This gruesome story is particularly ironic in the context of this essay. The transgression of Sodom wasn't homosexuality, but literally and brutally forcing human beings to fit an already existing rigid structure.

Human beings aren't merely male and female, heterosexual and homosexual. People are complex aggregates of hormones, genes, body structures, social mores, cultural contexts, and personal styles. As early as 1948 sex researchers such as Alfred Kinsey expressed sexual identity as a spectrum rather than two rigid categories. . . .

. . . [G]ender theorists are . . . increasingly understanding gender identity as a spectrum or multidimensional grid rather than two separate and discrete binary categories. It turns out that we humans are more than our chromosomes and hormones. The determinist argument of the "born that way" crowd reduces the humanity of all people by ignoring our complexity.

Another midrash (Mishnah Sanhedrin 4:5) teaches that while in Caesar's mint all the coins are the same, in God's mint each coin emerges unique. "Born that way" theorists want God's mint to be a slightly different version of Caesar's mint. This is sad. Human beings are wonderfully and miraculously diverse both in their individual selves and their cultures.

In addition, people change and transform over the course of their lives. Trans activist Kate Bornstein . . . has identified as a male, a female, and neither male nor female. How can the "born that way" argument square with Kate's authentic life experience? . . . Not only does the "born that way" argument avert its eyes from reality, it reduces the richness of authentic human difference into an unnatural and humanly constructed sameness and conformity. . . .

. . . I believe that . . . Jewish activists should challenge any notion based on determinism or binary categories. As Jews we claim the right to pursue our varied Jewish paths without coercion from the majority or claims of biological determinism; I suggest that as queer people and allies, we must do the same.

Joy Ladin (born 1961) is an American poet and the David and Ruth Gottesman Professor of English at Stern College of Yeshiva University. A graduate of Sarah Lawrence College who received an MFA from the University of Massachusetts, she received her doctorate from Princeton University. Ladin is the first openly transgender person to teach at an Orthodox institution.

Joy Ladin, *The Soul of the Stranger* (Waltham, MA: Brandeis University Press, 2019), 32–33.

The ideas that gender is a human invention and that gender can change may seem startlingly new, but they are there in the opening chapters of Genesis. Adam's version of gender consists of a single binary, man and woman. But in the verse that follows his response to first seeing Eve, gender is transformed, as the Torah expands the gender binary to include the mothers and fathers, wives and husbands, who will populate the future. The Torah does not envision transgender identities, but the idea that gender can not just change, but change radically, in a single generation, is at the heart of the biblical genesis of gender.

Above all, Genesis lays the ground for accepting people who don't fit the binary gender categories by reminding us that people don't have to be gendered to be human. As we saw, when God creates human beings at the end of Genesis 1, they are created without gender, because the differences between male and female bodies have not yet been given meaning; in the second creation story in Genesis 2, humanity is again created without gender, because God at first only created Adam, who, because he is unique, cannot have a gender.

By showing us that we do not need gender to be human, the Torah not only offers a basis for the acceptance of the humanity of transgender people. It also frees us to recognize the ways in which transgender people do not fit binary gender-categories, to notice that there are women who have facial hair and men who don't, women without breast tissue and men with plenty, women who are over six feet tall and men who are under five feet, women who don't have uteruses and men who don't have testicles, women with low voices and men with high voices. When we remember that, as the first two chapters of Genesis show, our humanity does not depend on gender, we can acknowledge, without fear or shame, the aspects of ourselves that don't fit the gender to which we have been assigned and the ways in which thinking of ourselves as only and always male or female limits our understanding of who we are and what we can be. In this way, the biblical account of the genesis of gender lays the ground for accepting the dazzling variety not just of transgender people, but of humanity.

VII | Peoplehood

Writing in the journal *Sh'ma* in honor of the ninetieth birthday of Mordecai Kaplan, Emil Fackenheim acknowledged what Kaplan had seen all along and what Fackenheim and others had only come to appreciate later in life: the Jewish people had to be the Archimedean point from which all Jewish thought would emerge. Fackenheim praised Kaplan for realizing this long before he did and for advancing this position so forcefully, and he saluted Kaplan for his "indomitable love for *amcha* [the Jewish people]."[1]

Of course, Fackenheim was correct when he associated Kaplan with this position. After all, in his 1934 preface to *Judaism as a Civilization*, Kaplan wrote that in an address he had delivered in 1909 before the alumni of the Teacher's Institute of the Jewish Theological Seminary at the behest of Solomon Schechter, he "developed the thesis that the future of Judaism demanded that all Jewish teaching and practical activity be based on the proposition that the Jewish religion existed for the Jewish people and not the Jewish people for the Jewish religion. That thesis marked a Copernican revolution in my understanding of Judaism."[2]

By his own admission, Kaplan had begun to make the Jewish people central to his thinking by 1909. This emphasis in his thought only grew through the influence of his colleague Horace Kallen and others throughout the first decades of the century. By 1934, Kaplan was able to articulate the importance of the Jewish people for Jewish thought and life in his *Judaism as a Civilization*. Yet Kaplan only coined the term "peoplehood"—and even then, rather offhandedly—in the early 1940s, as he grasped for an expression of "*'am yisrael'* the people of Israel" that went beyond what he regarded as the chauvinistic-aggressive meaning of "nationalism" in the political lexicon of the post–World War II era.[3] It was only in 1949, in his *The Future of the American Jew*,

1. [Emil Fackenheim, *Sh'ma* 4, no. 79 (October 18, 1974): 145.]

2. [Mordecai Kaplan, *Judaism as a Civilization* (New York: Macmillan, 1934), xxx.]

3. [For an extensive description of the development of the term and Kaplan's role in its formulation, see Noam Pianko, *Jewish Peoplehood: An American Innovation* (New Brunswick, NJ: Rutgers University Press, 2015), 14–66.]

that he fully defined the phrase "Jewish peoplehood." His definition of "Jewish peoplehood" is an "ethnic consciousness that makes a group into a people" and that causes individual Jews to realize that they are part of "an indivisible corporate entity"[4] came to dominate much of twentieth-century American Jewish life and thought. However, the popularity of this notion could not prevent dissenting voices from questioning the adequacy of the meaning Kaplan assigned to this term. "Jewish peoplehood" was destined to be a topic of robust conversation and disagreement among American Jewish thinkers from virtually the first moment Kaplan advanced this idea.

In the last part of this book, we attempt to show how exchanges and arguments over Jewish peoplehood have taken place over the past eighty years. The first selection comes from Kaplan himself and presents the substance of how he conceptualized the term. The Zionist and ethical-naturalistic dimensions of the term as he presented it are unmistakable, as is his conviction that Jewish peoplehood as he understood it would contribute to the revitalization of Judaism in America and provide a source of healing to a world recently torn apart by war.

The next selection is taken from the work of Simon Rawidowicz, who rejected the "Zionocentric" thrust of Kaplan's thought. While he shared much of Kaplan's commitment to Jewish peoplehood, Rawidowicz refused to affirm the centrality of the land of Israel in Judaism and insisted that the diaspora was an equal partner with Israel in the life of the Jewish people. He championed the indivisibility of Jewish peoplehood, with the land of Israel and the diaspora as coequal partners in the Jewish enterprise. George Steiner departs from Rawidowicz, and the passage excerpted from his writings is not only fiercely anti-Zionist but asserts that Jewish peoplehood—the Jewish people's "homeland"—centers on the "text" rather than any physical locale.

The American-born Arthur Cohen, who had studied and dialogued with Kaplan during his years as a student at the Jewish Theological Seminary and beyond, emphasized the voluntary nature of Jewish peoplehood in an American setting, where the corporate political nature of the Jewish community had completely dissolved. In the excerpt chosen for this volume, Cohen maintains that Jewish peoplehood rests on a theological basis that speaks of Israel "as a special instrument of God"—a formulation far removed from that of

4. [Mordecai M. Kaplan, *The Future of the American Jew* (New York: Macmillan, 1942), 63.]

his erstwhile teacher and dialogue partner Kaplan. Cohen offers a theological alternative to an approach that makes peoplehood a starting point, and he instead comes to a sense of identification with the people Israel as the result of a personal creedal commitment.

Closely allied to though distinct from Cohen's work is the writing of the Orthodox philosopher Michael Wyschogrod. Raised as a boy in the *Torah 'im derekh eretz* philosophy of German-Jewish Neo-orthodoxy,[5] Wyschogrod maintains that Jewish peoplehood is embedded in the carnal election of Israel by God. His emphasis on "the body of faith" runs counter to the contemporary Western tendency to promote an ideal and abstract notion of chosenness.

The prominent feminist theologian Judith Plaskow, in her pathbreaking *Standing Again at Sinai*, takes direct exception to the linkage Wyschogrod draws between "election and Jewish peoplehood." While she regards "the covenant at Sinai" as "the root experience of Judaism," Plaskow notes that women are "invisible" at the moment of Sinaitic revelation. The failure to include women and others in all their particularity in the Jewish community is an egregious wrong that contemporary notions of Jewish peoplehood must rectify. Plaskow demands the creation of a more expansive and less inherently hierarchical conception of Jewish community and peoplehood.

The iconoclastic scholar and contemporary Jewish commentator Shaul Magid argues that traditional notions of Jewish peoplehood are outmoded in a postethnic America where intermarriage in the Jewish community and the larger world abounds. Drawing on both sociological and theological sources, he asserts that new notions of the "Jewish collective" must emerge to ensure Jewish survival. Steven M. Cohen and Jack Wertheimer disagree directly with Magid and maintain that the contemporary American Jewish community should not surrender to the postethnic reality of modern-day America. Instead, they argue that traditional notions of Jewish peoplehood, with all that such notions entail, should be championed.

Arthur Hertzberg and Paula Hyman, writing for a symposium sponsored by the American Jewish Committee in the aftermath of the assassination of Israeli Prime Minister Yitzhak Rabin in 1995, indicate how difficult, if not impossible, the reality of a united Jewish people is to achieve in light of the

5. [The *Torah 'im derekh eretz* philosophy of German-Jewish Neo-Orthodoxy affirmed the worth of both religious and secular culture and education.]

political divisions that mark the contemporary Jewish world. Dianne Cohler-Esses and Lewis Gordon further complicate the question of Jewish peoplehood by bearing witness to the sociological and racial dimensions that mark and inform this subject. The writing of Cohler-Esses as a Jew of Syrian descent and that of Gordon as a Jew of color require that the positions on Jewish ethnicity and solidarity of other thinkers in this part of the present book not be reduced to simplifications. They indicate that Jewish peoplehood constitutes a multiracial and multiethnic reality.

Finally, Part Seven ends with an excerpt from the 2016 work of scholar Noam Pianko. He points out that Plaskow and other scholars challenge "the very idea that there could be one static essence that defines the Jewish people" and, like Magid, he calls for a "fundamental modification in the vision of Jewish collectivity." Indeed, Pianko contends that the utility of the concept of "peoplehood" may have run its course and calls for its abandonment in favor of what he labels "the Jewishhood project." While his is undoubtedly not the last word on the topic, he does point the conversation in what may be novel directions. Thus our sources see Kaplan's neologism "peoplehood" introduced, expanded, and challenged over the course of eight decades.

In his 1964 essay "Confrontation," Joseph Soloveitchik argued that Jews are "the bearers of a double charismatic load, that of the dignity of man and that of the covenantal community."[6] Developing his theme, he made an assertion that has been at the heart of American Jewish musing on peoplehood over the decades: "There is no identity without uniqueness."[7] The fabric of Jewish identity and the meaning of uniqueness in an American setting continue to intrigue, inspire, unite, and divide Jews in North America.

To be a Jew in the twentieth century
Is to be offered a gift.[8]

6. [Joseph B. Soloveitchik, "Confrontation," *Tradition* 6, no. 2 (1964): 17.]

7. [Soloveitchik, "Confrontation," 18. Soloveitchik's views of Jewish peoplehood in light of the creation of the State of Israel, including his distinction between a covenant of fate and a covenant of destiny, are succinctly expressed in a 1956 lecture. See Joseph B. Soloveitchik, *Kol Dodi Dofek: Listen My Beloved Knocks*, trans. and ed. David Z. Gordon (New York: Yeshiva University, 2006).]

8. [Muriel Rukeyser, "Letter to the Front," in *The Collected Poems of Muriel Rukeyser*, ed. Janet E. Kaufman, Anne F. Herzog, and Jan Heller Levi (Pittsburgh: University of Pittsburgh Press, 2005), 643.]

The opening words of Muriel Rukeyser's 1944 poem may serve as a coda to this exploration of the American Jewish conversation. The thinkers in this and the preceding parts of this collection have all contributed to an unending discussion. They ask: What is to be done with this gift? What is its value? What should we make of it? Is it to be rejected, neglected, bequeathed? Thinking about the nature and significance of the gift in the twenty-first century is now well under way.

For a biographical sketch, see Part One, p. 5.

Mordecai M. Kaplan, *The Future of the American Jew* (New York: Macmillan, 1949), 63–72.

"A people" is not an abstract category; it is, like the term "personality," a concrete and identifiable phenomenon. Like all such phenomena, it can be recognized by means of its effects rather than defined. What essentially distinguishes a people from any other societal group, and what alone constitutes the common characteristic of groups designated as peoples, is their own identification of themselves as such. An individual is a person, when and because he knows himself as such; a group is a people, when and because it knows itself as such.

Thus, the first implication of the foregoing conception of peoplehood is that it is ethnic consciousness which makes a group into a people. Ethnic consciousness is not some mysterious entity that hovers over a people. It is the experience which every individual has, when he senses or becomes aware of the existence of the people he belongs to as an indivisible corporate entity. That experience expresses itself as consciousness of kind, like-mindedness, or "we-feeling." The Jews throughout the Middle Ages, and down to modern times, constituted a people despite their dispersion, because they identified with Jewish peoplehood all that was summed up in the term "Jew."

. . . With the advent of Emancipation and Enlightenment came the need to reconstitute and redefine the oneness and indivisibility of the Jewish people. Their advent has brought about the following radical changes in Jewish life: the various local Jewries now form an integral part of various nations: Jewish culture has given way to the cultures of those nations; the Jewish civil law has been abandoned. Jews no longer are unanimous in identifying what it is that renders them a distinct group.

. . . *If Jews are to reconstruct their lives as individuals and as members of a distinct society, they have to convert their present sense of oneness (which is constituted almost exclusively of an awareness of common danger and common suffering) into a sense of peoplehood and into an imperative to keep the corporate entity of the Jewish people one and indivisible.* The sense of peoplehood would help to rally the resources of Jewry for improving the lot of the Jew materially and spiritually. Materially, the status of peoplehood would contribute to the political security and freedom of the Jews and to their economic stability and prosperity; spiritually, it would revive their cultural creativity, enable them to play an original rather than an imitative role in human civilization and make their collective experience an aid to personal happiness and social welfare for themselves and their fellowmen.

How is the status of Jewish peoplehood to be realized? The answer is that, in the world as it is constituted today, it has to be realized on three levels....

1. *The first or basic level of Jewish peoplehood would have to take the form of commonwealth status.* Such status implies the occupation of a definite territory and self-government, both of which requirements will have to be met in Eretz Yisrael. A Jewish homeland in which either requirement is lacking is a self-contradiction.... *The Jewish Commonwealth in Eretz Yisrael need not and should not be a sovereign nation.* For that matter, the very survival of humanity now calls for the surrender, by every nation, of part of its sovereignty. The Jewish Commonwealth in particular should avoid becoming involved in international intrigue.

... In Jewish tradition, a nation was thought of primarily as an organization of religion and culture. The matter of power, particularly in relation to other nations, was entirely secondary. That is the sense in which we called ourselves a nation. "Israel is a nation only by virtue of its Torah," is the way R. Saadyah sums up Jewish nationhood.[9] Nowadays, however, the term "nation" connotes first and foremost an organization of power, in a combative sense. Religion is altogether precluded, and culture or civilization is decidedly secondary.... The recent World War has intensified, rather than weakened, the national tendencies to self-assertion and aggression. For the Jews to continue to use the term "nation" with regard even to Eretz Yisrael Jewry is to expose themselves to misunderstanding and vile slander.... Jews of the Jewish Commonwealth in Eretz Yisrael would be bound by loyalties and interests which are not binding upon the rest of world Jewry. Nevertheless, they and the Jews of the Diaspora would be members of the Jewish people, held together by common religio-cultural loy-

---

9. *Emmunot Ve-Deot* III, 7. [Saadyah Gaon (882–942) was one of the greatest Jewish philosophers and rabbis of the Middle Ages.]

alties and interests. The Jews in the Diaspora, however, would owe political allegiance solely to their respective countries. . . . This level of Jewish peoplehood, however, provides these opportunities only for those Jews who would live in the Jewish homeland. . . . The status of Diaspora Jewry would still remain as ambiguous as ever. We must think, therefore, in terms not only of Eretz Yisrael Jewry but of Jewry as a whole, and formulate other levels of the status of peoplehood, in addition to the one of commonwealth.

2. *The second level takes the form of the social structure of Diaspora Jewry advocated by the late Simon Dubnow.*[10] Dubnow tried to fit Jewish group life into a pattern of cultural pluralism, such as was envisaged by the minority rights clauses of the treaties after the first World War. According to that conception, the Jews, although continuing to reside in the lands of the Diaspora, are to constitute a distinct politico-cultural community with proportionate representation in the government, with their own communal institutions and system of education.

It is at once apparent that this interpretation of Jewish status is a program designed to promote the material and spiritual interests of Jews in countries where minority groups would be granted certain political group rights. . . . For Jewish peoplehood to function in the manner advocated by Dubnow, during the first decades of this century, as a political and cultural community with minority representation in the state, the majority group would have to sanction such a status. That sanction has been accorded only where there have been a number of minority nationalities with clearly marked cultural traits. In the Western democracies, however, no such *modus vivendi* would be welcomed either by Jews or Gentiles.

3. *The third level would fit the status of Jewish peoplehood into such a pattern of political monism combined with religio-cultural pluralism as exists in the United States.* In this country, there are no majority groups which are, or desire to be, represented in the state as national-cultural groups. All citizens share as individuals in the cultural, economical, and political life of the nation. With their personal liberties adequately protected by law and custom, they feel no need for separate political representation based on cultural differentiations. Nevertheless, *the very recognition of personal rights has resulted in the development of voluntary communal*

10. Simon Dubnow (1860–1941) was a Russian Jewish historian and activist who advanced an ideology of Jewish autonomism that promoted Jewish self-rule in the diaspora.

and religio-cultural institutions. This makes religio-cultural pluralism compatible with political monism.

This religio-cultural pluralism is not one that divides the population into disparate and mutually exclusive groups. All share in the common American culture, but each is free to develop additional cultural interests based on family tradition, religious affiliation, ethnic origin, race, or any other natural factor. As long as the interests of such groups are not antagonistic to those of the nation as a whole, they are accepted as legitimate. In such a pattern the Jews would constitute a religio-cultural group with a commonwealth nucleus in Eretz Yisrael.

This involves the formulation of a new societal concept. Its acceptance depends first and foremost upon the Jews themselves. This is undoubtedly the most difficult step to be taken, if they are to achieve that self-renewal which is to give them a new lease on life. But once the Jews determine to regard themselves as a people with a homeland, the rest of the world will in time come to accept them at their own self-valuation. All that is necessary is for the Jews to be convinced that there is nothing, in this new concept of a Diaspora people with a commonwealth nucleus, that can reasonably be regarded as incompatible with whole-hearted loyalty and devotion to the United States or to any other nation.

The nuclear function of the Jewish Commonwealth in Eretz Yisrael vis-à-vis the rest of the Jewish people would not be to exercise authority, either religiously or spiritually. It would be to exercise only such cultural and spiritual influence as the values which it would evolve would exert of their own accord.

The status of the Jews throughout the world as one indivisible people would have to be recognized as a social concept that carries with it both rights and duties: rights implying freedom to foster a degree of group individuality and duties implying the responsibility of translating that individuality into concrete social institutions.

... An American Jewish community, which would be animated by the status of Jewish peoplehood, would foster Jewish educational and cultural activities designed to make the collective experience of Jewish living in past and present a means for personal and social self-fulfillment. It would encourage Jewish community collaboration with other liberal elements in the American population for realizing in American life the highest ideals which Jews have learned from their own history and religion. It would lift Jewish religion above the dogmatic and ritualistic formalism into which it tends to degenerate, when divorced from the secular interests of Jewish life, and make it again a source of inspiration and morale in our heroic struggle for self-emancipation and self-realization.

... *Such peoplehood is religious, for the essence of religion is the human quest for salvation.* Therefore, it has all the advantages, and none of the disadvantages, of denominational status which an earlier generation sought as the solution of the Jewish problem. It is in the mainstream of the spiritual tradition of our people, and can avail itself of the resources of the Jewish religious tradition. This religious conception of peoplehood saves religion itself from sterile dogmatism and formalism. The religion, which seeks to make of peoplehood a way of salvation for the individual and society, is the only kind of religion that can make the world safe for democracy.

Simon Rawidowicz (1897–1957) was born in Poland and educated in Germany. A brilliant Hebraist and a prodigious scholar of classical Jewish texts and history as well as secular philosophy, Rawidowicz took an active part in Jewish public affairs. He taught in a variety of academic settings in both the United Kingdom and the United States before becoming the first Chair of the Near Eastern and Judaic Studies Department at Brandeis University. His academic writings and popular essays are regularly consulted by scholars today.

Simon Rawidowicz, *State of Israel, Diaspora, and Jewish Continuity: Essays on the Ever-Dying People* (Waltham, MA: Brandeis University Press, 1986), 62–63.[11]

In the beginning, Israel's message was that of a universal optimism-salvation, happiness and perfection for all peoples. "The mountain of the Lord's house will be established in the top of the mountains"[12] means: the peoples of the world will also share alike, with Israel, in the blessing of the Messianic age. Many well-known and understandable factors compelled post-Exilic and medieval Messianism to become more one-sided and directed exclusively toward the redemption of Israel; optimistic toward Israel, pessimistic toward the world. In more recent times, most Jewish ideologies and political movements were dualistic inasmuch as they saw a world divided, Israel and world torn apart—nay, still more: Israel itself was to them no more. Thus, to give one illustration, Jewish Reform on both sides of the Rhine, nineteenth-century liberalism, was optimistic as far as the world's future was concerned, pessimistic for the survival of Israel as a nation with all national attributes. This same dualistic attitude was taken up by all kinds of assimilated Jewish revolutionaries in Eastern and Western Europe. Later, two Jewish ideologies fought each other in Europe: one was most optimistic for the remnant of Israel in Zion and pessimistic as far as the Jewish people in the Diaspora was concerned, while the other reversed this dichotomy, maintaining that

11. [This article was originally published in English in *Judaism* in 1967, an abridged version of a 1948 Hebrew essay.]
12. [Isaiah 2:2.]

only Diaspora Jewry had a future in some liberal or socialistic order. Both made the fundamental mistake of dividing Israel into two parts. Israel must always be considered one and indivisible—*yisrael ehad*. As long as one part of Israel lives in a hell, the other cannot live in paradise. I therefore say: we may not split up Israel into two spheres of reality. Israel is one. Neither may we approach the Jewish problem from an optimistic or pessimistic angle. Optimism and pessimism are only expressions or indications of our fears, doubts, hopes, and desires. Hopes and desires we must have; fears and doubts we cannot escape. Yet, what we need most at present is a dynamic Jewish realism which will see our reality, the reality of the world, our problem, the problem of the world, in its entirety, without any dualism hell-paradise or whatever. Such a Jewish realism will also show us the real meaning of that fear of the end which is so inherent in us. A nation dying for thousands of years means a living nation. Our incessant dying means uninterrupted living, rising, standing up, beginning anew. We, the last Jews! Yes, in many respects it seems to us as if we are the last links in a particular chain of tradition and development. But if we are the last—let us be the last as our fathers and forefathers were. Let us prepare the ground for the last Jews who will come after us, and for the last Jews who will rise after them, and so on until the end of days. If it has been decreed for Israel that it go on being a dying nation—let it be a nation that is constantly dying, which is to say: incessantly living and creating—one nation from Dan to Beersheba, from the sunny heights of Judea to the shadowy valleys of Europe and America. To prepare the ground for this great oneness, for a Jewish realism built on it, is a task which requires the effort of Jewish scholarship and statesmanship alike. One nation, one in beginning and end, one in survival and extinction! May it be survival rather than extinction, a beginning rather than an ignominious end—one Israel, *yisrael ehad*.

George Steiner (1929–2020) was a French-born literary scholar, cultural critic, and philosopher who came to America in 1940. He received his undergraduate education at the University of Chicago and earned an MA from Harvard University before receiving his doctorate from Oxford University. He was at the Institute for Advanced Studies in Princeton, New Jersey, for a number of years, and while he has lived outside the United States for the great majority of his career, his influence in American intellectual and academic circles was immense.

George Steiner, "Our Homeland, the Text," *Salmagundi* 66 (Winter–Spring 1985): 4–25.

In the founding secular manifesto of Zionism, Herzl's *Judenstaat*, the language and the vision are proudly mimetic of Bismarckian nationalism. Israel is a nation-state to the utmost degree. It lives armed to the teeth. It has been compelled to make other men homeless, servile, disinherited, in order to survive from day to day. . . . The virtues of Israel are those of beleaguered Sparta. Its propaganda, its rhetoric of self-deception, are as desperate as any contrived in the history of nationalism. Under external and internal stress, loyalty has been atrophied to patriotism, and patriotism made chauvinism. What place, what license is there in that garrison for the "treason" of the Prophet, for Spinoza's refusal of the tribe? Humanism, said Rousseau, is "a theft committed on *la patrie.*" Quite so.

There is no singular vice in the practices of the State of Israel. These follow ineluctably on the simple institution of the modern nation-state, on the political-military necessities by which it exists with and against its nationalist competitors. It is by empirical need that a nation-state sups on lies. Where it has traded its homeland in the text for one of the Golan Heights or in Gaza . . . Judaism has become homeless to itself.

But this, of course, is only a part of the truth.

To many among the few survivors, the interminable pilgrimage through persecution, the interminable defenselessness of the Jew in the face of bestiality and derision, were no longer endurable. A refuge had to be found, a place of physical gathering in which a Jewish parent could give to his child some hope of a future. The return to Zion, the fantastic courage and labour which have made the desert flower, the survival of the "Old Newland" (Herzl's famous phrase) against crazy political and military odds, have made a wonder of necessity. The overwhelming majority of Jews in Israel, of Jews in the Diaspora, seek neither to be prophets nor clerics deranged by some autistic, otherworldly addiction to speculative abstractions and the elixir of truth. They hunger, desperately, for the common condition of man among men. They would, like all other men and nations, vanquish their enemies rather than be oppressed and scattered by them; if harsh reality dictates, they would rather occupy, censor, even torture than be occupied and censored and tortured as they have been for so long. What mandarin fantasy, what ivory-tower nonsense, is it to suppose that alone among men, and after the unspeakable horrors of destruction lavished upon him, the Jew should not have a land of his own, a shelter in the night?

I know all this. It would be shallow impertinence not to see the psychological, the empirical force of the argument. Moreover, is the return to Israel not foreseen, indeed ordained, in the very texts I have cited? Is Zionism not as integral a part of the "prescribed" mystery and condition of Judaism as were the terrible times of sufferance . . . and dispersal?

The Orthodox answer is clear. Both currents of prevision are to be accomplished. The prescriptions of suffering have long been made manifest. And so shall be the homecoming to the promised land. But not before the messianic hour. The imperiled brutalized condition of the present State of Israel, the failure of Israel to be Zion, prove the spurious, the purely expedient temporality of its re-establishment in 1948. There were, then, armed men about and politicians. The Messiah was nowhere in sight. Thus the State of Israel, as it stands today, neither fulfills nor disproves the Mosaic and prophetic covenant of return. The time is not yet.

Personally, I have no right to this answer. I have no part in the beliefs and ritual practices which underwrite it. But its intuitive and evidential strength can be felt to be real.

The survival of the Jews has no authentic parallel in history. Ancient ethnic communities and civilizations no less gifted, no less self-conscious, have perished, many without trace. It is, on the most rational, existential level, difficult to believe that this unique phenomenon of unbroken life, in the face of every destructive agency, is unconnected with the exilic circumstance. Judaism has drawn its uncanny vitality from dispersal, from the adaptive demands made on it by mobility. Ironically, the threat of that "final solution" might prove to be the greatest yet if the Jews were now to be compacted in Israel.

But there is a more central intimation. One need be neither a religious fundamentalist nor a mystic to believe that there is some exemplary meaning to the singularity of Judaic endurance, that there is some sense beyond contingent or demographic interest to the interlocking constancy of Jewish pain and of Jewish preservation. The notion that the appalling road of Jewish life and the ever-renewed miracle of survival should have as their end, as their justification, the setting up of a small nation-state in the Middle East, crushed by military burdens, petty and even corrupt in its politics, shrill in its parochialism, is implausible.

I cannot shake off the conviction that the torment and the mystery of resilience in Judaism exemplify, enact, an arduous truth: that human beings must learn to be each other's guests on this small planet, even as they must learn to be guests of being itself and of the natural world. This is a truth humbly immediate, to our breath, to our skin, to the passing shadow we cast on a ground inconceivably more ancient than our visitation, and it is also a terribly abstract, morally and psychologically exigent truth. Man will have to learn it or he will be made extinct in suicidal waste and violence.

The State of Israel is an endeavor . . . to normalize the condition, the meaning of Judaism. It would make the Jew level with the common denominator of modern "belonging." It is, at the same time, an attempt to eradicate the deeper truth of unhousedness, of an at-homeness in the word, which are the legacy of the Prophets and of the keepers of the text.

In Jerusalem today, the visitor is taken to the "Shrine of the Scrolls" or, as it is also known, "House of the Sacred Books." In this exquisite building are kept some of the Dead Sea scrolls and priceless biblical papyri. It is a place of poignant, if somewhat sepulchral, radiance. One's guide explains the hidden hydraulic mechanism whereby the entire edifice can, in the event of shelling or bombardment, be made to sink safely below ground. Such precautions are indispensable. Because nation-states live by the sword. But such precautions are also a metaphysical and ethical barbarism. Words cannot be broken by artillery, nor thought live in bomb-shelters.

Locked materially in a material homeland, the text may, in fact, lose its life-force, and its truth values may be betrayed. But when the text is the homeland, even when it is rooted only in the exact remembrance and seeking of a handful of wanderers, nomads of the word, it cannot be extinguished. Time is truth's passport and its native ground. What better lodging for the Jew?

Arthur A. Cohen (1928–86) was educated at the University of Chicago and the Jewish Theological Seminary, although he was never ordained. An encounter with Milton Steinberg put this Jew from a nonreligious background on an intensely theological, if unconventional, course. A novelist and editor who wrote on a wide range of intellectual and religious topics, Cohen was also a prominent public intellectual who wrote frequently on theological matters. With Paul Mendes-Flohr, he coedited the influential *Contemporary Jewish Religious Thought*.[13]

Arthur A. Cohen, "Why I Choose to Be a Jew," in *An Arthur A. Cohen Reader*, ed. David Stern and Paul Mendes-Flohr (New York: Charles Scribner's Sons, 1986), 33–40.[14]

The irresistible forces of history no longer *compel* the Jew to choose Judaism. In many cases, however, he is choosing to repudiate Judaism or to embrace Christianity. I do not say the numbers are alarming. That they exist at all is, however, symptomatic. It is only the exceptional—those who are searching deeply or are moved profoundly, who ever reject or embrace. The majority tend more often to undramatic indifference—to slide into the routine of maturity without asking questions for which no meaningful answers have been offered.

Given the freedom to choose I have decided to embrace Judaism. I have not done so out of loyalty to the Jewish people or the Jewish state. My choice was religious, I chose to believe in the God of Abraham, Isaac, and Jacob; to acknowledge the law of Moses as the Word of God; to accept the people of Israel as the holy instrument of divine fulfillment; to await the coming of the Messiah and the redemption of history.

13. [Arthur A. Cohen & Paul R. Mendes-Flohr, *20th Century Jewish Religious Thought: Original Essays on Critical Concepts, Movements, and Beliefs* (Philadelphia: Jewish Publication Society, 2009). Perhaps Cohen's most significant theological work was *The Natural and the Supernatural Jew* (New York: Pantheon Books, 1962). He edited a highly significant anthology of essays in post-Holocaust Jewish thought entitled *Arguments and Doctrines* (New York: Harper & Row, 1970).]

14. [This article originally appeared in *Harper's Magazine* in April 1959.]

First, I chose to believe in the God of Abraham, Isaac, and Jacob. This is to affirm the reality of a God who acts in history and addresses man. Although this God may well be the same as the abstract gods formulated by philosophers, he is still more than these—he is the God who commanded Abraham to quit the land of the Chaldeans and who wrestled with Jacob throughout the night. . . .

My second belief is an acknowledgment that *the Law of Moses is the Word of God.* The Bible tells us that the Word of God broke out over the six hundred thousand Hebrews who assembled at the foot of Sinai. That Word was heard by Moses— he who had been appointed to approach and receive. The word became human —in its humanity, it undoubtedly suffers from the limitation of our understand- ing—but it lost none of its divinity.

The third of my beliefs is, as I have indicated, simply an element of God's reve- lation in Torah—that *the Jewish people has been chosen as a spiritual instrument of God.*

The Jews did not request the attentions of God. There is significant truth— truth moreover which the rabbis of the Talmud endorse—in the popular cou- plet: "How odd of God, to choose the Jews." Odd, and unsolicited. The ancient rabbis disclaim particular merit. If anyone possessed merit, they repeat, it was not the generation that fled Egypt and braved the wilderness for forty years, but the generations of the Biblical patriarchs—Abraham, Isaac, and Jacob. They had no organizer such as Moses, nor strength of numbers, nor the miracles of the well, manna, and quail. They made a covenant with God on sheer trust. The gen- eration of Sinai was *compelled* to become the people of God or perish. A God of History grows impatient with delay. The God of Israel was profoundly impatient on Sinai.

This tradition of election should not be confused with racial pride or an at- titude of arrogant exclusion toward others. The Jew believes neither that the truth flows in his blood nor that the gentile cannot come to possess it. Judaism is exclusive only in the sense that we affirm we possess important truth which is available to all—everyone can join but only on our terms.

The election of Israel is not a conclusion drawn from history—the survival and endurance of the Jews through twenty centuries of destructive persecution could be no more than blind accident. At best it could be construed as a com- pliment to the resiliency and stubbornness of the Jewish people. Judaism has insisted however—not as a declaration after the fact, but as a principle of its very existence—that it is both a holy nation chosen by God to be his own and a suffering nation destined to endure martyrdom for his sake. . . .

Israel is thus called not only to be the example to the nations, but, being the example, is tried all the more sorely for its transgressions. . . . It is precisely the fact of Jewish suffering which makes its election and mission all the more pertinent to the modern world. To have believed and survived in spite of history is perhaps the only evidence which Judaism can offer to the accuracy of its conviction that it is called to be a holy community.

Michael Wyschogrod (1928–2015) was educated in the Orthodox Adas Jisroel school in Berlin as a boy and emigrated to the United States in 1939. He then enrolled at Yeshivas Torah Vodaas in Brooklyn, New York, and studied at both Yeshiva University and the City College of New York. Wyschogrod was awarded his PhD in philosophy at Columbia University in 1953 and served for many years as head of the Philosophy Department at Baruch College. An Orthodox Jew, Wyschogrod was also an expert on Christian theology and an active participant in Jewish-Christian interfaith dialogue.

Michael Wyschogrod, *The Body of Faith: Judaism as Corporeal Election* (New York: Seabury Press, 1983), 175–76, 184.

Judaism is a carnal election.

God did not formulate a teaching around which he rallied humanity. God declared a particular people the people of God. He could have brought into being another kind of people of God, membership in which would have been a function of the individual's faith and/or virtue. This is how the Church came to understand its election. As the new Israel, it saw itself as the people of God that had replaced the old Israel. Whereas membership in the old Israel was bestowed by birth, membership in the new Israel was open to anyone who embraced the message of the Church.

But this is not the nature of Israel's election. This election is that of the seed of Abraham. A descendant of Abraham, Isaac, and Jacob is a Jew irrespective of what he believes or how virtuous he is. Being a Jew is therefore not something earned. This reflects the fact that the initial election of Abraham himself was not earned. It is true that in rabbinic literature Abraham is depicted as having "discovered" the one God when it occurred to him that a complex world could not have come into being by chance. But none of this is mentioned in the Bible. We are simply told that God commanded Abraham to leave his place of birth and to go to a land that God would show him. He is also promised that his descendants will become a numerous people. But nowhere does the Bible tell us why Abraham rather than someone else was chosen. The implication is that

God chooses whom he wishes and that he owes no accounting to anyone for his choices.

Israel's election is therefore a carnal election that is transmitted through the body. And to many, this is a scandal. Is it the body that makes someone dear to God or the spirit? Shouldn't we evaluate a person on the basis of his character and ideas rather than his physical descent? These are difficult questions to answer but we cannot evade coping with them.

We must first understand that we cannot sit in judgment over God. It is not incumbent on him to justify his actions to man. It is not for us to teach God what is fair but for him to teach us. If it was his decision to make Abraham his beloved servant and the descendants of Abraham his beloved people, then it is for man to accept God's will with obedience.

. . . He chose to elect a biological people that remains elect even when it sins. God is therefore involved with the sins of the elect, since the elect people become immersed in sin and purified in repentance.

How does the sin of the elect manifest itself both as sin and as sin of the elect? If the Jewish attraction to Marxism was sin, it was the sin of the elect because it took the form of thirst for righteousness. And the same is true for Jewish secular liberalism. If secular Zionism was sin because it rejected God as the source of Jewish redemption, it was the sin of the elect because, however secular its rationale, it was a longing for the holy soil of Israel. Even in sin, Israel remains in the divine service because the spiritual circumcision that has been carried out on this people is indelible.

For a biographical sketch, see Part Six.

Judith Plaskow, *Standing Again at Sinai: Judaism from a Feminist Perspective* (New York: Harper and Row, 1990), 25–28, 97–107.

Entry into the covenant at Sinai is the root experience of Judaism, the central event that established the Jewish people. Given the importance of this event, there can be no verse in the Torah more disturbing to the feminist than Moses' warning to his people in Exodus 19:15, "Be ready for the third day; do not go near a woman." For here, at the very moment that the Jewish people stands at Sinai ready to receive the covenant—not now the covenant with individual patriarchs but with the people as a whole—at the very moment when Israel stands trembling waiting for God's presence to descend upon the mountain, Moses addresses the community only as men.... At the central moment of Jewish history, women are invisible. Whether they too stood there trembling in fear and expectation, what they heard when the men heard these words of Moses, we do not know. It was not their experience that interested the chronicler or that informed and shaped the Torah.

Moses' admonition can be seen as a paradigm of what I have called "the profound injustice of Torah itself." In this passage, the Otherness of women finds its way into the very center of Jewish experience. And although the verse hardly can be blamed for women's situation, it sets forth a pattern recapitulated again and again in Jewish sources.... To accept our absence from Sinai would be to allow the male text to define us and our connection to Judaism. To stand on the ground of our experience, on the other hand, to start with the certainty of our membership in our own people is to be forced to remember and recreate its history, to reshape Torah. It is to move from anger at the tradition, through anger to empowerment. It is to begin the journey toward the creation of a feminist Judaism.

Jewish feminists, in other words, must reclaim Torah as our own. We must render visible the presence, experience, and deeds of women erased in traditional sources. We must tell the stories of women's encounters with God and capture the texture of their religious experience. We must expand the notion of Torah to encompass not just the five books of Moses and traditional Jewish learning, but women's words, teachings, and actions hitherto unseen. To expand Torah, we must reconstruct Jewish history to include the history of women, and in doing so alter the shape of Jewish memory.

... Jewish feminists cannot transform the place of women's difference within the people of Israel without addressing the larger system of separations in which it is embedded. This system can be approached from a number of directions. In the context of the reconceptualization of Israel, however, it is the notion of chosenness that is the chief expression of hierarchical separation and therefore the most important focus for discussion. As a central category for Jewish self-understanding that is emblematic of other gradations, chosenness provides a warrant and a model for ranked differentiations within the community and between Israel and others. If Jewish feminism is to articulate a model of community in which difference is acknowledged without being hierarchalized, it will have to engage with traditional Jewish understanding of difference by rejecting the idea of chosenness without at the same time denying the distinctiveness of Israel as a religious community.

... Michael Wyschogrod's theology is helpful in clarifying the import of chosenness, ... for Wyschogrod tries to give meaning to the idea of chosenness without either overstating or fleeing from its implications.

... This formulation of chosenness, because it continues to insist on the favored status of the Jews even while it avoids imputing to them special merit, clarifies the fundamentally hierarchical nature of the concept of election.

... Most reinterpretations of election have focused on the relation of Jews to the wider society—seeking to reconcile chosenness with equality and participation in a pluralistic culture. Feminism, however, calls attention to the function of chosenness in relation to Jewish self-conception and the internal dynamics of the community. Feminist objections to the idea of chosenness center not just on its entanglement with external hierarchical differentiations but with internal hierarchies as well. ...

Only a Jewish community that permits and desires its members to be present in their particularity and totality can know in its fullness the relationship to God that it claims as its center.

What must replace chosenness, then, as the model for Jewish self-understanding is the far less dramatic "distinctness." The Jewish community and the subcommunities within it, like all human communities, are distinct and distinctive.

Jewish experience has been variously shaped by gender, by place of dispersion, by language, by history, by interaction with other cultures. Just as the total Jewish experience is always located within a wider world, so the experiences of Jewish subgroups have taken place in some relation to a larger Jewish life and self-understanding. The term distinctness suggests, however, that the relation between these various communities—Jewish to non-Jewish, Jewish to Jewish —should be understood not in terms of hierarchical differentiation but in terms of part and whole.

. . . Jewish women, Sephardim, Ashkenazim, Paradesim, Malabarim (groups of Jews in Cochin, India) are part of the larger Jewish community as Jews are part of a larger heterogeneous culture. The parts are distinct. They have their own history and experience, and depending on their character, their own institutions, religion, practices, and beliefs. It is the content of this distinctness that creates an internal sense of group identity and community and also that allows the group to distinguish itself from others.

. . . Awareness of the wider communities to which any community belongs fosters an appreciation of distinctness that need not be rooted in hierarchy or in projection onto others of rejected aspects of the self.

. . . If the different groups and subgroups that make up a community or nation are parts of a greater whole, there is no whole without all the pieces. . . . Unless Jewish history and community include the history and experience of women, Jews in India, Jews in the Arab world, it is not truly "Jewish" history or "Jewish" community but male Eurocentric Jewish history and community. This exclusion is destructive not only to the groups ignored but also to the rich tapestry of Jewish life that grows in distinctness and beauty with the distinctness and beauty of its various portions. The creation of Jewish communities in which differences are valued as necessary parts of a greater whole is the institutional and experiential foundation for the recovery of the fullness of Torah. . . . What is true of communities is also true of selves. . . .

. . . Jewish women, as we gain equal access to Jewish communal life, deny our own experience for normative male practice and discourse. Those whose differences might have enriched and challenged the greater communal life learn to forget or keep hidden pieces of themselves.

We are brought back to the spiritual injury that such forgetting entails, and to the potential for liberation in a different model of community. To be wholly present in our lives in all our power is to touch the greater power of our beings that is the final unity within which all particulars dwell. To deny our complex peculiarity, as individuals or communities, is to diminish our connection to the God known in and through the experience of empowered selfhood. The community or self that spends its energy repressing parts of its totality truncates its creative power and cuts itself off from its full possibilities. A Jewish community that defines itself by walling itself off from others without and within marshals strength at its boundaries to the detriment of the center. It nourishes selves that must deny parts of themselves and thus cannot bring their uniqueness to the enrichment of a common life. To create Jewish communities that value particularity is to create places where Jews in their complex wholeness can bring their full power to the upbuilding of Jewish community and the other communities in which Jews dwell. It is not in the chosenness that cuts off but in the distinctiveness that opens itself to difference that we find the God of Israel and of each and every people.

Shaul Magid (born 1958) is the Distinguished Fellow in Jewish Studies at Dartmouth College. Ordained an Orthodox rabbi in Jerusalem and the recipient of an MA from the Hebrew University of Jerusalem and a doctorate from Brandeis University, Magid has also taught at the Jewish Theological Seminary of America and Indiana University. His academic work has ranged from Jewish mysticism to contemporary Jewish thought and history. Magid also writes often on contemporary Jewish affairs and has long been associated with the Jewish renewal movement.

Shaul Magid, *American Post-Judaism: Identity and Renewal in a Postethnic Society* (Bloomington: Indiana University Press, 2013), 17–21, 34.

America is steadily being transformed from a multiculturalist and ethnocentric society to a postethnic society, and this change undermines, or at least problematizes, the place of ethnicity in American identity that dominated the second part of the twentieth century. This does not suggest that ethnicity has disappeared, or will disappear, and that America will become a society divided purely by class. "Ethnicity," depending on how the term is defined, will survive but will become something other than purely a consequence of ascription or descent. A multiethnic or polyethnic society will produce new ethnicities that are created by a combination of descent and consent, ascription and affiliation. . . .

If postethnicity is indeed a growing reality, and if Jews in America are so integrated into their social structure that asking them to reject it would be tantamount to asking them to become an anomaly in order to "survive" might we think about how this postethnic turn can suggest new structures of Jewish identity? That is, how can "survival" be reformulated in a way that enables the entire notion of identity to be calibrated anew? My point is not to argue that our understanding of the future of Jews, Judaism, and Jewishness in America should be driven solely by the realities of the American cultural landscape (that is, that the "ought" should, by definition, be determined by the "is"). One could surely argue quite forcefully (and many have tried to) that the existence of a burgeoning postethnic America should compel Jews to create an even stronger ethnic anchor in order to prevent Jewishness and Judaism from becoming hopelessly buried in the multiethnic mix of American society. This is exactly what . . . Steven Cohen and Jack Wertheimer argue. . . . What I am suggesting, however, is that while the "is" of postethnicity poses certain challenges, it also poses certain potentially productive opportunities to rethink the very notion of the "ought." . . . Such a situation does not require new articulations of older ideas but new models of understanding the very categories in question. Put differently, the new reality is not simply one more obstacle to be overcome (the traditional argument) or one more dimension of modernity that Jews must creatively respond to in order to survive under traditional parameters of survival (the progressive argument). Rather, postethnic America is, to borrow a term used by Zalman Schachter-Shalomi for different purposes, a "paradigm shift" that demands a totally new approach to the very notion of survival, to the very contours of what we mean by "Jewishness" and "Judaism" in contemporary America. . . . My point is only to begin with the premise that postethnicity is with us for the foreseeable future, and Jews must learn how to think within its boundaries and not simply deny its existence or remain wed to old-paradigm "oughts" in order to create models for survival, continuity, and renewal.

The question as to whether the instability of identity and ethnicity is a phenomenon limited to the individual or whether it extends to the very fabric of the Jewish collective is pertinent. That the individual Jew is in a state of flux in America is not a new observation. The important question is with regard to the collective. The debate among sociologists, cultural theorists, and historians who study American Jewry is generally about the collective future of Jews and Judaism in America. Much of it begins with the assumption that being Jewish in America is no longer a liability. . . . For some this is the blessing under which hides a curse. While some argue that the Jewish collective has already collapsed, others argue that notwithstanding the danger posed to Jewish individuals, the community remains stable, intact, and thriving and continues its process of Americanization, managing the tension between tradition and acculturation. I submit that the Jewish collective in America (as previously construed) is in a state of collapse, but unlike those who view this change in purely negative terms I suggest this collapse is largely dependent on the lens through which it is viewed, that is, how we understand the criterion of the "Jew" and the makeup of the Jewish collective.

The Jewish collective in America will survive; it will just look different than before. The normalization of intermarriage combined with a fairly new phenomenon of the intermarried Jew remaining part of a Jewish community and bringing his or her spouse and children into that community raises new issues about the very construction of a Jewish collective that includes non-Jews. . . . This postethnic approach considers young men and women who own multiple narratives, family histories, and affiliations without a sense of disparity. It includes many who choose to live in multiple ethnic communities without seeing that choice as a contradiction. . . . In my view, the age-old criterion of Jewishness as rooted almost exclusively in familial history and affinity cannot survive the multiethnic family that no longer requires one to choose ascribed allegiance. One can contest and/or lament the reality that is emerging, and even try to institute measures to prevent it, but one cannot turn a blind eye to the changing contours of Jewishness in contemporary America.

. . . Those who maintain that Jewishness can only be determined by ascription, that is, by external criteria defined by particular communities, and that Judaism is meant solely for Jews, will never acquiesce to this seemingly anarchic and radical rethinking of Jewishness and Judaism in a postethnic era. Yet it is, in my mind, a worthwhile endeavor to explore this phenomenon for the simple reason that this is increasingly where American Judaism lives. While the "is" should not, by definition, determine the "ought," those who reflect on the "ought" certainly need to give it careful and serious consideration, especially in a Jewish society in which religious, political, and cultural hegemony is absent.

74

**Steven M. Cohen and Jack Wertheimer,
"What Is So Great about Post-Ethnic Judaism"/
"Whatever Happened to the Jewish People"**

Steven M. Cohen (born 1950) and Jack Wertheimer (born 1948) are prolific academic researchers who have been two of the most prominent analysts and thinkers on the modern American Jewish scene. Cohen received his doctorate in sociology at Columbia University while Wertheimer earned his PhD there in Jewish history. Wertheimer is Professor of American Jewish History and served for many years as provost of the Jewish Theological Seminary of America. Cohen taught at Queens College and the Hebrew University of Jerusalem, and he served as Research Professor of Jewish Social Policy at Hebrew Union College-Jewish Institute of Religion. According to a 2018 statement from HUC-JIR, Cohen resigned from his position on the faculty of HUC-JIR in the wake of an internal investigation by the institution in response to several complaints that he had engaged in sexual misconduct.

a. "What Is So Great about Post-Ethnic Judaism," *Sh'ma* 41, no. 678 (March 1, 2011): 5–6.

b. "Whatever Happened to the Jewish People," *Commentary* 121, no. 6 (June 2006): 37.

A.

Shaul Magid is right to draw attention to post-ethnic trends in America. But whereas he applauds the shift to a porous, self-constructed, and voluntary ethnicity, we doubt it is "good for the Jews." We take wary cognizance of post-ethnicity and urge American Jews to contend with it, rather than surrender.

Moreover, where Magid sees Jewish exemplars of post-ethnicity as the vanguard, we regard the many Jews who continue to identify with the Jewish religion and people as the nucleus for renewal. Among our neighbors in the Greater New York area, where one-third of America's Jews reside, are large numbers of Orthodox Jews and quite a few committed Conservative, Reform, Reconstructionist, and post-denominational Jews who care about the Jewish people; to their ranks, we may add the hundreds of thousands of Jews from the former Soviet Union and their now-adult children, and thousands more from Israel, Iran, and South Africa who share the same commitments.

By contrast, we do not anticipate that the children of intermarriage will lead a Jewish revival, particularly since the large majority are not receiving a Jewish education. Much to our dismay, only a small proportion identify as Jews or with Jews. . . . It is a sad fact that within two or three generations, intermarriage, in the large majority of cases, will be a way out of Jewish life.

Our main objection to Magid's argument, though, is its ideological defeatism. . . . Why should we accept the ignorant judgment of those who regard long-established norms of endogamy as racist, when we know that in-marriage (including the marriage of born-Jews to Jews-by-choice) still serves as a powerful predictor of Jewish engagement and demographic continuity, no less than it did in the past?

As for the sources of renewal, Jewish creativity is (still) predicated on a grounding in the religion and culture of the Jewish people, a civilization that is genuinely distinctive and profoundly different from cultural trends of the moment. Overwhelmingly, . . . today's innovative leaders have emerged from deep experiences of Jewish peoplehood. They disproportionately are children of in-married parents. They have been formed by intensive formal and informal educational programs, and especially by study in Israel. Those of us who wish to build a strong and authentic Jewish life dare not communicate to our children that everything is up for grabs, that their Jewish descent is non-binding, and that Jewish living is merely one option among a broad array of lifestyle choices.

Magid's analysis has the propensity to dismiss everything that was held sacred in the past as "socially constructed." But is "Jewish peoplehood" in our times a mere "social construction," lacking any moral, political, cultural, or religious force? Sixty-five years after the Holocaust demonstrated the interconnected fate of all Jews, sixty-two years after the State of Israel was established as a heroic achievement of the Jewish people, and but a few decades after the epic struggle to free Soviet Jewry, a magnificent expression of Jewish solidarity, is Jewish peoplehood suddenly finished, all because America has gone post-ethnic of late?

No. . . . Jewish identity was predicated for much of our history on the biblical command to behave as a "kingdom of priests and a holy people," a neat formulation of the inseparability of Judaism and Jewish peoplehood. Our dual identity as a people-nationality-ethnicity with its own religion has enabled Jews to create a remarkable civilization. It has left room for nonbelievers to connect as Jews, even if they are not moved by religious practices. It has enabled Jews in the past and present to travel anywhere in the world and find *landsleit*, fellow Jews who share similar preoccupations, liturgies, and memories. And it has given Jewish life an international dimension that has vastly enriched our discourse, our cuisine, our music and art, let alone our self-understanding.

Shaul Magid's perception of rising post-ethnic Judaism may be accurate, though not as prevalent as he claims. The post-ethnic Judaism he envisions puts us at risk of abandoning a critical aspect of our "thick" Jewish culture, our obligation and familial ties to the Jewish people in Israel and around the world—in effect, trading our Jewish birthright for a thin gruel. That bargain, let us recall, was taken by Esau, not by his brother Jacob.

B.

Jews are not solely the agglomeration of adherents of a particular faith, each seeking personal meaning: they are a people whose primary mark has been the conviction of a unique corporate role in history—the mark, to use classical theological language, of chosenness. To retreat from peoplehood is to repudiate what has been at the core.

Even from the point of view of the individual, the loss of this core can be devastating. To see oneself as part of a larger collective entity is to situate oneself in a history of 3,200 years and more, imparting a sense of transcendent connection, purpose, and destiny. It buttresses faith, enhances religious activity, lends significance to communal affiliation. For a sense of how intrinsic, how almost innate, this connection to peoplehood was within living memory, and how thoroughly inseparable from specifically religious ideas, here is how Eugene B. Borowitz, a Reform theologian, wrote about it in 1965:

> Jewish peoplehood is an indispensable part of Jewish religious thought and Jewish religious practice. A specifically Jewish religious life means, therefore, life in and with the Jewish people, the Covenant community.... When at least ten Jews congregate to pray, they ... represent all Israel, past and present, here and everywhere.[15]

In slightly altered terminology, one could cite abundant sources to the same

15. [Eugene B. Borowitz, "The Individual and the Community in Jewish Prayer," in *Rediscovering Judaism: Reflections on a New Theology*, ed. Arnold Jacob Wolf (Chicago: Quadrangle Books, 1965), 124.]

effect from secular Jewish authorities no less impelled by the idea of a communal Jewish mission. But whatever the language in which the idea of peoplehood is couched, it is impossible to believe that many forms of Jewish collective endeavor can survive without it. In the end, the decline of Jewish peoplehood is symptomatic of a decline of morale, of national self-respect. A people no longer proud of what and who it is, no longer dedicated to caring for its own, cannot long expect to be held in high regard by others, or to move the world by its message.

75

Arthur Hertzberg, from *Rebuilding*
Jewish Peoplehood

Arthur Hertzberg (1921–2006) was a prominent Conservative rabbi and leading American Jewish intellectual and activist. He was a graduate of Johns Hopkins University and received his doctorate in history from Columbia University. Hertzberg also taught for many years at Columbia, Dartmouth College, and New York University, and was a president of the American Jewish Congress. He was particularly well known as the author of *The Zionist Idea*.

Arthur Hertzberg, from *Rebuilding Jewish Peoplehood: Where Do We Go from Here? A Symposium in the Wake of the Rabin Assassination* (New York: American Jewish Committee, 1996), 51.

I see no possible compromise between those who think that Jewish political decisions should be made rationally and pragmatically and those who think that their views represent the clearly articulated will of God. We have become, at very least, two peoples.

The only possible basis for unity is an agreement to join together for some tasks in which both elements might share, such as resisting anti-Semitism. I am not very hopeful that even this will work well, because there is now almost nothing on the Jewish agenda, from the question of the West Bank, to the rescue of Russian Jews (many of whom are not Jews according to halakhah), to state aid for parochial schools, on which the agendas of these two Jewish communities are in agreement.

We might be able to strengthen the nonfundamentalist, nonmessianic majority of the Jewish people by deepening a common education in classic Jewish texts and traditions, but even the Bible and Talmud are different—radically different —when studied on the basis of fundamentally different religious premises.

. . . I foresee a contemporary version of the convulsion of at least a century in which the followers of Shabbtai Zvi split off and were excommunicated.[16]

16. [Shabbtai Zvi (1626–76) proclaimed himself to be the messiah when he arrived in Constantinople in 1666. The Jewish world was roiled over these claims, and Shabbtai Zvi and his followers were ultimately excommunicated and condemned by the vast majority of the Jewish community for what were seen as false messianic claims.]

Paula Hyman (1946–2011) was a prominent student of French Jewish history and famed as a pioneer in and scholar of Jewish feminist history. As an activist and scholar, she shaped the latter field in significant ways. Hyman received her undergraduate degree from Radcliffe College, and Columbia University awarded her a doctorate in history. She was a professor at Columbia, the Jewish Theological Seminary, and Yale University.

Paula Hyman, from *Rebuilding Jewish Peoplehood: Where Do We Go from Here? A Symposium in the Wake of the Rabin Assassination* (New York: American Jewish Committee, 1996), 55.

Unity of the Jewish people is not an end in itself. There are times when conflicting visions of Judaism and the Jewish future cannot be reconciled, if we are to remain true to our values. Should Zionists in 1897, for example, have bowed to the overwhelming sentiment in the Jewish world that opposed their reading of the Jewish past and program for the Jewish future? Should anti-Zionists of that time, in the West or the East, have moderated their opposition in the name of Jewish unity, when they considered either their own civic equality or interpretation of Judaism at stake? Should Jews committed to achieving peace for Israel and her Arab neighbors in 1995/6 mute their voices so that a bland "unity" may be achieved? Should American Jews privilege the fundamental belief of Orthodox leaders that women be denied some forms of participation in communal public events over the deeply felt commitment of the majority to the absolute value of gender equality?

There are many areas of Jewish life where our differences are so significant that we cannot recognize other Jews as our partners in community. Many of us cannot enter into a dialogue, for example, with those who consider Baruch Goldstein a hero.[17] We cannot discuss politics with those who are confident that God determines political strategy. A tribal people such as the Jews are like a

17. [Dr. Baruch Goldstein perpetrated a massacre in the Cave of the Patriarchs in Hebron in 1994, killing and wounding more than one hundred Muslims at worship there.]

family. You can't choose your relatives, but you can favor some over others. And a few you can choose not to invite to the party.

This is not to say that we should read out of our community all our political and religious antagonists, or speak only with those with whom we are in agreement. It does suggest that all participants in shared communal debate must accept the rules of rational and civil discourse. As a community divided along multiple fault lines, we must set limits upon ourselves in the way we speak to and about those with whom we disagree.

Dianne Cohler-Esses (born 1960) was the first woman from the Syrian Jewish community in Brooklyn, New York, to become a rabbi. Ordained by the Jewish Theological Seminary in 1995, Cohler-Esses has served in a number of Jewish communal positions. She now serves as Associate Rabbi and Director of Lifelong Learning at Congregation Romemu in New York.

Dianne Cohler-Esses, "A Common Language between East and West,"
Journal of Feminist Studies in Religion 19, no. 2 (Spring 2003): 111–18.

In this multicultural age, I have found it fashionable to be a Syrian Jew. Jews of European descent have been fascinated with stories of my community and especially the fact that I left it to become the first Syrian Jewish female rabbi and the first non-Orthodox Syrian rabbi, male or female. Not knowing how to approach this strange world, they often relate to being Sephardic through a familiar symbol. "That's so exotic!" they exclaim. "Does that mean you eat rice on Passover?" "Yes," I answer, exasperated that the sum of my culture is reduced to the luxury of eating grains on a spring holiday. . . .

When I first graduated from college, having just fled the Syrian community, my first job was to run an oral-history project of the immigrant elders of the Syrian community. The stories I was privileged to listen to for the next four years taught me to respect the historical heart of this community, a heart I had previously rejected. I came to understand the elders' story as a part of my own. For example, the following story reaches back to the 1930s. Mal Dweck, of the Syrian community in Bensonhurst, Brooklyn, spoke of an incident that took place at the home of an Ashkenazi friend during his teenage years. By the time my colleagues and I interviewed him, in the early 1980s, Mal was blind from old age.

We had little gatherings at her [the friend, Sylvia's] house. . . . Now, I could not read Yiddish. I knew how to read Hebrew letters, but I could not read Yiddish. . . . My skin was dark. I looked like an Italian. So Sylvia said to her grandfather that I'm Jewish. He says to her, "Baloney, this guy's no Jew." She says to him,

"Yes, he is." She says to me, "Go prove it." And so he says to me, "Come prove it." So he says, "Here. Here's the Jewish Forward. Read it." But I told him, "I can't read this, Mr. Goldner, I can't read that. But I'll do better than that." I said, "You wanna hear the prayer for wine? Which prayer you wanna hear?" So I started rattling. "Enough, stop!" Grandpa says. "You're Jewish but you don't look it!" Grandpa says. "Well I am. I'm a Syrian Jew." Says Grandpa, "What the hell is a Syrian Jew?"

This story issues a challenge. What is the American Jewish community's notion of Jewish identity? Is it informed only by the majority of its population? Perhaps broadening those conceptions might inject new possibilities into Jewish identity. . . .

The only Jewish world available to me—as a searching, questioning woman—was the Ashkenazic world. This new land embodied for me all the Western notions I had come to hold as true and liberating: choice, equality, education, and individualism. Instead, I discovered another culture that had its own limitations and was as blind to the consequences of those limitations as the culture I grew up in. . . . I was in shock. . . . In the place I came to search for my Jewish roots, my own roots were invisible. I found that, in all the classes I took, the Jews of the East disappeared after they left Spain, as if they disappeared entirely off the historical map. In response to my questions as to why the history of the Mizrahi Jews was not included in courses on modern Jewish history, I received one of two answers: "Because the Jews of the East haven't entered the modern period," or, "Because my students are Ashkenazic, becoming rabbis of Ashkenazic congregations. They don't need to know or teach about the history of the Jews from the East." After that, I was silent concerning my own history. Not only was I an oppressed minority, I was essentially a minority of one. . . . I knew then that I really was a stranger in two worlds. Although I had become a stranger to the world I came from, I could never feel at home in the world I had entered. . . .

When I am in the community of my origins, I represent the West. I am a kind of outlaw, a strange, genderless creature who has chosen a male profession. I am the one who has left, who has betrayed community and history, who has rejected everything the community stands for. And yet members of that community danced at my wedding (having survived an egalitarian ceremony) and came to the celebrations of my children's births (even a covenant ceremony for my daughter!). Despite all the broken rules, still to them I am a Syrian Jew. Still I belong to them. As long as the rabbi part of me is unrecognized, they will acknowledge me and celebrate with me, or at least the life-cycle events of my family.

When I am among the Ashkenazis, I represent the East—exotic, dark-skinned, rice-eating on Pesach—a traveler from another world. They want some of my exoticism; they often envy it. Truly I am Sephardic, some tell me. I relate much more to that culture than to Ashkenazic Jewry, they say. I do not tell them that being Sephardic is more than eating rice on Passover . . . that one cannot claim a Mizrahi identity unless one has grown up with its ethos, with a culture that binds.

And to myself, I still yearn to be accepted by the community that raised me, that gave me history and identity—yet I cannot live on its terms. So I live in an Ashkenazic world, speaking the language of the West, a language still foreign to me. . . . I pretend to speak the language, but it is not native. I practice it when I am alone so that my friends and colleagues will not guess that I am posing as a Westerner and as a rabbi. . . .

. . . I often experience being pulled painfully taut by two competing and contradictory histories, those of the East and the West. Perhaps when, or if, I can give rise to a new internal vision in which each does not contradict the other, I can begin to speak a language common to East and West. . . . Perhaps there will be a day when a Jewish voice will be raised with the deep understanding of the vast multiplicity of the Jewish people, offering the world vision in healing the painful and violent terrain between East and West, a prophetic vision in which the lion can lie with the lamb and East and West do not have to destroy one another.

Lewis Gordon (born 1962) is Professor of Philosophy at the University of Connecticut. Born of a Jamaican Jewish mother, Gordon received his undergraduate degree from Lehman College, City University of New York. He earned his PhD in philosophy at Yale University. Gordon has also taught at Purdue, Brown, and Temple Universities. At Temple, he was Director of the Institute for the Study of Race and Social Thought, as well as founder of the Center for Afro-Jewish Studies. A renowned scholar of W. E. B. DuBois and Frantz Fanon, Gordon has written in numerous areas of philosophy and social thought.

Lewis Gordon, "Foreword," in Diane Kaufman Tobin, Gary A. Tobin, and Scott Rubin, *In Every Tongue: The Racial and Ethnic Diversity of the Jewish People* (San Francisco: Institute for Jewish and Community Research, 2005), 9, 13–15.

. . . I found myself in a political debate with a white secular Jew. The debate, ironically, emerged from my intervening to challenge the presumption, in an online debate on Israeli and Palestinian politics, that Israelis were an exclusively white Jewish population versus peoples of color (the Palestinians). I argued that most Jews living in Israel could be characterized as people of color and that there are Jews worldwide who both do not and *cannot* be identified as white. After all, most Israelis have Sephardic and Middle Eastern heritage. Why, the challenger posed, would Jews of color want to acknowledge their Jewish background? I was confronted here with a new kind of question, one which I had not seen broached to white Jews, but which I'm sure some might have faced: *Why do you choose to continue being a Jew?*

An odd feature of the question is the presumption that choice is somehow more a question for a black Jew than it is for a white one. Something insidious lay beneath it, for I suspected that the challenger did not treat his Jewish identity as something over which he had a choice.

In my reply, I pointed out that I had spent most of my life as a secular Jew, as someone who adamantly did not want to be involved in Jewish religious life, because I saw a double standard imposed upon African and African Diasporic Jews that was not faced by white Jews. Black Jews had to be religious and meet all kinds of criteria that white Jews, in fact, did not have to meet. White Jews, in other words, could be secular. The underlying theme was that white Jews are really Jews no matter what. So, I had consciously focused on being a born Jew as a fight against that prejudice. . . .

I have been fortunate enough to meet communities of Jews in a variety of settings because of my work as an intellectual. When I taught at Brown University, most of my classes had one or sometimes several Jews of color. In one small seminar, eight of ten students were Jewish, although only two of the students were white. I have received letters from many Jewish communities, but none has had an effect on me as much as the community of Be'chol Lashon (In Every Tongue), a program organized by Diane and Gary Tobin of the Institute for Jewish and Community Research in San Francisco. Knowing much about the diversity of Jewish communities worldwide is one thing. Sitting in a room with nearly a hundred representatives of such communities is another matter. I participated in the 2002 Be'chol Lashon International Think Tank, where I was able to see the beautiful tapestry of Lemba Jews from South Africa, Ethiopian Jews, the Abayudaya of Uganda, Ibo (also known as Igbo, derivation of Hebrew) Jews of Nigeria, Egyptian Jews, Cuban Jews, Spanish and Portuguese Conversos who have returned to Judaism, Ashkenazi Jews, Sephardic Jews, and Israelites. Some of the participants were also Jews from mixed marriages involving Jewish mothers; others were children of Jewish men who sought connection with their Jewish family; many were "converts." I place conversion in quotation marks because many were also born Jews who felt the need to affirm their identity through practices of converting to a particular movement. Some were Asian, and others were Native American. Some were lesbians, and some were gay men. All were in active struggle *with* and *for* this way of living that we call Judaism. It became clear to me, as I participated . . . that something special was being realized by this wonderful community of hope—namely, a new stage in the history of Jewish people. It is post-denominational and pan-denominational, post-racial and pan-racial. It is what Judaism has always been—we are a people.

Peoplehood involves taking seriously the diversity of Jews and the complexity of our history. It involves taking on the fallacies that have been imposed on our past in the service of a false, homogeneous identity that has encouraged bigotry.

Noam Pianko, *Jewish Peoplehood:*
An American Innovation

Noam Pianko (born 1973) holds the Samuel Stroum Chair in Jewish Studies at
the University of Washington. A graduate of Brown University, Pianko earned his
PhD at Yale University and has authored a number of important works on modern
Jewish intellectual history.

Noam Pianko, *Jewish Peoplehood: An American Innovation* (New Brunswick, NJ:
Rutgers University Press, 2015), 112, 114, 134–37.

Finally, perhaps the most important Jewish studies challenge to the idea of
a unified Jewish past and a united commitment to a common mission derives
from Jewish feminism. How can a story of a unified people claim to encompass
and represent all of its constituents when half of the purported group has been
marginalized from the sources and historical narratives . . . defining that collective essence? . . .

Theologian Judith Plaskow put forth the fundamental limitations of Jewish
sources as core texts for defining the Jewish people in *Standing Again at Sinai*. By
focusing on the absence of women at this founding moment of Jewish collectivity in religious sources, the revelation at Sinai, Plaskow illustrates the extent to
which Jewish sources and rituals are defined by the experience of men. There is
also a fundamental problem, she insists, in the biblical image of God as male,
one that cannot be overcome in all subsequent definitions of Jews and Judaism.
In attempting to reconstruct Jewish belief and practice to integrate women's
experiences, Plaskow argues for new interpretations (*midrashim*) and rituals to
reimagine and actively reshape the past, present, and future of Jewish life and
community.

With notions of peoplehood so deeply rooted in the asserted memory of the
past, a feminist approach demands a significant reevaluation of the historical
significance and future mission of the collective. More fundamentally, feminism challenges the very idea that there could be one static essence that defines
the Jewish people. Instead, articulating peoplehood itself must be an ongoing
process of rediscovery and explanation that constantly seeks to overcome hier-

archies and biases by giving voice to historically marginalized members of the collective. . . .

Divergent approaches to Jewish peoplehood today—Jewish communal conversations; studies of nationalism, ethnicity, race, and peoplehood itself; and Jewish studies—leave us [then] with two fundamentally different views of Jewish collectivity in the past, present, and future. On one side, Jewish communal conversation emphasizes an unchanging understanding of Jewish collectivity with a strong emphasis on boundary preservation and support for the state. On the other side, [other] approaches to Jewish peoplehood historicize the concept and question the practical possibility and moral validity of any group identity steeped in the nationalist paradigm and/or fixed collective boundaries. There is a fundamental divide between essentialists and constructivists, particularists and universalists, and statists and diasporists, and there are good reasons why Jewish peoplehood as it is currently conceived does not provide a comfortable meeting ground for the two camps. But Jewish peoplehood—or something like it—will remain an important idea, albeit one that needs to be redefined. Is there a way to bridge the gap between these camps, or at least draw from both—the peoplehood proponents and the cultural constructivists—in order to rehabilitate Jewish peoplehood in a new key? . . .

I offer Jewishhood as a new term to serve as a touchstone for conceptions of Jewish collectivity in a new key. In hopes of sparking a productive conversation about the meaning of Jewish collectivity, rather than offer the new key word I propose to explore the term as one alternative model to peoplehood—one that respects the critical nature of groupness within Jewish tradition and Jewish life, without privileging the nationalist paradigm as the default and outdated model for the ties that bind Jews to one another.

Jewishhood is a self-consciously constructed term intended to highlight the three key elements of peoplehood in a new key. The Jewish in Jewishhood makes the study of Jewish collectivity a reflection on an evolving story of what Jews do, rather than an affirmation that Jews exist as a discrete group. The conceptual vocabulary of Jewishhood is not positioned to make essentialist claims about the nature of the collective; instead, the term Jewishhood acknowledges family resemblances in Jewish expressions without erecting rigid boundary markers. *Hood* (decoupled from the nouns *people* and *nation*) signifies a shift from nationhood to neighborhood, underscoring local, diverse, and multiple natures of community building and a sense of group solidarity, and drawing our attention to local aspects of Jewish interaction and belonging that together constitute global Jewish collectivity. Most radically, peoplehood in a new key will not necessarily include people at all. Instead, a robust conception of Jewish collectivity can be imagined in the vocabulary of project—again, reflecting a fundamental modification in the vision of Jewish collectivity from who Jews are to what Jews do.

The Jewishhood project is not proposed here as the replacement term for Jewish peoplehood, but as the basis for a new conversation that acknowledges the extent to which a very limited and singular definition of Jewish collectivity has come to both dominate communal vocabulary and eclipse the potential evolution of new concepts reflecting contemporary trends—concepts that might even more closely resemble premodern versions of how Jews are linked to one another. Jewishhood certainly sounds jarring, without any clear precedent in English. But peoplehood must have sounded quite strange to the ears of English speakers during its formative years in the beginning of the previous century. Playing with the language of Jewish collectivity in English is, in a sense, itself an important part of the legacy of the peoplehood innovation in American Jewish life. The pioneers of peoplehood recognized that only a new vocabulary of collective Jewish identity could change people's thinking: new key words reshape how individuals imagine their own sense of self and their relationship to broader groups. A process of generating new key words, then, is not only about terminology; the conscious and unconscious shaping of new key terms allows communities to imagine collective connections in radically new ways. . . .

In thinking about peoplehood in a new key, I am keenly aware of a tension. There is a need for a new key term to challenge the hegemony of an existing key word for describing the criteria and boundaries of Jewish collectivity. How can a new key word be introduced that also challenges the very idea of a singular all-encompassing term articulating a specific set of assumptions about collectivity? Indeed, one open question is whether the Jewishhood project is itself too singular. Including the definite article carries over the supposition from Jewish people and the Jewish nation that there is one set of unifying and shared boundaries. Jewishhood projects would more profoundly break from the nationalist paradigm by emphasizing the inherently plural and often incompatible visions of Jews' primary goals, practices, politics, and allegiances.

My hope is that whatever language we use going forward moves beyond unity, solidarity, and rigid boundaries to integrate fragmentation, conflicting visions of Judaism, and permeable boundaries of Jewishness into definitions of the Jewish people past, present, and future. Such a shift in conceptualizing the meaning of the Jewish people would address the limitations of the term as it was defined in the modern period and preserve the possibility of reclaiming the ability of some term to reinvent itself in conversation with shifting paradigms of individual and group identities. It is my hope that this shift will also help address the polarization that has developed between peoplehood advocates, who view their role as making a case for Jewish unity, and peoplehood critics, who question the historical validity of collective claims and treat group solidarity with suspicion. Jewishhood is thus an idea meant to bridge oppositional thinking about Jewish peoplehood between those threatened by critical scholarship and those driven by critical scholarship to make interventions by discrediting the theoretical basis of particular group loyalties.

. . . The escape velocity needed to redefine peoplehood may be too great to salvage that terminology. However, it is not too late to salvage Jewish collectivity itself.

Jewishhood provides a terminological and conceptual model potentially more effective and more consistent with contemporary realities than peoplehood. Jewish communal policy shaped by Jewishhood projects, rather than peoplehood, might undermine·some specific strategies for galvanizing peoplehood currently supported by American and Israeli institutions, but placing pressures on institutions to change is not the same as advocating the end of everything that we currently know as peoplehood. The ultimate goal of building a sense of shared connection and co-membership in a group that transcends time and place remains the aim; the optimal path, however, and the institutions necessary to reach toward that objective, may look quite different than the contemporary Jewish communal landscape. Jewishhood would likely not, in fact, immediately bolster support for the Federation movement or positively transform attitudes among American Jews toward Israel. But refocusing the conversation with new terminology and emphases might spark a revitalization of Jewish collective life and institutions—perhaps even to the level of creativity, growth, and innovation that accompanied Jewish peoplehood in the last century. It is only in the context of the acknowledgment that Jewish peoplehood is indeed a relatively new and thus negotiable concept—open to reinvention and transformation— that a workable vision of collectivity can emerge and function as an essential part of the wide expanse of Jewishness.

Further Reading

This volume includes excerpts from over seventy books and articles. Readers are encouraged to explore further the writings of these thinkers. Here we list titles by authors other than those excerpted in this volume. In our view, these titles represent significant contributions to American Jewish thought. They are not organized according to theme, since a number of them relate to several topics covered in this volume. The number of excellent works of and about American Jewish thought far exceeds our capacity to encompass them in a volume of this kind. It is our hope that if you consult these works, a picture of the range and depth of the field may emerge. In some cases, authors whose work appears in this book have edited volumes included on this list.

Aaron, David H. "Engaging Literary Voices to See the Universal in the Particular." *Reform Jewish Quarterly* 66, no. 3 (Summer 2019): 154–78.

Artson, Bradley Shavit. *God of Becoming and Relationship: The Dynamic Nature of Process Theology.* Woodstock, VT: Jewish Lights, 2013.

Biale, David. *Power and Powerlessness in Jewish History.* New York: Schocken, 1986.

Biale, Rachel. *Woman and Jewish Law: The Essential Texts, Their History, and Their Relevance for Today.* New York: Schocken, 1995.

Brous, Sharon. "Joy and Jeopardy." *Judaism* 54, nos. 3/4 (Summer 2005): 151–56.

Cohen, Aryeh. *Justice in the City: An Argument from the Sources of Jewish Tradition.* Brighton, MA: Academic Studies Press, 2012.

Cohen, Gerson D. "The Blessing of Assimilation in Jewish History." In *Jewish History and Jewish Destiny,* by Gerson D. Cohen, 145–56. New York: Jewish Theological Seminary, 1997.

Cosgrove, Elliot N., ed. *Jewish Theology in Our Time: A New Generation Explores the Foundations and Future of Jewish Belief.* Woodstock, VT: Jewish Lights, 2010.

Dorff, Elliot N. *Knowing God: Jewish Journeys to the Unknowable.* Northvale, NJ: Jason Aronson, 1992.

Eilberg, Amy. *From Enemy to Friend: Jewish Wisdom and the Pursuit of Peace.* Maryknoll, NY: Orbis Books, 2014.

Eisen, Arnold M. *Rethinking Modern Judaism: Ritual, Commandment, Community.* Chicago: University of Chicago Press, 1998.

Eisenstein, Ira. *Judaism under Freedom.* New York: Reconstructionist Press, 1956.

Elazar, Daniel J. *Kinship and Consent: The Jewish Political Tradition and Its Contemporary Uses.* Ramat Gan, Israel: Turtledove, 1981.

Erlewine, Robert. *Monotheism and Tolerance: Recovering a Religion of Reason.* Bloomington: Indiana University Press, 2010.

Fine, Lawrence, Eitan Fishbane, and Or N. Rose, eds. *Jewish Mysticism and the Spiritual Life: Classical Texts, Contemporary Reflections*. Woodstock, VT: Jewish Lights, 2011.

Gillman, Neil. *Sacred Fragments: Recovering Theology for the Modern Jew*. Philadelphia: Jewish Publication Society, 1990.

Goldstein, Elyse, ed. *New Jewish Feminism: Probing the Past, Forging the Future*. Woodstock, VT: Jewish Lights, 2009.

Goodman, Saul L., ed. *The Faith of Secular Jews*. New York: Ktav, 1976.

Gordis, Robert. *Judaism for the Modern Age*. New York: Farrar, Straus, and Cudahy, 1955.

Green, Arthur, and Mayse, Ariel Evan. *A New Hasidism: Branches*. Philadelphia: Jewish Publication Society, 2019.

Halivni, David Weiss. *Revelation Restored: Divine Writ and Critical Responses*. New York: Westview Press, 1997.

Hammer, Jill, and Taya Shere. *The Hebrew Priestess: Ancient and New Visions of Women's Spiritual Leadership*. Teaneck, NJ: Ben Yehuda Press, 2015.

Hartman, Tova. *Feminism Encounters Traditional Judaism: Resistance and Accommodation*. Waltham, MA: Brandeis University Press, 2007.

Held, Shai. *The Heart of Torah: Essays on the Weekly Portion*. Philadelphia: Jewish Publication Society, 2017.

Katz, Steven T. *The Impact of the Holocaust on Jewish Theology*. New York: New York University Press, 2005.

Kepnes, Steven, ed. *Interpreting Judaism in a Postmodern Age*. New York: New York University Press, 1996.

Kepnes, Steven, Peter Ochs, and Robert Gibbs. *Reasoning after Revelation: Dialogues in Postmodern Jewish Philosophy*. With commentaries by Yudit Kornberg Greenberg, Susan E. Shapiro, Elliot R. Wolfson, Almut Sh. Bruckstein, and Edith Wyschogrod. Boulder, CO: Westview Press, 1998.

Kristol, Irving. *On Jews and Judaism: Selected Essays*. Edited by Gertrude Himmelfarb. E-book: Mosaic Books, 2014. Accessed on Kindle.

Kushner, Harold S. *When Bad Things Happen to Good People*. 2nd ed. New York: Schocken, 1989.

Kushner, Lawrence. *The River of Light: Spirituality, Judaism, and the Evolution of Consciousness*. Woodstock, VT: Jewish Lights, 1990.

Lamm, Norman, and Walter Wurzburger, eds. *A Treasury of "Tradition."* New York: Hebrew Publishing Company, 1967.

Lerner, Michael. *Jewish Renewal: A Path to Healing and Transformation*. New York: Harper Perennial, 1994.

Levenson, Jon D. *Creation and the Persistence of Evil: The Jewish Drama of Divine Omnipotence*. Princeton, NJ: Princeton University Press, 1988.

Mintz, Adam, and Lawrence Schiffman, eds. *Jewish Spirituality and Divine Law*. New York: Yeshiva University Press, 2005.

Mittleman, Alan. *Human Nature and Jewish Thought: Judaism's Case for Why Persons Matter*. Princeton, NJ, and Oxford: Princeton University Press, 2015.

Morgan, Michael L. *Beyond Auschwitz: Post-Holocaust Jewish Thought in America*. Oxford: Oxford University Press, 2001.

Ochs, Peter, and Nancy Levene, eds. *Textual Reasonings: Jewish Philosophy and Text Study at the End of the Twentieth Century*. Grand Rapids, MI, and Cambridge, UK: Eerdmans, 2002.

Ochs, Vanessa L. *Inventing Jewish Ritual*. Philadelphia: Jewish Publication Society, 2007.

Rackman, Emanuel. *One Man's Judaism*. New York: Philosophical Library, 1970.

Rashkover, Randi, and Martin Kavka, eds. *Judaism, Liberalism, and Political Theology*. Bloomington: Indiana University Press, 2014.

Reines, Alvin J. *Polydoxy: Explorations in a Philosophy of Religion*. Buffalo, NY: Prometheus Books, 1987.

Rose, Or N., Jo Ellen Green Kaiser, and Margie Klein. *Righteous Indignation: A Jewish Call for Justice*. Woodstock, VT: Jewish Lights, 2008.

Samuelson, Norbert M. *Revelation and the God of Israel*. Cambridge: Cambridge University Press, 2002.

Schwarzchild, Steven. *The Pursuit of the Ideal: Jewish Writings of Steven Schwarzchild*. Edited by Menachem Kellner. Albany: State University of New York Press, 1990.

Seidenberg, David Mevorach. *Kabbalah and Ecology: God's Image in the More-Than-Human World*. New York: Cambridge University Press, 2015.

Shapiro, Susan. "Failing Speech: Post-Holocaust Writing and the Discourse of Postmodernism." *Semeia* 40 (1987): 65–91.

Silver, Abba Hillel. *Where Judaism Differed: An Inquiry into the Distinctiveness of Judaism*. Philadelphia: Jewish Publication Society of America, 1957.

Steinberg, Milton. *Anatomy of Faith*. New York: Harcourt, Brace, and Co., 1960.

Strassfeld, Michael. *A Book of Life: Embracing Judaism as a Spiritual Practice*. New York: Schocken, 2002.

Tirosh-Samuelson, Hava, ed. *Women and Gender in Jewish Philosophy*. Bloomington: Indiana University Press, 2004.

Tirosh-Samuelson, Hava, and Aaron W. Hughes, eds. *Jewish Philosophy for the Twenty-First Century: Personal Reflections*. Leiden: Brill, 2014.

Umansky, Ellen M., and Dianne Ashton, eds. *Four Centuries of Jewish Women's Spirituality*. Boston: Beacon Press, 1992.

Walzer, Michael, Menachem Lorberbaum, Noam J. Zohar, Madeline Kochen, Ari Ackerman, and Yair Lorberbaum, eds. *The Jewish Political Tradition*. 3 vols. New Haven, CT: Yale University Press, 2000–2018.

Wiener, Shohama, ed. *The Fifty-Eighth Century: A Jewish Renewal Sourcebook*. Northvale, NJ: Jason Aronson, 1996.

Wine, Sherwin T. *Judaism beyond God*. Farmington Hills, MI: Ktav and Society for Humanistic Judaism, 1995.

Wolfson, Elliot R. *Language, Eros, Being: Kabbalistic Hermeneutics and Poetic Imagination*. New York: Fordham University Press, 2005.

Wolpe, David J. *In Speech and in Silence: The Jewish Quest for God*. New York: H. Holt, 1992.

Yerushalmi, Yosef Hayim. *Zakhor: Jewish History and Jewish Memory*. Seattle: University of Washington Press, 1996.

Index

Bible/biblical text (*continued*)
the Holy, 107; identity, 286; imagery,
198; interpretive tradition, 72–73;
Israel's election, 276–77; obligation, 83;
prophecy, 44; quotations from, 20n16,
57, 61, 102n17, 104n18, 107n24, 107n28,
134, 135, 146, 152n22, 180n7, 181n9, 182,
201, 222, 268n2, 278; racism, 201–4;
renewal, 182; revelation, 39, 49–51, 52–54,
64–65, 76; selfhood, 67–68; Tabernacle,
102; Textual Reasoning, 132; women in,
227; Word of God, 274
binary categories, 252–54
black Jews, 295–96
Blumenthal, David R., 183–84
Bonhoeffer, Dietrich, 19n13
Bornstein, Kate, 252–53
Borowitz, Eugene B., xxi, xxiv, 66–69, 72,
75–76, 287
Boyarin, Daniel, 200–205, 245
Boyarin, Jonathan, 200–205
Braiterman, Zachary, xxixn16, 167n1
Brous, Sharon, 301
Bruckstein, Almut Sh., 302
Brunner, Emil, 50
Buber, Martin, xxiv, 16n8, 17, 32, 37, 38, 50,
66, 131, 178–79, 191
Buddha/Buddhism, 22, 50
Butler, Judith, 21n46, 190–91

Camus, Albert, 19
Canne, John, 150
Cantor, Aviva, 213
Cantor, Georg, 103
Carroll, Lewis, 232, 240
Catholic Israel, 60–61
Chanukah, 162–65
chavurah movement, 86–87
Chicago, Judy, 121–22
chosenness, 204, 276–77, 279, 281, 287
Christianity, 20, 22, 23, 152, 158–59, 200–201,
204
citizenship, 155–57

City of David, 182
classical Judaism, 76–77
Cochin, 280
Cohen, Arthur A., xxiv, 167, 273–75
Cohen, Aryeh, 301
Cohen, Gerson D., 301
Cohen, Hermann, xxiv, 66, 75, 133, 144–45,
179
Cohen, Steven M., 283, 285–88
Cohler-Esses, Dianne, 292–94
collective, 92, 202, 283–84, 287–88, 297–300
colonialism, 190–91, 201
commandments, 39–40, 45, 47–48, 52–53,
56, 103, 177, 222–25
Commentary (magazine), xxv, 40, 156, 209–11
commonwealth, 264–66
communal life: Covenant, 66–69; Cover's
bridge metaphor, 79–80; halakhic
man, 57; Jewish diet, 118–20; Jewish
renewal, 91–92; Jewish thinking, 132;
and obligation, 81; peoplehood, 287–88,
298–300; pluralism, 265–66; public
sphere, 158–59; revelation, 75–77; unity,
290–91; women, 227–28, 280
complementarity, 195
conditional Zionism, 209–10
Conservative Judaism, 30, 163, 219
context-free and context-bound truths,
135–37
Cosgrove, Elliot, 331, xxixn15
covenant/Covenant: in American Jewish
thought, 2; as bilateral relationship,
75–77; Jewish renewal, 114; Jewish self,
66–69; *peshat*, 128; power, 34; Sinai,
58–61, 278; and women, 224, 232
Cover, Robert, 41, 78–80
Cox, Harvey, 19n11
creation, 97–98, 121–22
Cromwell, Oliver, 150–51
cultural identity, 201–5
cultural pluralism, 265–66
culture-bound concepts, 142–45
cumulativism, 62–64

Greenberg, Blu, 229–31
Greenberg, Hayim, 154
Greenberg, Irving, xxi, xxiv, 35, 124n3,
    185–87, 188
Greenberg, Steven, 239–42, 251–52
Greenberg, Yudit, 131, 302
Greenstein, Edward L., 30–32
Gush Emunim, 193, 201
Gutierrez, Gustavo, 152n5

Haam, Ahad, xxiv, 148–49, 178
Ha'aretz (newspaper), 198
Haberman, Jacob, xxixn5
hakhel, 110
halakhah: change, 58–60; Cover on, 78–80;
    debate, 140; defined, 55n12; feminism,
    78–80, 217–20, 226–28, 229–31; halakhic
    man, 55–57, 94–95; interpretative
    tradition, 63; Jewish community, 76–77;
    paradigm shift, 112; postmodernism,
    70–74; sexual identity, 251–52
halitzah, 221–22n10
Halivni, David Weiss, 302
Hamas, 193–94
Hamilton, William, 18n10, 19
Hammer, Jill, 302
Handelman, Susan, 70–74
Hartman, David, xxi, xxiv, 138–41
Hartman, Tova, 302
Harvey, Warren Zev, xxixn14
Hasidic teaching, 113
haskalah, 70
havurah, 91, 107
Hayot Hakodesh, 109–10
healing, 115–17
Hebrew Bible, 53–54, 201
Hebrews, 134–37, 143
hegemony, 201–3
HeHasid, Yehudah, 240–41
Heine, Heinrich, 148
Herberg, Will, xx, xxiii, xxiv, xxixn12, 49–51,
    86
hermeneutics, 63–64, 123–24, 201

Hertzberg, Arthur, 289
Herzl, Theodor, 209–11, 270–71
Heschel, Abraham Joshua, xx, xxiii, 9–12,
    39–41, 86, 96–98, 124n3, 159
Heschel, Susannah, xxii, 87n7, 217–20, 233
heterogeneity, 190
heteronomy, 70–71, 75–76
heterosexuality, 239
hevlei mashiach, 108
hiddenness of God, 14
hierarchical differentiations, 279–81
Himmelfarb, Gertrude, 156
Himmelfarb, Milton, 41n5
Hirsch, Samson Raphael, xxiv, xxixn5,
    36–41
Hoffman, Lawrence, 88
Hole, Judith, 226n13
Holocaust, 167, 171–73, 176–77, 178–79,
    188–89, 210
homosexuality, 239–42, 243–47, 251–52
Horeb, 58
Hughes, Aaron, xxixn14, 303
humanism, 23–24
humans and God, 75–77
humor, 139–40
hurban, 20
Huss, Boaz, 85n2
Hutner, Yitzhok, xxv, 46
Hyman, Paula, 30n24, 213, 290–91

identity: American Jewish community,
    292–94; Covenantal, 67; Diaspora,
    201–5; and diversity of Jews, 295–96;
    and ethnicity, 282–83, 286; gay and
    lesbian, 243–47; gender and sexual,
    251–52; obligation, 81; Palestinian
    national, 186; and peoplehood, 298–99;
    re-exploration of Judaism, 116; and
    uniqueness, 260
idolatry, 16, 22, 30–31, 224
imagery, 27–29
imitatio dei, 35
imperial mode, 79

Maccabean revolt, 163–64

Magid, Shaul, xxiv, xxxn17, 87n8, 282–84, 285–87

Maimon, Avraham, 47n7

Maimonides, 44, 56, 62

man and God, 5–12, 17, 18–20, 43–45

man's freedom from God, 21–22

Marshall, Stephen, 151

masculine orientation of liturgy, 30–32

maternal experience, 83

Matt, Daniel C., 103–5

maximalist and minimalist interpretations, 58–60

Mayse, Ariel Evan, 302

meditation, Jewish, 113

Mendelssohn, Moses, xxiv

Merkabah, 110

messianism, 66–68, 146, 150–51, 182

metaphysics, 134–35

methodolatry, 232–33

Michaelson, Jay, 243–47

Michel, Sonya, 214

midrash, 72–73, 104

Milton, John, 47

mindfulness, 128–30

minority groups, 265

Mintz, Adam, 302

mishkan, 107

Mishnah, 132, 138–39

Mittleman, Alan, 302

mitzvot, 75, 81–82, 112, 177, 244

Mizrahi Jews, 293–94

modern culture, 39–40, 143–46

modernity, 77, 78–83, 112, 118–19, 123, 154–55, 219, 283

modern Judaism, 50–54, 60, 218–20, 233

modern man, 18–19

monism, 144, 154–55, 265–66

monotheism, 27–29, 31

morality, 63–64, 70, 71, 132–33, 194–95, 202

Morgan, Michael, xxiv, xxixn6, 167n2, 302

Morris, Benny, 198–99

Mosaic law, 62–63

Moses, 40, 44, 107, 274, 278–79

multiculturalism, 154–57

mysticism, 116–17, 246

myth of Holocaust and redemption, 171–73

narratives of destruction, 237–38

nationalism, 164–65, 185–86, 190–91, 209, 257, 270–72, 298–99

"The National Prospect," 156

nationhood, 263–67, 268–69

nation-states, 80–81, 191, 270, 272

neoconservatism, 156

neo-Hasidism, 87

neshamah, 110

Neturei Karta, 204

Neusner, Jacob, 171–73

New Historians, 198

New Testament, 52, 200, 204

Niebuhr, H. Richard, 50

Niebuhr, Reinhold, xx, 49

Nietzsche, Friedrich, 19, 143–44

Noahide covenant, 66

nomos, 78–80

Novak, David, xxiv, 75–77, 124n3

oath of hastening the end, 174, 174n3

obedience, 71–72

obligation, 47, 68, 81–83, 237, 251

Ochs, Peter, xxiv, 124n3, 131, 302, 303

Ochs, Vanessa, xxiv, 303

olam-shanah-nefesh, 108–9

oness, 251–52

Oral Torah, 44–45, 46, 63, 72–74, 128–29, 222

Orthodoxy, 219, 240

otherness, 11, 29, 47, 93, 96, 226–28, 238, 278

Otto, Rudolf, 94n15

Oz, Amos, 194

Ozick, Cynthia, 221–25, 226–27

paidaic mode, 79

Palestine, 186–87, 189, 190–91, 192–95, 198, 201–3, 207–8, 295

theology *(continued)*
  59; and power, 35; predicate, 36–37;
  prepositional, 37–38; queer, 243–47;
  radical, 18–20; and Sinai, 73; and the
  Torah, 43–45; Wyschodrod's, 279
thought-concepts, 22–23
tikun hanefesh, 117
tikun olam, 117
Tillich, Paul, xx, 15
time, 96–98, 107
Tirosh-Samuelson, Hava, xxivn14, 303
Tobin, Diane and Gary, 296
Torah: commentary of Yehudah, 240–42;
  Diaspora, 204; as divine, 43–45; and
  feminist Judaism, 228, 231, 278–80;
  gender in, 254–55; Giving of, 40; and
  God, 30; halakhic change, 59–60;
  halakhic Judaism, 112–14; laws of, 45,
  163; Oral, 44–45, 46, 63, 72–74, 128–29,
  222; particularism, 200; renewal, 80,
  109–10; revelation, 39, 46–48, 62–65, 274;
  scholars, 139–41; Sinaitic, 64–65; spiritual
  growth, 101–2; *svara*, 249; Textual
  Reasoning, 132–33; women in, 221–25;
  Written, 45, 46, 64, 103–5, 222
torah kelulah, 129–30
Torah min ha-shamayim, 43
Torah she-be'al peh, 44
Tosafists, 62
Tosefta, 138–39, 138n9
tradition: abuse, 183; change, 109; Covenant,
  66–69; divine power, 34; education, 289;
  election, 274; ethnocentric Judaism,
  204; feminism, 218–20, 227–28, 229–31,
  233–34, 278–79; gender hierarchy, 240;
  and God, 30–31; halakhic change,
  60; imagery, 28; Jewish diet, 118–20;
  Jewishhood, 298; Jewish renewal, 113;
  nationhood, 264; peoplehood, 267;
  and politics, 158–61; postethnicity, 283;
  queer rabbis, 249–50; queer theology,
  244–45; rabbinic interpretation,

62–63; reconstituative ethics, 237–38;
  re-exploration of Judaism, 115–16;
  revelation, 44–45, 63, 138–41; spirituality,
  99–101; Textual Reasoning, 132–33
transgender people, 252, 254–55
tremendum, 167
"true realities," 147
truth, 135–37, 144–45
Turner, Frederick, 201
"Two Nations" notion, 156

Umansky, Ellen, xxiv, 30n22, 86, 303
"The Unfreedom of the Jewish Woman"
  (Weiss-Rosmarin), 213
unity, 121–22, 289, 290–91
universalism, 118, 143–44, 200, 204, 210
Universe, 134–35

Varnhagen, Rachel, 147
verbal revelation, 77
vertical metaphors, 101–2

Wach, Joachim, 94n15
Walzer, Michael, 124, 150–53, 303
Waskow, Arthur, 118–20
Weinberg, Sheila, 121–22
Weiss-Rosmarin, Trude, 213
Wertheimer, Jack, 283, 285–88
Whitehead, Alfred North, 33
white Jews, 295–96
Wiener, Shohama, 303
will to live, 5–8
Wine, Sherwin T., 303
Wisse, Ruth R., 192–96
Wolf, Arnold Jacob, 86
Wolfe, Alan, 210
Wolfson, Elliot R., 123, 302, 303
Wolpe, David J., 303
women: absence at Sinai, 278–79, 297;
  female images, 25–29; gender binaries,
  254–55; gender equality, 290; gender
  hierarchies, 240; in Judaism, 217–20,